Across Eurasia

Toby D. Smith

Blue Mountain Press

Library of Congress Control Number: 2017918279

ISBN 978-0-9996892-0-2 (paperback)
ISBN 978-0-9996892-1-9 (e-book)

Edited by Joel E. Smith
Cover photograph by the author

Blue Mountain Press
Philadelphia, Pennsylvania
www.bluemountainpress.net

Manufactured in the United States of America

FOR FAY AND STEVE

"I like to be free, I like to move where I want, go when I want to," he had told me in that tent in the middle of the Arctic Ocean. "My definition of the word 'adventure' is to 'invent life.' That's my advice to everyone: 'Invent your life. Be happy. Do what you want to do.'"

- Will Steger, *Crossing Antarctica*

Across Eurasia

PART I

…[the chaplain's] voice was quite steady when he said: "Have you no hope at all? Do you really think that when you die you die outright, and nothing remains?" I said: "Yes." He dropped his eyes and sat down again. He was truly sorry for me, he said. It must make life unbearable for a man, to think as I did.

- Albert Camus, *The Stranger*

1

A PANSY WHO LONGED TO BE A ROSE

"I'm from Baltimore originally," said the teenager sitting next to me, "but heading west to visit my girl." His grin faded. "And the baby."

"Congratulations," I said.

"She's already a month old," he added, "but I ain't even seen her yet."

Such was the paradox of travel. While on the road, I had noticed, travelers often seemed to befriend strangers more readily than their own neighbors.

"Are you excited about starting a family?" I asked.

"Sure," he said. "But, I also feel like I ain't even lived yet."

I nodded. I had been struggling with a similar family versus freedom dilemma. I felt unsure whether I must choose one, or if I could have both. That uncertainty was part of the reason I sat aboard this westbound Greyhound bus.

The teenager fell silent and returned his gaze to the setting sun that silhouetted the Pocono Mountains in purple against a pinkish swath of evening sky. The Poconos, I recalled from my bookworm days, comprised the southern portion of the

Catskills, from which many early American artists drew their inspiration. Washington Irving's description from *Rip Van Winkle* came to mind as we rose and fell with the forested slopes.

"They are a dismembered branch of the great Appalachian family," Irving writes. "When the weather is fair and settled, they are clothed in blue and purple, and print their bold outlines on the clear evening sky; but sometimes, when the rest of the landscape is cloudless, they will gather a hood of gray vapors about their summits, which, in the last rays of the setting sun, will glow and light up like a crown of glory."

After the sun slipped below the horizon, the teenager turned towards me. "What's your story?" he asked.

Like the Poconos, my roots nestled firmly in Pennsylvania. A few miles south of our route lay Reading, the city of my birth. My family tree sprouted in the adjacent countryside from fertile farmlands and had unfurled since the early 1700s across rural villages and boroughs such as New Jerusalem, Dryville, Topton, and Kutztown. My ancestors had immigrated to the area from Germany's Palatinate region. In Germany, inhabitants referred to themselves in their native language as the "Deutsch" people, and their land as "Deutschland."

Once in Pennsylvania, however, Europeans referred to Germans as "Dutch," and so my ancestors became known as the Pennsylvania Dutch. The Amish and Mennonite sects were considered Plain Dutch for their simple clothes and lifestyles. My Lutheran ancestors were Fancy Dutch only because their dress and custom were less orthodox than the Plain, who shunned technology and still travel by horse and buggy. Many locals and some members of my family retained the same Pennsylvania Dutch dialect that my ancestors had spoken for three hundred years.

When my maternal grandmother turned forty, she wept at the thought of it. A year later, my grandfather died. "Ach," my grandmother said after his unexpected passing. "Now I got something to cry about."

My grandmother was left to raise my nine-year-old mother

and my three aunts alone in her 1820 stone farmhouse in the village of New Jerusalem. Though I was later raised farther south in the state of Maryland, there were frequent visits to the old Pennsylvania farmhouse, and every Christmas my parents and sister and I gathered with my aunts and uncles and cousins in my grandmother's bustling kitchen and oversize living room to eat and laugh and celebrate another year.

At these gatherings, my Aunt Fay and her husband Steve Marko planted the seeds of inspiration for my travels to exotic lands. They shared stories of their adventures in Nepal, Tibet, India, Eastern Europe, and later Portugal and Morocco. I dreamed of one day visiting all such lands.

My strongly accented grandmother and her fieldstone farmhouse, both well-built, enduring, and strong in character, together formed an integral part of the foundation of my formative years. Despite my bucolic beginnings, I felt a westward pull. As writer William Least Heat-Moon mused, "the open road is a beckoning, a strangeness, a place where man can be himself." I understood this calling. I had always been curious about the larger world.

By my late teens I began to crave the anonymity of the road. I longed to lose myself amidst the mass of humanity, be stripped to my bare essence, and learn something about myself that I had been unable to while living at home. In my early twenties my family versus freedom dilemma emerged. Recently, another larger question had been gnawing at me that I had been so far unable to fully grasp. These threads, I knew, were why I had found myself amongst this assortment of bus riding strangers.

"I'm from around here," I said to the teenager after a long pause, "but heading west. I've got some things to sort out." He nodded and left me to my thoughts as the bus droned on through gathering gloom and into the heart of Appalachia. The setting sun lit up a deep-gray wisp of cloud atop the next looming ridge like a crown of glory.

During the night, the Greyhound crossed the Susquehanna River. Soon after I was born, my parents brought me to their tumble-down mobile trailer home along the river's banks. We lived together in the doublewide while my father attended college in nearby Selinsgrove. My mother often swam in the broad waters before driving to her nursing job in her '57 Volkswagen Beetle. That fall we relocated to Penn State where Dad began a two-year stint studying animal behavior. Afterward, we moved to Michigan for two years so he could complete his education in ecology. Following his graduation, we returned to Pennsylvania with my new baby sister in tow.

As recession swept the land and with job prospects slim, my parents rented a shabby farmhouse down the road from my grandmother's 1820 stone farmhouse. Across the two-lane stood a house my grandmother's parents once owned, which was a couple cornfields away from the farm my grandfather's parents tended in the 1940s.

Nine months later, my father landed a position in Maryland. With that prospect, the four of us relocated to a cedar shake farmhouse on three acres a half-dozen miles south of the Mason-Dixon Line, an eighteenth-century surveying marvel that separates Maryland from Pennsylvania.

Aboard the Greyhound, nothing indicated our bus was rolling parallel to the historic boundary. Yet it was there, I knew, and I wondered how different my life would have been had we stayed on the Pennsylvania side. Would I speak remnants of the dialect peculiar to my Dutch-Deutsch kin? Would I crave scrapple and boova shenkel and all things sour?

My thoughts shifted to the part of Maryland I had recently left behind—the area where I grew up and my parents still lived. Our farmhouse centered in the heart of the Piedmont. From *pied*, French for foot, and *mont*, hill, the rolling foothills retained a mix of forest, farms, and rural folk, but did not quell my parents' penchant for travel.

Most weekends we explored a new corner of our adopted state. On summer vacations we packed the baby blue 1978 Chevy Malibu Classic station wagon and toured another slice of America—New England one year, the Deep South another, eastern Canada once, back to Maine, and out West twice.

The trip that most changed my life was our six-week drive across the country. For that journey, Dad transformed an empty Ford cargo van into a comfortable, carpeted paradise. The Piedmont's undulations paled compared to jagged snow-covered spires of the continent's backbone, and I knew at age thirteen that I must one day live near mountains like the northern Rockies.

When the Greyhound driver hit his brakes too hard I was jolted back to the present. As the bus rolled through the darkness, I contemplated the events that had brought me west.

The year prior, at age twenty-six, I had worked my first summer in Alaska as a bartender at a remote lodge on the banks of the Nenana River. A co-worker, Barbara, flew home before the season ended but left her car behind. She asked if I would drive her silver Probe from Alaska and return the car to her in Oregon. It was an opportunity to explore the length of the Alaska Highway, and I eagerly accepted.

After dropping off the Probe I met Barbara's friend Hilery, who needed to get to Seattle to retrieve her Volkswagen microbus. We three road tripped up the coast together, skinny-dipping at hot springs and sharing our poems along the way. Upon arriving in Seattle I met Hilery's friend Geo, who showed us the underground party scene and hip happenings.

A few weeks later, in early October, I boarded the train and returned to the East Coast. I soon reunited with Tamara, my on-again, off-again girlfriend. My departure for Alaska had driven a wedge between us. I had dreamt of visiting Alaska for years, but my time there still felt to her like abandonment. Over the following winter, Tamara and I fell apart again. We seemed unable to get past our differences.

She wanted commitment and the sound of small children squealing in the backyard. So did I, but too often, other sounds distracted me. Lyrical sirens beckoning me from the road promised adventure and exoticism. Sometimes, I felt compelled to leave behind the woman who loved me. In time the siren songs would fade, the yearning for nurturing would grow, and Tamara and I would reunite. And again, the sirens would beckon. I knew the pattern could not endure. I wanted a family, and craved the love Tamara offered. I also wanted freedom to explore new horizons.

In late spring, she moved to Boulder, Colorado. I was stunned. Prior to a road trip we had made together two summers prior, she had never been west of West Virginia. On that joint venture we had visited our friends Bob and Matt while driving to Montana in my parents' Ford van. When Bob later invited Tamara to visit him and Matt in Boulder, she thought a change might do her good.

Though we were not together it felt as though she had left me, and I fretted over my options. One day I took action. I locked my third floor apartment, abandoned my broken Chrysler on the corner, and boarded the Greyhound that I found myself sitting upon.

Sometime in the night, the hiss of airbrakes woke me. Cabin lights came up, and a few passengers stirred. The teenager grabbed his gear, nodded to me, and exited to change buses. I continued to the end of the line, and two days later found myself back in Seattle.

Geo took me in, and together we explored the city's rave scene. One night we ventured to an all-night bonfire in the outlying hills. A six-foot, ebony-skinned, budding shaman sporting orange striped coveralls, black-framed glasses, and twirling dreadlocks danced around the flames much of the night. In early morning hours we struck up a conversation. Glenn was drawn to myth, tribal tradition, and the spiritual arts. He sought to uncover ancient ways of knowing largely forgotten by western culture. Over coming weeks at Capitol Hill coffee shops and downtown markets, Glenn also shared tales of Mexico, a place I had not visited or given much thought.

"Let's meet in Monterrey," he said one morning over coffee

as if suggesting a movie to watch. After considering this idea for a few minutes, I agreed to meet him in one month in the northern Mexican metropolis.

The next evening, I tried to call Tamara at Bob and Matt's house using Geo's touch-tone telephone. After several more attempts, I reached her. She sounded well. She agreed to my proposed visit, so a few days later I backtracked by bus from Seattle to Bozeman, then down to Boulder. On my way there I considered cancelling my plans with Glenn.

When I arrived, however, I found Tamara immersed in the summer social scene. We were not entirely off it seemed, but not quite on. With Tamara distracted by admirers, I opted to keep my promise to Glenn.

After a few days in Boulder, I hopscotched by bus to San Diego, walked across the bridge spanning the Río Tijuana, traveled to the bottom of Baja, boated across the Sea of Cortez, and negotiated the northern deserts to Monterrey.

I met Glenn at the airport, and after visiting his friends Triunfo and Martina, the two of us made a side trip. From the main road, a narrower one of flattened cobble-like stones ventured beyond the village of Matehuala. The road wound through the desert past burros and chickens and shacks where passengers on occasion stepped on or off the decrepit bus that shook enough, as Glenn noted, to mix a can of paint. We climbed into the mountains along cliff edges as slanting rays of afternoon sun cast long shadows over distant plains and arid foothills. At a tunnel entrance we stopped, and boarded a smaller bus to negotiate the dim mile and a half hand-cut rock and dirt passageway.

As we emerged from the other end of the tunnel, darkness descended upon the ruins of Real de Catorce. Named for fourteen royal Spanish soldiers killed long ago by Chichimeca warriors, the silver mining town once held a theater, bullring, mint, import shops, and forty thousand residents. When the price of silver plummeted the cobblestone streets fell silent, Catorceños abandoned their stone homes, and nopal cacti sprouted from creviced walls. Pilgrims still flocked to the statue depicting Saint Francis of Assisi housed inside La Parroquia de la Purísima Concepción cathedral, hopeful he would cure their ailments. The few hundred villagers remaining in Real mostly catered to this annual influx.

At the first boarding house, or *hostal*, we asked if any rooms remained. A man lit a match and led us to the basement. Some boys followed us, and we asked them if they knew of other rooms, perhaps one with electricity. A bent old man in a nearby doorway told them he and his wife had one for sixty pesos. We took the room.

In the hallway I chatted with a young woman from Monterrey named Sarah. Outside on the street corner her brother Paco and his girlfriend Maríe congregated with a few other locals. All had gathered in Real for the Independence Day holiday. Maríe offered us homemade tuna casserole. Paco and I shared Mexican cigarettes. We each took turns over the next few hours dashing to the cramped shop one street over to buy oversize bottles of local beer, and drank and smoked and talked as though we had known each other all our lives.

Evening settled upon us, and beneath the brilliance of a full moon we all left the corner and drifted past intricate stone walls and crumbling ruins to Plaza Hidalgo. There, locals and Mexican visitors milled about in preparation for the evening's festivities. A line of musicians filed past. One woman sold mescal Jell-O shooters. When two officials stepped into the plaza gazebo, the crowd gathered closer. At eleven, after a few words, everyone shouted "Viva Méjico!" over and over.

Afterward, Sarah led me to the abandoned bullring and pulled from her bag bottles of Squirt and vodka. Claudia, a shapely twenty-one-year-old brunette with deep brown eyes, joined us. She spoke English as well as Spanish, and was learning French. Claudia and I talked into the night.

"I want to see the world," she said as the eastern horizon brightened. "But if I do not marry by twenty-three, my family will be angry."

"Why?" I asked.

She shrugged. "It is the way of my country."

"I too want to see the world," I murmured. Thanks to my upbringing I had seen much of my own land, but there were many others yet to explore. I had never wanted a desk job or nine to five routine, or to work for the weekends and loathe my weekdays. I did not want to frequent tourist spots, comb souvenir shops, or sleep at resorts.

What I wanted was to be a traveler. I yearned for a life of simplicity and exploration. I wanted to live out of a rucksack and lose myself in other countries and sleep in places few had ever heard of. I wanted to immerse myself in other cultures and meet people different from me and be submerged in their languages and ideas and histories. Yet like Claudia, I worried that I would stop before really starting. I did not want to lose Tamara, but wondered how long she would wait. It seemed Claudia and I faced a similar dilemma.

Sarah and the others had disappeared. Claudia and I wandered back to the *hostal* but found the entrance locked for the night. We threw pebbles at Paco's window until Maríe unlocked the heavy wooden door from inside to let us in.

The next evening Glenn and I met at a restaurant around the corner. Sarah and Paco and Maríe and Claudia were just leaving, but invited us to their sparse yet spacious shared room for coffee. As the grounds brewed, the moon rose beside the nearby cathedral steeple.

We talked of life's yearnings. Glenn shared an allegory, as was his nature, which he attributed to Kahlil Gibran. Once, Glenn began, there was a pansy who longed to be a rose. The other pansies ridiculed him. "You should be content with your lot in life," the queen of the pansies said, "and be happy." The pansy was undeterred. He longed to see sights and treasures lying beyond the garden wall, and prayed to the gods of nature that his wish be granted.

One day his dream came true, and he became one of the roses, swaying in the breeze, looking upon another world. He had never been happier.

An hour later a windstorm swept through the garden and toppled all the roses. Being so low to the ground, the pansies were spared. The queen chided the pansy. "You ought to have been happy as a pansy," she told him. He was not convinced. There are some things in life worth dying for, he believed, and he possessed the courage to not be content with what he was allotted. He had seen sights the other pansies never would, and for that he was grateful. He held no regret as he lay dying in the garden.

"That is tragic," Sarah said, "and lovely." She turned to me. "What do you want from life?"

I thought a moment. I too wanted to be a rose, and be true to myself. I tended to seek approval, try to please others to gain acceptance, and place my own ambitions last. I no longer wanted to be like that. I wanted to follow my heart.

"I want to see sights I've never imagined before," I said. "And when I come home, be loved for who I am. That might be all I really want."

2

RENACIMIENTO

Glenn and I parted, and from the village of Real de Catorce I circled north to Boulder to reunite with Tamara for a friend's wedding. Afterward, we both returned to the East Coast to pick up where we had left off months before. She still wanted children, more than ever. Her prospects with me remained risky, however. I craved the road even more, and she feared further abandonment. Over the winter, Tamara and I again fell apart. By spring, she found someone else.

One day, Glenn telephoned. "Meet me in Monterrey," he said. After contemplating this for a few days, I again agreed to meet him there in a month. A couple weeks later Tamara heard I had already left for Mexico, but intercepted me on my way out of town.

"Guess I'll see you in six months," she said. This time, I was unsure. I knew one of us needed to break our pattern.

I had decided to detour to New York City on my way to Mexico, for Central Park can be delectable in spring. My childhood friend Frank dropped me at the Baltimore station, where I shook his hand and said good-bye.

A few hours later in New York I found a bunk in a sparse hostel hidden on a Chelsea side street. Franco, a Basque, sat on the bunk above mine. We traded our backstories. While he wrote in my notebook, I contemplated the auspicious transition from Frank to Franco, from the familial to the unfamiliar.

"Toby Mexikora daa hillabete pasatzera. Espero dut ongi egongo dela," Franco had jotted. *Toby is going to Mexico for a month. I hope he will be alright.*

I later researched the Basque language. I learned that the Indo-European family of languages includes English, Spanish, Hindi, Portuguese, Bengali, Russian, and hundreds of others all descended from a common ancestor. Euskara, as the Basques call their tongue, is a language isolate, in that it has no known link to any other language. A few other isolates remain in the world because all languages related to them went extinct, but Euskara consists only of itself, with no known relatives, extinct or extant.

Franco too was an isolate, I thought. Even in New York, a melting pot mecca of eight million, he was one of a handful speaking Euskara.

The next afternoon I wished Franco well and resolved to visit him if I found myself in the Pyrenees Mountains. An hour later I boarded a Greyhound bound for Cleveland. At four in the morning I transferred to another, which stopped at Columbus and Dayton. I waited in Cincinnati. Next, my bus continued into Kentucky.

Elvis memorabilia cluttered the Memphis gift shop. Bloody derelicts staggered past the staging area. One of them offered me his neon green Walkman for five dollars, which I declined. Outside, an old guy muttered about the cops who beat him up and took his watch and money. Another detailed how often dead bodies turned up in Las Vegas highway medians, how he once got carjacked there, and that last week these guys in New York tried to sell him crack and prostitutes.

A southbound at last departed Memphis, but crammed into the seat, the night was long with few snatches of sleep. When the company lost the Laredo-bound bus, I waited impatient in Dallas at half past six in the morning. Long ragged lines filed past towards Miami and Los Angeles with departure times well after mine. Finally my bus called at Laredo. After walking across the litter-strewn riverbed via the bustling border bridge and into Nuevo Laredo, I found a mangled mini-bus along the Guerrero thoroughfare and made Monterrey by nightfall.

Glenn and I reunited, and after visiting Triunfo and Martina we traveled much of the night to once again reach Real de Catorce, this time for Easter Sunday. On the way we found bits of sleep beneath a full moon. From the village of Matehuala, we climbed into distant silhouettes. At the far end of the tunnel, golden Maxfield Parrish-like lighting bathed the mountaintops while bells atop La Parroquia cathedral chimed.

We camped this time. After pitching our tent outside town beyond the bullring and uphill from the abandoned church and old graveyard, we returned downtown for coffee. Mexican hippies sold jewelry on the corner. Locals rode past on mules. Music emanated from a lone decrepit car. Two teenage girls curious about Glenn, the *negrito* as locals called him, asked to take our photo.

An ex-pat traveling alone around Mexico in her Volkswagen van stopped to talk. "I left Germany in '72," Doris told me as she brushed aside a shock of blonde hair offsetting sharp features. "I've traveled all over this world over the years, but I'm not finished searching. God knows I've walked away from a few relationships because they were stifling. What I seek is someone who can be there and love me for who I am. Yet let me breathe when I need to." I nodded. I wanted that too.

As Doris continued on her way, I was reminded that something else—that same indescribable something I had felt on the Greyhound bus—had been tugging harder at me. The essence of that yearning, I noticed, felt more within reach in Real. Perhaps some part of the answer awaited me in this crumbling Mexican village.

The memory of my mother pulling weeds from one of her flowerbeds came to mind. My eight-year-old self stopped to watch her work.

"Mom," I had asked. "Is there a God?"

"Of course," she said. "God is everywhere."

I was not so sure.

Twenty years later I asked my father what he thought. "Of course there's a higher power," he said. His answer surprised me. He was a scientist and rationalist, after all.

I was baptized as a Lutheran, yet had never believed in the idea of a single, all-powerful God. I had also never accepted that a man executed by the Romans was the Son of God who chose to die for my sins. I did not doubt that Jesus actually existed. I believed that a Jewish carpenter was born in a stable, wandered about with a message of peace and love, and for political reasons was crucified by Pontius Pilate. I also believed that some version of the stories in the Bible occurred. As Huston Smith in *The World's Religions* points out, Christianity "is founded not on abstract principles but in concrete events, actual historical happenings." However, since I never accepted Jesus as the path to salvation, I had not identified myself as a Christian since pre-adolescence.

Life is a complicated journey, and billions of us rely upon religion for meaning. It is all the extras—gods, figureheads, rituals, and rules—that people attach to the divine that did not resonate with me. I felt that whatever entity created the earth and sky and this and all universes is beyond human comprehension and description. Since humans need a way to reference the indescribable, I grew comfortable with whichever terms people agreed upon. For me, "God" or "Allah" or "Brahma" or "higher power" were interchangeable.

Yet, I realized that while an incomprehensible, description-defying creator of universes appealed to my rational sensibilities, the explanation left my soul wanting. A lack of meaning and purpose had begun to plague me. I saw little sense in ambition or achievement. If we live this one short life and nothing afterward remains, I wondered, why strive for greatness? I worried that my life was evolving into one of futility and emptiness.

The hippies packed and left the ruins of Real. Another German, Olaf, happened past. Thin but well-built, a mass of unkempt hair perched atop the trimmed sideburns framing his chiseled face. A single yellowed tooth amidst his otherwise perfect set served as subtle reminder that even Germans are imperfect.

While we chatted, a man driving a battered gray Land Rover stopped on the cobblestones. "Iremos al desierto mañana, a las ocho," he said through the open window. *We'll go to the desert tomorrow, at eight.*

He continued onward. As Glenn explained, the faithful flocking to Saint Francis inside La Parroquia cathedral were not the only pilgrims traveling to Real. From the language of the ancient Aztecs came *peyotl,* from which derives the name of a small, spineless cactus. The peyote crown consists of disc-shaped buttons containing a psychoactive alkaloid called mescaline. For more than five thousand years local Tonkawa, Mescalero, Lipan Apache, and later Comanche and Kiowa had gathered the hallucinogenic cactus from surrounding highlands. The Huichol still pilgrimage to Real.

Modern-day seekers could hire trucks for journeys over winding rock-strewn tracks deep into the desert. After hours riding in back on a hard wooden bench, pilgrims walked into the emptiness and upon finding a crown chewed the button or boiled it into a tea. Hopefully, the driver returned the next day.

As one shaman has explained, peyote is the crossing of the souls. It is everything there is. Without peyote, nothing would exist. Native Americans treated toothaches, pain in childbirth, fever, skin diseases, rheumatism, diabetes, and blindness with peyote. It was effective against a dozen strains of penicillin-resistant bacteria. Members of the <u>Native American Church</u> <u>who ate the cactus</u> during all-night communal sessions did not feel a high, but rather <u>underwent intense inward reflection.</u>

As we walked back to camp, I wondered whether this was the reason I had returned to Real. Olaf threw his sleeping bag into the dirt and I lit a small fire of dried cactus that flared then flickered. We listened to the silence, until a dusty white pickup raced into our camp. A ragged band of Mexicans descended. *What are your names?* We wondered who they were too, until one flashed a La Policia identification card. *Where are you from? Do you have marijuana?* We shook our heads. *Peyote?* No. *Anything?* Nothing.

Fear flashed through me. We had broken no laws that we knew of. Desert wind blew Olaf's sleeping mat into the fire as they frisked and searched us. Two of the men grabbed the mat and pinned it down with rocks. After I emptied my pockets, a man placed each coin one at a time back into the pouch. Glenn produced a ticket stub, ten pesos, and an expired condom. At first the man did not know what the latter was, but then laughed. The raid was over.

A Mexican version of the Keystone Kops pushed their truck from the sand, after getting it stuck and it almost not starting from leaving the lights on, and left. Much relieved, I smiled as we settled back into the sands. The eastern sky brightened, stars faded, and the brilliant orb of a full moon eased above the ridgeline. This sacred Wírikuta, as the Huichol call the desert around Real, held endless surprise. The Huichol believe the world was created at Wírikuta, and is where the sun made its first appearance. Likewise, I could not imagine what the next appearance of the sun might bring.

Doris joined Olaf and Glenn and I downtown at nine the next morning. The man in the gray Land Rover reappeared. We will meet instead at ten, he said. Another man in a bluish Land Cruiser asked if we wished to go into the desert.

We debated what to do. The previous night around the fire,

we had discussed the idea of pilgrimaging into the desert. The journey sounded tempting, but we felt unprepared and ill-equipped. We carried limited gear, and the sun and heat could be punishing.

Two Italians chanced along. As the four of us conferred, the Italians loaded the gray Land Rover. Though cheaper, the driver of the gray Land Rover took passengers to a village halfway out, from where seekers must arrange their own transportation deeper into the desert. Whether or not the Italians understood this was unclear.

"Vámonos!" called the driver of the bluish Land Cruiser. *Let's go!*

Feeling rushed, we decided the journey was not for us. A young woman sat nearby. Glenn and the young woman conferred. "Don't worry," she said to him. "The desert always provides. You may undergo your journey here."

I met Olaf, Doris, and Glenn in the shade of the solitary tree at our camp. From our vantage, we could see a nearby dirt path that branched into the barren mountains like gnarled tree roots. Now and then locals on foot or upon mules trudged into the emptiness. In the distance, a farmer and his mule plowed a patch of seared land, back and forth, beneath the brunt of high desert sun. We settled into the sand and partook of the gift that the young woman had bestowed upon us.

Glenn had told me earlier about the Huichol who believed that during peyote rituals they interacted with fire, deer, and eagle ancestor spirits, part of their trinity of Corn, Blue Deer, and Peyote deities descended from the sun god Tao Jreeku. As animists they saw no separation between the spiritual and material worlds.

"Souls exist in humans, animals, plants, rocks, mountains, and rivers," Glenn had said. Anything, even a stone, contained a resident spirit able to evoke or address a question.

I wondered whether the abandoned church, alone and empty, held any answers for me. I left the group, descended the hillside, and drifted over a stone path leading into the old graveyard. Sun-bleached gravestones leaned in all directions or lay flat atop the dirt. The church interior felt cool and eerie. Wind rattled a loose door and broken window. For a moment the ceiling breathed. Faded angels and saints on the peeling walls came alive. With wings flapping, they shook their fingers in admonishment. Amidst the wind's moans rose the voices of the heralds circling overhead. All asked the same question—the very one that had been plaguing me for so many months.

Far off, I heard bells of La Parroquia cathedral chime in commemoration of Easter Sunday. The peals reminded me of the statue of Saint Francis housed within La Parroquia, to which the other brand of pilgrim in Real gravitated. In the thirteenth century, Saint Francis created the first live Christmas Nativity scene. Within a hundred years every church in Italy displayed one. Hand-painted *santons* grew popular in Provence; in Germany and Austria figurines were cut from wood; Poland favored elaborate *szopka*; the Pennsylvania Dutch *putz* evolved into elaborate villages. In Mexico, depictions of the *Nacimiento*—Spanish for Nativity—filled entire rooms with hundreds of hand-made clay, wax, and wooden figures.

The devout streaming into La Parroquia on Easter Sunday celebrated Christ for a similar reason that Christians displayed Christmas Nativity scenes. Easter marked Christ's rebirth, or a divine *Renacimiento*.

Glenn and I had also talked about the world before the rise of the world's dominant religions, when every tribe celebrated its own set of timeworn practices. Various versions of shamanism, of which peyote ritual was one remnant, permeated all indigenous cultures and served as a milestone roadmap. Among the most important ceremonies were those which initiated the child into adulthood as part of a symbolic rebirth, or individual *renacimiento*.

Doris waited in the old graveyard while I stood inside the abandoned church. When I returned outside, we rested in the shade of a stone wall. My mind reeled. The mountain swirled. A crooked tree nearby transformed into an oversized ostrich and ran away. Two Mexicans riding past on a single mule trotted into one wall, bumped into another, and laughed as they zigzagged over the hill and into the desert. The mountain shuddered and sighed.

I told Doris what I had seen.

"What did the voices say?" she asked.

"They said 'what will you choose?'"

I understood the heralds' message. Though I had rejected Christian dogma, perhaps there was another option that would better connect with me. Every historical religion contained a core message worth contemplating. The heralds, in essence my manifested subconscious, were right. I must make a choice.

Hands, feet, and clothes covered in wind-blown sand and hair caked in dust, we climbed the hill to find Glenn and Olaf laughing in the shade. The farmer still plowed as we feasted on oranges and papaya. Olaf mashed an overripe banana and avocado together with a squeeze of lime.

"Oh, der grilled banana would be *so* good," he said again. He couldn't get the idea out of his mind.

Atop the barren ridge above our encampment, the wind at times blew strong enough to hold us upright if we leaned into it. Primordial mists clung to surrounding valley walls. With Doris and I as witness, Glenn and Olaf danced naked in the breeze as the sun sank into a brilliant orange haze.

At first light, Glenn and I said good-bye to Olaf and Doris. We missed by minutes the bus back through the tomb-like tunnel, the only way into or out of Real by road, so we walked instead through the tunnel. On occasion a dangling bulb provided some light, but mostly we groped our way through the darkness. When the dirt-covered walls shook from passing vehicles, we hugged the walls with inches to spare.

In time a point of light appeared. Blinded, disoriented, and bloodied where the rocks had cut us, we emerged from the tunnel mouth under the gaze of open-mouthed Mexicans. Strangely, neither of us recalled entering the narrow passage days before by bus. It truly felt as though everything had begun in the womb of Wirikuta.

When we reached the village of Matehuala, Glenn turned north to Monterrey and I south towards an uncertain future. In San Luis Potosí, I scrambled aboard an overcrowded second-class Mexico City-bound train. I glided through desert browned by searing sun. At each stop dozens of vendors selling snacks and vegetables turned the stifling carriage into a madhouse. One boy fingered a bass guitar. His younger brother played rhythm. Evening sun drifted into orange dust-filled clouds. The lights of the carriage did not work, so we sat in the darkness. Often the locomotive sat idle on the sidings as lengthy working trains snaked past with a hypnotic clicking of the wheels. Mexican pop played from kids' boom boxes deep into the night.

When someone yelled "Méjico!" I drifted from a dream. The carriage stood empty. I climbed down from the deserted train and walked into the station. The hands on the clock read three twenty, so I lay on one of the hard wooden waiting room benches to await sleep.

There were few others I knew who would give up a comfortable apartment, quit a decent job, sell their car, put everything into storage, say good-bye to family and friends, and board a bus bound for Mexico with no concrete idea of what was to come. I had no trust fund, no inheritance, and little money, but also no debt. Apolitical by nature, agnostic, and recently free of all organizational affiliations, I was in many ways a blank slate.

"I could not simplify myself," explained the suicidal Nezhdanov in Turgenev's *Virgin Soil*. We cling to our attachments, thus life grows increasingly cluttered unless we manage our beliefs and belongings. Like Franco the Basque, I was an isolate. Like Saint Francis, I leaned towards simplicity. Like the ancients, I yearned for transformation. I was not sure where I was going or what my choices were, but knew I wanted to be one of Glenn's roses and see what lay beyond the garden wall. It seemed my own *renacimiento* had begun.

3

THE TRANCENDENTALISTS

From Mexico City, I made my way to Oaxaca. After a few days in the fishing village of San Agustinillo on the edge of the Pacific, I ventured to Chiapas. In Guatemala, I wandered from Totonicapán to Lake Atitlán, and across El Petén to Tikal. The only way out of Guatemala without backtracking overland through the vast jungle of El Petén was to hire a boat for a journey down the Río Usumacinta. On the Mexican side of the river, I circled north from Palenque towards the border.

Eventually I worked my way back to Boulder. "Stay here!" friends said when I arrived. I was tempted, and debated whether to continue to Alaska. My previous decision to go there continued to divide Tamara and me.

Yet, Alaska still made my heart beat faster. Twenty-four hour daylight, snowy peaks that reflected light from a hidden sun at two in the morning, the stillness, or a sudden appearance of Northern Lights in late August—all such marvels drew me onward. I heard the sirens call again. I repacked my gear, and headed to the northern frontier.

I spent the rainy summer living in a one-room twelve by

twelve-foot wood frame cabin without running water that nestled amongst white and black spruce of the outer Alaska Range. At over twenty thousand feet, North America's highest peak reigned over the region. Indigenous Athapaskans called her Denali.

Huge, grand, and magnificent, Alaska brimmed with mountains, glaciers, wolves, caribou, luminous skies, rainbows, oil, gold, salmon, individuality, solitude, space, and great bodies of water. The land of midnight sun was not for everyone. For some, she was everything.

Yet magnificence can also come in smaller forms, including placid pools such as Walden Pond where Henry David Thoreau sought his own identity. "I went to the woods because I wished to live deliberately," the nineteenth-century author wrote in *Walden*. His words inspired me, and I tried to do likewise in the Alaskan wilderness. I longed, as Thoreau wanted, "to front only the essential facts of life, and see if I could not learn what it had to teach, and not, when I came to die, discover that I had not lived. I did not wish to live what was not life, living is so dear; nor did I wish to practise resignation, unless it was quite necessary."

Another of Thoreau's notions—that a man who does not keep pace with his companions perhaps hears a different drummer—accompanied my long walks in the mountains. Through the summer, I wondered just which path I would follow—a traditional work ethic, or a perpetual search for relevance through travel.

Thoreau's own journey began at Harvard College, I recalled, where he discovered the writings of Ralph Waldo Emerson. Emerson had followed in the footsteps of his Unitarian minister father, who died of stomach cancer when Emerson was eight. Later, two of Emerson's younger brothers died of tuberculosis, and when his first wife died at age twenty only two years into their marriage, also of tuberculosis, doubts crept in to undermine his faith.

As Virginia Hanson in *The Sage From Concord* notes, Emerson thought it unwise and unnatural to belong to any religion, and ultimately he was unable to conform to traditional orthodoxy. At age twenty-six, he resigned from his ministry.

I had sidestepped the misfortunes that Emerson experienced, but his crisis of faith intrigued me. Traditional religions had never resonated with me, and I found no comfort in their teachings. I had never found a cause, or faith, worth choosing. By not choosing, I felt incomplete. This emptiness made the question posed by the heralds in the abandoned church feel all the more urgent. It seemed that my doubts had provoked a journey of discovery.

Emerson's doubts led him to writing. After a period of reflection he published *Nature*, which laid the foundation for America's first significant intellectual movement—transcendentalism. As Virginia Hanson observes, the New England Transcendentalists—of which Emerson was the guiding spirit—gave impetus to America's intellectual and spiritual foundation, without which the new nation would still surely be impoverished.

Emerson's meetings with like-minded intellectuals gave rise to the Transcendental Club. Among them were Margaret Fuller, who encouraged prison reform and the emancipation of slaves, championed education and employment rights for women, and published the first major feminist writings in America. Near the end of a return voyage to America, Fuller's ship struck a sandbar and she and her husband and son were lost at sea. Emerson sent his friend, Henry David Thoreau, to search the shore but only the boy's body was ever found.

Grandson of the leader of the first student protest in the American colonies, Thoreau found no inspiration in law, clergy, or business. When Thoreau contributed his first essays and poems to Emerson's periodical *The Dial*, they were revised passages from journals he had kept at Emerson's suggestion. Thoreau took another of Emerson's ideas to heart when he moved into a small, self-built cabin along the banks of Walden Pond, where he wrote his signature work, *Walden*.

In Emerson's closing years he traveled west and there met John Muir. From Emerson's perspective, Muir was the prophet-naturalist he had long hoped for. Muir became known as the patron saint of the American wilderness and motivated presidents and Congress to preserve landscapes that have inspired millions.

These and other leaders comprised the spiritual heart of transcendentalism. This informal protest against culture and society maintained that reality could only be understood through intuition and the study of nature, for nature existed over, and was larger than, God. People must remove themselves from society's distractions, and through solitude and immersion in nature, awaken their spiritual awareness. Transcendentalists believed that people are at their best when self-reliant, independent, and whole with nature. On the other hand institutions—political parties, corporations, and organized religion—corrupt the individual.

The idea that social institutions could prevent the individual from reaching his or her natural potential became a cornerstone of my thinking. I embraced other thinkers, such as Franco-Swiss philosopher Jean-Jacques Rousseau. This concept from *The Social Contract* stands among his most enduring and gets to the heart of the matter most bluntly: man is born free, yet everywhere is in chains. In plain words, institutions thrive on control.

To be fair, humans have sought protection since the dawn of civilization from the suffering that war, disease, and famine bring. In time the palace guaranteed economic stability, the market offered goods and leisure, and the temple promised salvation. As all three evolved, they set heroes upon pedestals for worship by the masses and interwove their lives with myth so followers had role models to aspire towards. George Washington, Henry Ford, and Jesus come to mind. All institutions branded themselves with symbols and slogans, maintained bureaucracies, provided public assistance through education, philanthropy, or aid, and purchased real estate whether museums, malls, or mosques. All sought new followers, whether by conquering territory, advertising, or proselytizing. And all came with a price. The palace provided safety but imposed taxes, the market traded products for currency, and the temple offered immortality for a donation.

The history of civilization is the saga of these three institutions struggling for control, and the story of factions within each battling amongst themselves. The structures that rose above all others–whether the government-built pyramids at Giza, business-oriented skyscrapers of New York, or Catholic cathedrals in Rome–often reveal which institution dominated an era. In Christian lore even the Son of God struggled to overcome political, economic, and spiritual hurdles, for these three were the temptations of Christ.

In the modern era the state, corporation, and church still compose the infrastructure of society. All three require control over the individual in order to implement an agenda. By submitting, the individual gains a measure of security. Of the three, not unlike the transcendentalists, the church troubled me most. Too much proselytizing and too many examples of intolerance and murder in the name of a supernatural being had jaded me. For me, hypocrisy had come to outweigh the potential benefits of any historical faith.

Yet I wondered whether I had left some stone unturned. I suspected there might be more to religion than what sermons, books, and the media revealed. The heralds circling above me in the abandoned church had reinvigorated me. I wanted to experience firsthand the options available to me. I was looking for meaning in my life, and I wondered if perhaps one of the religious traditions might have an answer. I was ready to make a choice, but first needed to understand my options.

The short Alaskan summer soon wound down. Pockets of quaking aspen blazed golden amongst the spruce. Crimson tundra shrouded the lower flanks of snow-shrouded peaks. Labrador tea, prickly rose, and dwarf dogwood had long ceased flowering. By mid-September, the lodge and lounge where I worked were empty and the surrounding area abandoned but for a few hardy residents hunkered in outlying hills. The icy cold of a forty below zero winter would soon follow, and I did not relish that thought.

On the first of October I hitched a ride to Anchorage. Denali's icy sheen loomed against a blue bird sky. That night, through the taxi window en route to the airport, Northern Lights fluttered overhead.

While awaiting my outbound flight, my thoughts reverted to the heralds' question. The closest I had yet come to making a choice was the ancient Chinese philosophy Taoism. In a secondhand Seattle bookshop two years earlier, I had stumbled upon a translation of the *Tao Te Ching* by fifth-century BCE poet Lao Tzu. His Taoist philosophy struck a chord with me.

"The Tao is the way," Lao Tzu writes. Too vast for human comprehension, the Tao transcends all and cannot be perceived. "The farther you go, the less you know. Thus the sage knows without traveling; he sees without looking; he works without doing."

As Huston Smith describes in *The World's Religions*, water best describes the way of Tao. Supple though strong, water finds the path of least resistance yet carries mountains away. To embody these strengths is to act without strain and persuade without argument. Taoism's rejection of competition, position, and fame spoke to me. Like transcendentalism, Taoism sought harmony with nature, not dominance. Animist traditions and ancient Eastern traditions had long taught that nature and humanity could coexist—a concept I firmly believed.

The passive essence of the Tao, however, left me yearning. I needed a more assertive life philosophy. Unlike the sage, I needed to go into the world to find answers, and I was ready to travel to the ends of the earth to find them.

The East still held promise as a source of answers. A non-credit comparative religion class I had taken at a local community college sparked my interest in Buddhism. The Buddha taught that anyone could reach enlightenment in a single lifetime. His teachings encouraged a self-directed inner search, rather than reliance upon an invisible godhead for salvation. Perhaps the Buddha's teachings might provide a worthy path, I thought. To find out, I must witness practice in action. As Smith explains, original Buddhism, more philosophy than religion, demands such validation. On any question, the Buddha taught direct personal experience as the best test of any truth.

Since Buddhism originated in Asia, I decided my search must begin there. I picked Bangkok, Thailand as my Asian gateway on the grounds of affordability. The one-way four hundred-dollar fare was cheaper than any Southeast Asian destination. From there, it seemed I should be able to delve deeper into Asia.

I boarded the Bangkok-bound 747 with a mixture of trepidation and excitement. I wondered what my friends and family thought of me. Was my search worthy? Would I find any answers?

Onboard, striking Chinese attendants scurried about in skirts with long slits up the sides. When they had trouble getting a bag of rolls from an overhead cabinet, two of them asked me for help. I retrieved the bag with a pair of tongs.

"Oh, you my hero!" one said as the other laughed.

I returned to my seat, and partly inspired by the slit skirts bustling past, thought of Tamara. Before I left, she had tracked down the phone number of the lounge in Alaska where I worked. She called towards the end of one early autumn evening shift.

"Take me with you," she said. Another round of on-again drama loomed, I thought.

From the Old French *travaillier,* to torment, and the Middle English *travail*–to toil or make a laborious journey–the word *travel* originated as a Late Latin word for a Roman torture rack. For most of history, travel was a perilous endeavor. As in days of yore, I sensed a toilsome journey ahead. "One," I told Tamara, "best undertaken alone." For now, I decided, the freedom to seek out my answers must outweigh my notions of family.

Strauss' *Blue Danube* played through the speakers as cobalt-hued ocean passed beneath. Rows of cloud stretched towards bands of orange and yellow. Eventually, lights from cities of Japan slipped past. When the sun rose and cloud tops turned pink, we approached Taiwan. After a pause in Hong Kong, we passed Vietnam. To the northwest loomed the Himalaya, where even Denali would stand unnoticed. Beyond the highest mountains on earth stretched the Tibetan Plateau.

As the plane descended towards the nation of Thailand, a place of new mystery for me, a familiar transcendental adage that had accompanied me on my long walks through Alaska's mountains played in my mind.

"Go confidently in the direction of your dreams," Thoreau recommended. "Live the life you have imagined." This was the perfect inspiration for the journey ahead, I thought. For I was indeed about to embark upon the life–I hoped–that I had long imagined.

4

ASOK

Monsoon rains fell hard. A young stranger scurried along the sidewalk towards the open-air noodle stall where I sat. There was a vacant seat across from me, and I waved him toward it.

"Sawatdee," he said. *Hello.*

I nodded.

"Australian?" I shook my head. "Perhaps you are English?"

"No."

When I solved the mystery he smiled. "You are not like other Americans," he said. It was my turn to smile.

"My name is Asok," he said. "I am pleased to acquaint you."

The proprietress, frantically tending to customers, paused long enough for Asok to order vegetables and rice. He said he had been in Bangkok eight years, and was once a Buddhist monk, but no longer. His parents had sent him to the monastery in the north of Thailand when he was a boy. It was a way to educate one's son when too poor to feed him. But that was a long time ago. When he stopped speaking I pressed him for more details.

"It is a long tale," he said.

"But we are going nowhere in this rain."

He looked towards the deluge. The monsoons would move south in a few weeks but for now pounded roofs, battered awnings, and flooded the streets.

"Is this your first visit to Bangkok?" he asked.

I nodded. "I arrived this morning."

He leaned forward. "There is much to see, and much to avoid." He sat back as the woman set his meal down.

"I remember well my first days in Bangkok, after I left the monastery," he said. "What a place! The smells, noise, people, and poverty—all were overwhelming. I remember seeing two monks across the road. I wanted to rush to them, but the traffic was too much. And anyway, I was no longer of their world."

After a few bites he continued. "I found a tiny room near Bangalampoo and spread a few butter lamps, a picture of the Buddha, and some incense on the table. It was everything I had."

He smiled. "I thought of the Buddha. He gave up wealth, his wife, his child, and wandered penniless for years, but did not find what he was looking for. One day he rested beneath a Bo tree, where he faced three temptations. There he overcame fear, the weakness of doing what others told him he must, and—how you say—lust."

Asok's words resonated with me. I mentioned my quest as he finished his meal. He nodded. "This was why I left the monastery. Only by being out in the world could I understand what the Buddha underwent. But it was not so easy. I went into the street and found this place. I sipped my soup as the rains fell, like today, and watched the woman running this place gather everyone under cover as though we were all family. Here I was happy. I had found one way to overcome my fear of leaving the monastery."

Asok waved at the woman, who brought a piece of paper with scribbles on it. I handed her a few Thai baht, the local currency, before she darted away.

"Sawatdee," Asok said as he stood to leave. *Good bye.* "You too will find your way, as all must." With that he smiled, and plunged into flooded streets.

I wandered downtown. Thousands milled about and rushed past in buses, taxis, and tuk-tuks–noisy three-wheel contraptions buzzing city streets. Throughout the Chinatown district, throngs of Chinese-Thai sold everything from squid and snails to toys and kitchenware along narrow alleys piled high with goods. Only a sliver of space remained amongst the mountains of merchandise for pedestrians, pushcarts, and motorbikes to squeeze through. In the Pahurat neighborhood– known as the "Little India" of Bangkok–long-bearded Sikhs donning colorful turbans sold fabric and textiles. At Sampeng Market the crowded alleys, called *soi,* were awash with the aroma of fish and incense and spices.

During that first night in Thailand, rains pounded the corrugated tin roofs with newfound fury. The city sweltered, but my dusty hotel room fan hung immobile. Broken frayed wires poked into the air. Water dripped from the puckered plaster into a bucket beside my mattress. Black ants stormed the Vietnamese candy wrappers I tossed onto the wood floor.

Thunder crashed so loud my ears rang. The lights in my windowless room went dark. I curled into a naked, bewildered ball. Like Asok, I found the city's noise, traffic, and immensity overwhelming. A summer in the silent Alaskan wilds had not prepared me for the bustle of Bangkok. Another clap of thunder shattered the room. I had not seen family for six months, and didn't carry much more with me than Asok had when he first arrived. Like him, I longed for some element of familiarity. When another flash of lightning flickered through the room, I could see enough to reach for a stitch of clothing. I wrapped the garment around me as feeble protection, and waited for the storm to pass.

In the morning, I awoke not to the sound of monsoon rains, but to the muffled din of an awakening city. Dame Freya Stark captured the feeling perfectly. "To awaken quite alone in a strange town," the intrepid British writer observed, "is one of the pleasantest sensations in the world." I was indeed alone, and in a place quite beyond my imagination.

Rejuvenated after feasting on Chinese donuts and tea, I walked into the city's core. With no more baht for a taxi or tuk-tuk I wandered on foot but soon became lost. In a small park I rested. One of the homeless women picked lice from the head of another. Others wearing tattered wraps joined them. A woman with swollen feet offered me a ball of rice. I hesitated, but accepted. Another with soiled skin wished to share vegetables and seaweed with me. I glanced nervously at the woman's stained hands, but her generosity won my heart.

I ate with the homeless women, and then continued deeper into the sprawling city. At last I found a money exchange. I placed the worn baht in my breast pocket and stepped into warm sunshine. My next task was to find a noodle stall.

A young Thai woman stopped. "Your eyes," she said, "are brilliant."

Slightly embarrassed, but intrigued, I paused.

She said her name was Lili, and invited me to her brother's home for lunch. I demurred, for city people seemed always to want something.

"You will see," she smiled. "We are very friendly, always open and hospitable. Do not worry."

Curious to see a bit of Bangkok from the inside, I agreed to accompany her. Besides, her words and smile proved disarming.

"We must take taxi," she explained. "The buses are too slow—no good." When a taxi stopped she waved him on. "And some taxis too much. It is hard to know." When a green one paused she opened the door. "We go now," she decided.

We raced through narrow streets that twisted and turned until stopping at the foot of a tall building. Lili pointed to a swimming pool near the entrance. "You may come and swim whenever you wish," she said. Inside she greeted the doorman, a guard, a woman selling food, and another woman behind a broad reception desk who gave her a key which on the ninth floor Lili slipped into a door.

"Thirsty?" I accepted a can of Thai soda. "Hungry?" She offered a guava fruit from the miniature icebox. I handed her a piece. She laughed.

"Is okay," she said before taking a bite. "Settles the stomach after spicy food. Relax!"

A snappily dressed man entered and, surprised but happy to see us, introduced himself as Vhetoy Santos, Lili's uncle. He said he had a meeting scheduled there in a few minutes with Mr. Bali, a Muslim from Brunei, and could not stay.

"Eat! Please," Vhetoy said.

He mentioned that things had not gone well the night previous. Mr. Bali had won seventy thousand dollars at a nearby casino, and normally Vhetoy would receive ten percent. "But Mr. Bali is greedy. He will spend and spend at the casinos, but you ask him for a dime and he ignores you." A mere two hundred dollars was all Vhetoy received as his commission.

"Someday I will get my seven thousand dollars. Honestly, you see." Vhetoy pulled the two crisp one hundred-dollar bills from his pocket and leaned forward. "Might you be interested in doing business with us? I have worked in casinos across the world. Malaysia, Kathmandu, Las Vegas. What games of chance are you familiar with?"

I shook my head.

"None? How about blackjack?" Vhetoy pulled a deck of cards from his briefcase. "Do you believe in luck?"

I lied. "Yes."

Vhetoy executed a card trick, and produced my chosen card despite myriad shuffles and cuts of the deck. "This is not luck," claimed Vhetoy. "The house always wins."

"What is it I am to do?" I asked.

"The holiday is coming, yes? I have a family, you see. And you have a long journey ahead. Times are hard. Rather than rely upon chance, it is better to have an arrangement.

"It is quite simple. You will meet me at the Hilton where I shall give you three thousand dollars of my money. You will sit at my table, for I am a dealer, you see, and we shall play blackjack. When you have won one hundred thousand dollars you will go directly to your room and split the money four ways. You will keep one share and put the other three into envelopes, one each for the banker, general manager, and me. The next morning at nine we will meet in the lobby, you will give me the envelopes, and you will be gone. You will be comfortable, and I have a family, you see."

Lili squealed.

"I know nothing of gambling or casinos," I said, yet my heart pounded. I had never known wealth.

"This is okay. I will teach you everything." Vhetoy dealt a hand. "Let me show. The person who comes closest to twenty-one without going over, wins." I held a ten and a seven.

"Do you want a card?"

"No."

Vhetoy held a King and six, for a total of sixteen. The dealer must always stop at seventeen, but at sixteen or less— Vhetoy drew a four.

"You see, you lose. This is luck. You will never win this way. But imagine you know what comes next? Like this." He dealt a second hand. I held a five and nine, and with a deft movement of the hand, Vhetoy revealed the top card, a seven.

"Do you want a card?" Vhetoy asked.

I smiled. "Twenty-one!"

"Ah, but we are not finished. In blackjack the dealer keeps one card hidden and one open. Would it be still better for you to know the dealer's card?"

"Of course," I responded. Vhetoy explained that when he showed a thumb it signaled an Ace. Each finger counted as two. A bare knuckle meant ten. In the next several hands I could not lose for I knew both of Vhetoy's cards plus the cards to follow.

"If I ask if you want coffee, that is the signal to stop. Do you understand?" I nodded. "Mr. Bali will be here soon. When he arrives, you must ask him to a game of blackjack."

"What?"

"You cannot be nervous. We must see how you will do. Just a dollar or two per hand. Here is two hundred dollars." I mumbled that I was not ready, but Lili touched my arm. Mr. Bali knocked and entered. Introductions went around. He was in a hurry, and was Mr. Vhetoy ready for their meeting? Lili began to say something, and all were quiet, until I heard myself speak.

"Mr. Bali, would you care for a game of blackjack?"

"Well," he said, glancing at his watch, "okay, but only for half an hour," and looked into my eyes.

Vhetoy dealt. "Gentlemen, what will you start with?" Mr. Bali produced a crisp roll of American bills. "I shall open with, oh, two thousand dollars."

My face felt hot. Though slow, I won steadily. Twenty-five thousand dollars, I thought. Soon all of Vhetoy and most of Mr. Bali's money lay in the center of the table, a pile of red, blue, and white chips. Mr. Bali raised fifty dollars, but I had no more chips. In the excitement I did not notice the stakes had gone far beyond a dollar or two per hand.

"Will you match Mr. Bali's raise?" Vhetoy repeated.

"I have no more chips," I replied.

Vhetoy smiled. "I will gladly extend you a line of credit."

I could not lose, yet the timing was too neat, the cheating too obvious. I felt for the baht in my pocket. Could it be that Lili had watched me leave the money exchange? Vhetoy again offered credit, and at last I responded. "No."

"Then," Mr. Bali stated, "I win." He pulled the chips in, cashed them, and took the same two hundred dollars he had given Vhetoy the night before.

"Gentlemen, and lady, I thank you for the game. Vhetoy, perhaps I shall see you later." With that he was gone.

Lili clicked her tongue and no longer sat so close. Vhetoy appeared angry. "What happened? You were nervous. I had told you before I would extend to you a line of credit." I remembered no talk of lines of credit.

Vhetoy ran late. Lili too had to go. Outside she flagged me a taxi. "You may still use the pool if you like," she said as I climbed into the taxi. I looked back through the taxi window as the driver pulled out of the parking lot. Lili disappeared inside the tall building. I wondered what had just happened.

As I neared my hotel, I felt as though I were coming home. Sidewalks were packed with vendors, wares, and shoppers. I could barely squeeze between racks of clothes and tables packed with merchandise. Goods were stacked on curbs, in the streets, and before every storefront. From among the crowds a man mumbled something in passing. I did not want to visit anyone's home or buy any hand-tailored suits, and was about to tell the man as much, until I recognized him from breakfast.

"Come," said the man. "Let us walk while we talk." I caught a glimpse of the shiny brochure he produced from his pocket.

"Will you eat?" the man asked.

I pointed at the brochure. "What is this place?" I asked.

The man smiled as we sat at a noodle stall. "It is the place of your dreams, where your every pleasure may be satisfied. I am on my way there now. We will go together."

I laughed. "I will do no such thing! And Buddha teaches…"

"I know well teachings of The Great One, my friend. But you may do as you please. Even Buddha succumbed to desire."

I shook my head.

"Why have you come to Bangkok?" asked the man. "Life is short, yes? When you are old and withered you will look upon your life and regret moments in time."

"No."

"Is this your first time to Bangkok?" I said nothing. The man placed his chopsticks on the edge of the bowl, sat back, and gazed upon me. "Have you never known the pleasures of a Thai woman, the finest in the world? This is why you have come to Bangkok, and why you have met me. Come."

I rode with him in a taxi along Ratchawithi past the Victory Monument. Men wearing crisp Armani suits welcomed us at the door. Inside the dimly lit lobby a bartender awaited customers. To the left, behind a glass partition, forty young women sat in rows beneath bright overhead lights. The "superstars" wore alluring outfits. The "second-class" ones wore pale green gowns. Each had a numbered tag pinned to her dress. A few waved, others fixed their hair or put on lipstick. The host, in his custom-tailored silk suit, asked who I preferred. "Surely some young lady must draw your interest?" I counted my remaining baht and looked again at the young women.

I met number twenty-five at the elevator's sliding wrought iron door, and we rumbled upward. She broke the silence.

"How many years are you?" she asked.

I looked up into a weary face. "Twenty-eight."

She laughed. "I am twenty-six!"

A few women sat on the hallway floor amidst playing children. She exchanged pleasantries, and they smiled back. Inside the room were a large bathtub and a bed with a single sheet and pillow. I sat on a bench in the corner. A woman in calf-high rubber boots and smock strode in and set half-full bottles of lotion near the tub. The young woman locked the door and tied her long black hair in a bun as water ran into the tub.

"What's your name?" I asked.

She smiled. "Usanee."

"Where do you come from?"

"Krabi."

I tried to imagine her life. "How long have you done this?"

"Five months. I was married once, for six years, but no more." She tested the water, unzipped her pale green gown, and played with her hair. When the gown slipped to the floor, I studied the cracks in the walls.

"Lie down." She massaged my back with the lotions. "Now into tub." She caressed my shoulders and neck for three-quarters of an hour. "Okay. Finished." I prayed that was the end of it. She wrapped the towel around her slim waist before sitting on the edge of the bed.

"Come here. Ready?"

At last I laughed.

"You want make love or not?" she asked.

"That's not why I came here."

"You don't like?"

"It's not that. You're very beautiful."

"Is okay. We still have time."

"It's hard to explain."

She seemed sad as I laced my boots.

"It's all right, Usanee," I said. "You've done nothing wrong."

When the elevator opened, two Americans stood with a pair of superstars, all laughing like old friends. Some of the young women behind the glass waved and smiled. Others primped their hair or smoothed their dresses. Usanee said good-bye, and was gone.

At the noodle stall, rats scurried out of the sewers. Rain filled the gutters and overflowed onto the sidewalks and drowned the streets. There is no sound in the world like raindrops meeting their end.

As the torrents tapered and sounds of the city filtered through, a familiar figure waded through calf-deep waters. Asok smiled as he sat down across from me. When the overworked proprietress paused, he ordered vegetables and rice.

"There is no place like Bangkok," Asok said, "but at times it overwhelms even the stoutest of souls. It is good to have your refuge."

I nodded, and looked into the flooded streets. I remembered the story about the Buddha that Asok had shared when we first met. I was no Buddha, but the unexpected parallel between my time in Bangkok and the Buddha's experience startled me.

"Asok," I asked, "what happened after the Buddha overcame his three temptations?"

He stroked his chin, and smiled. "Why," Asok said, "he achieved illumination, of course."

5

A NIGHT IN DHAKA

A few days later, Mr. Noi drove me to the train station in his sputtering tuk-tuk. It was a long time negotiating the sprawl of Bangkok aboard the overcrowded morning train. Labyrinths of decrepit dwellings upon spindly wooden stilts jutted over trash-strewn sewage-filled canals. The clickety-clack of iron wheels sounded on the tracks as damp air streamed through wide dirt-streaked windows. Endless coconut palms flashed by then yielded to saturated sawgrass-covered plains. When half a dozen peasants got off the train to return to flooded rice fields, I took their place upon the grimy floor.

The locomotive announced its late arrival at the airport with a sharp blast from twin whistles. I had decided that my search should begin in the Kingdom of Nepal, where one could trek amongst the highest places on earth. For centuries both Buddhist and Hindu influences had shaped the nation's ancient culture. The mountainous kingdom sounded, to me, like a spiritual enclave awaiting discovery.

As I learned from a Thai travel agent, Biman Bangladesh's Flight 061 departed Bangkok once daily for Kathmandu, the capital of Nepal. The flight arrived twenty-four hours later because Biman's bargain basement fare included a night in Bangladesh, among the world's poorest nations. Motivated by price, I bought a one-way ticket bound for Kathmandu.

An hour after liftoff, the pilot spun lazy ellipses over Rangoon, the capital of Burma, as security cleared the craft for landing. After touchdown, my plane sat on the tarmac until permitted to taxi to the gate, though only locals or those few in possession of a Burmese visa were allowed from the plane. A militaristic government and political isolation had pushed Burma from second wealthiest nation in the region under British colonial rule, to being among the world's most impoverished.

In time the coconut palms again fell away and disappeared beneath thick cloud. Within an hour we descended, this time through darkening skies towards Dhaka, capital of poverty-wracked Bangladesh. The aging DC-10 shook and shuddered. Heat lightning illuminated distant clouds. The plane bucked sharply to the left, bounced once, and then found solid ground with thrusters screaming.

I stumbled from the worn aircraft and filed into a crumbling, cramped waiting area. Inside the dinghy, haze-filled interior, half a dozen dark men smoking hand-rolled cigarettes gazed upon us. Some passengers glanced in slight alarm at the decrepit surroundings.

Dhaka sits where the sacred Ganges and Brahmaputra river deltas empty into the Bay of Bengal. Monsoon deluges regularly ravaged the city. I pulled from my rucksack the tattered Associated Press news article containing the only material about Bangladesh that I carried.

Bangladesh monsoon kills seven

Monsoon floods sweeping northeastern Bangladesh have killed at least seven people and made thousands homeless. "Four persons were killed in landslides and floods," Abdul Quader, relief and rehabilitation officer of Moulvi Bazar district, told Reuters. He said some 50,000 people were stranded by floods in the district.

Many of nearly 100,000 people stranded on flooded
Sandwip Island in the Bay of Bengal have been living
on boats, rooftops and trees for two days.

"We better get in line," said Kathy, my seatmate on the
flight. We joined a meandering queue that encircled the dim
room and terminated at the counter where the somber men in
strange wraps puffed the unfiltered tobacco that burned our
eyes. When Kathy announced with some urgency that they
were taking passports, I stuffed the headlines back into my bag.

When we reached the men demanding our passports, we
protested. The baleful men only stared back at us. The line
grew shorter and seats fuller until all foreigners had
surrendered their passports for a handwritten airline ticket
valid the next morning.

We followed a man upstairs, outside, and into the dank air.
Sweating in the heat, we awaited new commands. A twelve-
foot barbed wire-topped chain link fence surrounded the
perimeter. When a movement caught my eye, I peered into the
darkness. Hundreds of Bangladeshis clinging motionless to the
other side of the fence watched our every move. In a land
without luxuries, we were the entertainment.

A decimated bus pulled to the curb with open holes where
glass panes once were. Some of us squeezed on board, and I
managed a seat by one of the holes. As the bus began to move,
two young boys appeared from the darkness. They chased after
us.

"Meester, meester!" they screamed.

One running below my window looked into my eyes. They
pled for spare change.

"Baksheesh!" they yelled in a futile attempt to garner a few
coins. "Please, meester! Baksheesh!"

The steel gates rose long enough for the bus to pass. The
boys kept pace then fell behind, still running as we picked up
speed and joined the main road. Brightly painted trucks, buses,
and rickshaws honked and hurtled around every corner.

Somewhere in the heart of Dhaka we stepped into a dark

hotel lobby. After much confusion, a man asked for three volunteers. A few brave souls raised their hands, and the first room was assigned. Small alliances formed. Kathy and I joined Anish, a Nepalese student. One of the men led us to a room.

We stowed our gear then decided to go for a walk. In the lobby, however, someone stopped us. "No, no. Come, you eat," the man said.

In a side room with settings adorning three long tables, the men placed before us bowls of curried chicken and dal baht, a local rice and lentil dish. As other travelers arrived, the men scurried about attending to everyone's needs. With our bellies full we again attempted to venture into the humid darkness.

"Beyond the gate, sir," said one of our hosts, "you musn't go at night. It is too dangerous."

Cycle-rickshaws materialized from the darkness and glided past with a tinkling of bells. The wiry pedal pumpers and their passengers all stared. Two wooden shacks on the opposite side of the narrow lane held a few items for sale. Flickering candles illuminated a cross-legged man inside each. One of the Aussies inquired about cigarettes, but the Bangladeshis spoke no English. None of us had any taka–Bangladesh's currency–anyway. Other than the shacks and rickshaws, in all directions there was only the darkness of Dhaka.

At dawn our hosts knocked at each door, and after black coffee with white toast and squat bananas, Kathy and I ventured outside. Women wore sumptuously colored garments that contrasted with the drab, decaying buildings. Every cycle-rickshaw driver and passenger stared. Parades of children walking alongside asked for bits of spare change. "Baksheesh?" they asked. At one gridlocked intersection, for a moment there was scarcely a movement, and thousands of eyes fell upon us.

I had not anticipated being in Bangladesh, and the unexpectedness of the sights around us startled me. More so than Bangkok, Dhaka was a place of poverty and struggle. I had slipped back in time, it seemed, to Bangkok as I imagined the city to have perhaps appeared in the 1940s.

Farther along, a group of huddled men fixated on a ringmaster delivering his pitch in rapid Bengali. The crowd parted for Kathy and I. Two wooden boxes in the dirt sat near a mongoose secured by a short leash. The men raised their arms and handed the ringmaster money. He opened one box, and pulled out a long slithering cobra. The mongoose attacked the snake. As the creatures sparred, money again changed hands.

The ringmaster held the viper at eye level for Kathy and I to see. "No bite!" the men chorused before he slipped the cobra back into the box.

Kathy and I continued onward. At a nearby school, Kathy asked the headmaster whether we could see a classroom. A scarlet-clad woman led upstairs. Children leapt from their seats as we passed from room to room, all crowing in unison "Hi!" and "Goodbye!" These were the privileged few. The majority lived on the streets or worked long hours for a handful of taka.

An hour later, with few minutes to spare, we boarded the wretched bus for the return to the airport. Police with long sticks blocked Bangladeshi from converging as the gates closed behind us. We were handed our passports as we boarded our flight, and Dhaka soon fell behind. To the north, snow-covered peaks of the Himalaya glimmered through thick cloud.

I felt grateful to have witnessed a place such as Dhaka. Such was the benefit of travel. Even more so than Bangkok, the bit of Bangladesh I had seen was quite beyond my imagination. Should I return, I suspected that much would be changed.

After an abrupt landing in Kathmandu, we waited in long immigration lines. Outside the terminal, finally, Kathy and I hailed a taxi that negotiated narrow mazelike roadways. These twisted past wandering oxen, shops lit by candlelight, and locals clothed in brilliant attire. When the streets became too congested, we abandoned the cab and walked. A mellow vibe filled the air.

We found a guesthouse in the Thamel district. At a corner hideaway we ordered tall bottles of local beer and Newari along with Tibetan dishes: thukpa, a thick meat soup; fried vegetable pakora; peanut masala; and kachila—water buffalo—minced with oil and egg.

After dinner, our rickshaw driver peddled furiously through darkened streets and alleyways. Burning candles illuminated street side shops and pedestrians' glowing faces. Down a side alley, two girls in matching blue skirts and sweaters swung a rope. A third jumped in, laughing. One barefoot man sold flavored ice in a cone. Three boys ran past, yelling. They had invented a game.

At Durbar Square we met a lad who led us among the mixture of Buddhist and Hindu temples. Around every corner a man whispered from shadows.

"Hashish, opium. Whatever you need, sir."

I shrugged the men off. The aroma of incense wafted around me. Passing locals chatted in Nepalese. Eyes of the Buddha painted on the side of a whitewashed stupa watched over the square and red, blue, white, and yellow prayer flags fluttered. My senses already overloaded, I needed no other stimuli than the intoxicating smells, sounds, and sights of Kathmandu.

6

AROUND ANNAPURNA

Over the next week, Kathy and I secured the gear and permits we would need to trek through the Himalaya. One morning at dawn men loaded rucksacks and travelers' gear to the bus roof. An undercurrent of electricity filled the air. We at last were venturing into the highest mountains on earth. Trucks and buses careened by as we twisted up and out of the Kathmandu Valley along green sculpted terraces carved centuries ago by grandparents of grandparents of bent men tending flooded fields of rice.

In the village of Dumre, most passengers continued on the main road. Kathy and I managed seats on another bus heading north over a rough track that bisected villages filled with curious onlookers. At times the track disappeared beneath streams rushing down from Himalayan heights. Each time the driver lurched through a precarious crossing, we nearly tipped over into the valley below. At the first police checkpoint we wrote our identifiers into the register, and after a second inspection and final treacherous crossing, the bus climbed into the outpost village of Besi Sahar. Here the rough path ended, and the battered bus could go no farther.

Touts surrounded the bus as I climbed to the roof to hand dusty bags down to Kathy. Such men were ubiquitous across Asia, and earned their commissions by importunately luring potential customers into hotels and restaurants, onto guided tours, and inside shops. We threaded our way past the touts to sip well-deserved beers at a backstreet garden after the daylong nerve-wracking jostle through the mountains. In time, after the touts forgot us, we chose a guesthouse.

At dinner, two others joined us. Camilla, a Swede, and Jonathon, from South Africa, jabbered about finding a guide and porter. After a heated negotiation erupted between them and two Nepalese porters, Jonathon was ready to abandon the whole idea.

Our collective goal was to reach the city of Pokhara, one hundred sixty miles away. Kathy and I had decided to tackle the month-long walk without the support of porters, who earned their livelihoods by carrying goods into the mountains. Though we agreed to venture into the mountains as a team, we were only slightly stronger together than as individuals. To get to Pokhara we must climb to Thorung La, hoping for minimal snow at the eighteen thousand foot pass. From there we must descend into Kali Gandaki gorge, the deepest in the world. This would lead to the Annapurna Sanctuary, a place of perpetual snow and avalanche. Though the monsoons were over, we needed every day our permits allowed to walk out of the hills before the full brunt of winter descended.

Of the fourteen mountains in the world that exceeded eight thousand meters, eight touched Nepal. I intended to see as many as possible, especially Chomolungma, the highest, which stood on Nepal's northern boundary. The second highest, K2, lay in Tibet and Pakistan. Kangchenjunga, Lhotse, Makalu, and Cho Oyu, the third, fourth, fifth, and sixth highest, straddled Nepal's border. The seventh and eighth highest mountains, Dhaulagiri and Manaslu, resided solely within Nepal. Nanga Parbat in Pakistan was ninth, but the tenth highest mountain at over twenty-six thousand feet was Annapurna. The craggy massif included Annapurna I, Annapurna II, Annapurna III, Annapurna IV, Gangapurna, and Annapurna South. These comprised the peaks we must encircle to reach Pokhara.

Later that evening, Camilla and Jonathon hired a porter to carry their sleeping bags, winter clothes, and any items they would not need during daylight hours. Their porter Shantaman, or "PeeWee" as he preferred, grew up near the Annapurna Sanctuary.

At first light, the three loaded gear. After I ordered tea and toast from Parashu, our guesthouse host, I walked down to see the trio off. An hour later, Kathy and I followed. We picked our way across a rickety bamboo bridge spanning the raging Khudi Khola, paused at Bhulbule for refreshment, and then crossed the turbulent Marsyangdi Khola on another shaky span. All the while we marveled at terraced mountains filling the skyline.

I recalled the words of author Chris Townsend. "Walking is the best way to gain understanding of a place, to assimilate its rhythms and time scales," he notes in *Walking the Yukon*. "To sit still is to watch the land flow past, to walk is to move with it. Mechanized travel leaves the land behind, disconnecting us from it. One of the problems of modern times is that we are separated from the world that supports us by the speed with which we traverse it. Walking is the best way to know a place, perhaps the only way."

I could not agree more. Along our path Nepalese washed, cooked, and ate only a few feet away. Villagers dressed in all manner of homespun walked past with always a "Namaste"– meaning *I bow to the divine in you*–exchanged in greeting. In this world wheels and wires played no roles. Footpaths served as high country highways, for upon our arrival the only way through these mountains was on foot. Porters carried bags of rice, bottles of soda, building materials, furniture, thick timbers, anything and everything. Calves bulging, eighty pound loads supported by two thin shoulder straps and one tump line around the forehead, the stocky men trudged over the passes wearing only flip flops and a few tattered wraps.

Kathy and I overtook Camilla and Jonathon and PeeWee at the village of Ngadi as they lunched. We continued over the Ngadi Khola, passed through a settlement of Tibetan refugees, and climbed towards Utsa. All four trekkers fell behind me as scrub forests gave way to bright green rice terraces. Insects chattered but the rivers, now far below, grew silent. At last, I thought, I am walking among the highest mountains on earth.

After a dozen miles, at the village of Bahundanda, I stopped. I watched PeeWee pick his way up the four thousand foot ridge. When he reached Bahundanda, he smiled. His yellowish complexion, straight black hair, epicanthic eye folds, and prominent cheekbones revealed his Tibetan roots.

Many ethnic Gurung, of whom PeeWee was one, were a peaceful lot who herded sheep or grew rice, wheat, or millet. Using a wooden *mai* to level the ground, men yoked oxen to a *halo* to make rows while women and children following behind dropped seeds into the furrows. Some Gurung followed a different path. The same age as I and on his eighth circuit of Annapurna as a hired porter, PeeWee's career was well underway, which was more than I could say for myself.

The Gurung had not always been so docile. After Buddha's visit to the Kathmandu Valley and the subsequent spread of his philosophies during the reign of the Kirati, the Licchavi clan arrived. A melding of Kirati Buddhism and Licchavi Hinduism began. Chaitya temples, stupa shrines, and chorten monuments from the era litter Kathmandu's back streets even today. Afterward, the Malla kings came to power and initiated a five hundred-year Nepalese golden age. The opulence was financed by the trade of musk, wool, salt, yak tails, and Chinese silk between Tibet and India.

Prithvi Narayan Shah, ruler of the hilltop kingdom of Gorkha, in the eighteenth century dreamed of a unified Nepal. He took Kathmandu, moved his capital there, established the Shah dynasty, and became known as the founder of Nepal.

Needing more loot to slake soldiers' thirsts, the kingdom's expanding boundaries set it against the British Raj, then the world's most powerful empire. Britain was so impressed with the fighting ability of Gorkha warriors that the British East India Company recruited them along with ethnic Chhetri, Thakuri, Magar, and Gurung peoples into the Indian and British armies. Oblivious to the various ethnicities, Brits called the regiments Gurkhas.

In battle, Gurkha soldiers were legendary for their fierceness. It was about them that former Indian Army Field Marshal Sam Manekshaw said, "If a man says he is not afraid of dying, he is either lying or is a Gurkha." In the aftermath of colonialism, Gurung people along with Nepal's other ethnicities settled into the farming and trekking lifestyles that today dominate rural Nepal.

While waiting for the others, I unpacked my gear and found my alarm clock lying in pieces. I attempted to repair it, to no avail, and tossed it in the trash to be discovered later by a boy fascinated at the novelty of it. For the next few days I asked Kathy the time, clinging to the world I knew, but it was as if the Fates intervened to teach a lesson. I soon fell into a rhythm of rising with the sun, and retiring with falling darkness—as nature intended.

Over breakfast, Dinesh and Bisnu Raj told me about the upcoming Tihar festival. For five days Hindus paid homage to Laxmi, goddess of wealth. Devotees hung strings of marigolds, lit hundreds of oil lamps and candles, and threw firecrackers into the streets. Men gambled all night. Sometimes they lost their homes, and on occasion, their wives.

Kathy and I overtook Ginger and Dan and strolled with the honeymooners through Lili Bir, Kanigaon, Ghermu Phant, and Syange. Beyond a creaky suspension bridge the valley narrowed into a steep canyon where rivers rushed swift and loud past massive midstream boulders. In Shree Chaur, while we lunched, a troupe of gray langurs raced along the far edge of a rice paddy. The monkeys dashed through the underbrush, swung into the treetops, and then scaled the scrubby mountainside. A man with long gun in hand slunk after.

Waterfalls poured from the clouds. A gentle drizzle gave no sign of ending, and at the village of Jagat a hard rain fell. We stayed with Sushma, a lively innkeeper. Most trekkers left by five in the morning, hoping to make as many miles as possible, but the four of us held back, at least for now, and chatted over hot tea as rain dripped from the eaves.

Sushma played a trick. She told us she was forty-eight years old. We wondered aloud whether her youthful appearance derived from mountain air, simple living, or some secret of the hills. Then we caught her laughing to the side and her husband, who spoke little English but knew what she was up to, said with a smile that she was thirty-one. We all shared a laugh.

While I was in Alaska I had sought the solitude of untamed wilderness, where fulfillment derived from self-reliant isolation. In Nepal, one could not avoid humanity. Trekking was a social endeavor spent amongst villagers still living as their predecessors had centuries before. Travelers from around the world passed through the villages, which served as crossroads of information. The shift in social interaction in high mountainous environments was for me an unexpected and dramatic one. Before arriving in Nepal I had read of occasional crowds on the trails and nearly ventured elsewhere, concerned as I was about the quality of the experience.

I was reminded of Robert Pirsig's musings about quality in *Zen and the Art of Motorcycle Maintenance*, not really about maintaining motorcycles, but about living a meaningful life. If one "starts to look for options of Quality," Pirsig writes, "and secretly pursues these options, just for their own sake, thus making an art out of what he is doing he's likely to discover that he becomes a much more interesting person and much less of an object to the people around him because his Quality decisions change him too."

A rooster crowed, children called out, a flutter of wood smoke wafted upward. Porters and townsfolk walked the dirt pathway separating our guesthouse from the thatched roof huts a few feet away. Chrysanthemums and nasturtiums bloomed along the flagstone courtyard edges. Sushma chattered in Nepalese over the distant roar of a river churning through the valley.

Trekkers often hurried around this circuit. But, having myself rushed too quickly through many otherwise rewarding experiences, it was with relief that I found myself slowing down. Connecting with others was among the most powerful components of a meaningful life. I was learning that Nepal held far more than the snow-shrouded peaks and creaking glaciers I had come to see. For once where I wanted to be, and amongst a people far friendlier than I had imagined, I opted to savor, as Pirsig might suggest, the simple act of walking around Annapurna.

In the morning, we set out beneath burning sun and climbed cliff edges above the raging Marsyangdi. Beyond the village of Chamje, we crossed the blue-gray river upon a rickety bridge with worn floor boards ready to crumble. Marigolds and poinsettia trees grew wild, as did crimson bromeliads and pastel orchids thriving in damp pockets. At Tal, where donkeys and goats and chickens lay in the lone dirt street and troupes of monkeys swung from tree to tree, we stopped for the night.

Another long day awaited, and there was much talk between Kathy and Ginger about hiring a porter. Their loads, combined with the steep inclines and high altitude, were proving too much. I had strolled into Tal before noon; they arrived well after three, their energy spent. We encountered a brother and sister duo, Simrun and Joson, both looking weary and beaten. They asked around for available porters, and found one for hire.

"We've never been on a trek like this before," Joson said over dinner. Simrun laughed. "We've never even been on a hike before, and we pick one of the hardest as our first. There's no way we can carry these packs over Thorung La pass."

"I want to enjoy some of this," her brother added, "and this is killing me."

Soon after daybreak we ventured onward, but by Dharapani

I stopped for tea to let Ginger and Dan and Kathy catch up. They wished to reach the village of Chame by nightfall. Their ambition matched their determination. At a bhatti, a small tea shop, I stopped for lunch. There sat Simrun and Joson, both looking much happier without loads strapped to their backs.

When the others found me, we departed en masse. The trail climbed sharply. While waiting atop the steep rock staircase I glimpsed them below, struggling even before the start of the near vertical pitches. As I continued upward the roar of distant rivers faded. Only the familiar ring of a mule train plodding in the distance broke the silence.

I soon found the mules standing in the path. Inside a nearby teahouse, their drivers downed glasses of chhang—home-brewed rice beer. Snow-covered Manaslu, the tallest mountain I had ever seen, peeked through thick cloud. Her outline would dominate the skyline across the forested valleys as I walked northward.

While contemplating the surreal vista, it occurred to me that our goal of reaching Chame before dark looked more and more difficult, and I worried for the others. Many sections were barely passable even in daylight. Every year travelers died on these paths. Like fallen comrades, many I had met on the trail had retreated. The guy with the blown knee and the Norwegian whose father fell ill had both returned home. Then there were those descending with bouts of altitude sickness, the woman with the bandaged leg being evacuated on horseback, and the other wounded straggling back. With accommodations scarce, I debated how much to hold back in order to let the others catch up.

A few outlying buildings appeared, and Chame's center soon after. Manaslu glowed on the horizon. I kept an eye out but knew I would not see my companions that night. After paying extra for a large bucket of hot water in addition to one filled with cold, I poured the hot over my aching back. In the evening chill, steam rose from my sore muscles.

The only other travelers in the village, three Germans and Melissa, an American, joined me at dinner. A dozen singing and dancing Nepalese in the courtyard celebrated the Tihar festival. Melissa's guide Amir danced with anyone, explaining that though a member of the highest Brahmin caste, he did not agree with the system. He enjoyed dancing and drinking chhang and having fun. We gave the revelers money as custom dictated. They moved to the next home, circulated through the village, returned, and sang more songs about Hindu gods and Nepalese ways of life. I missed my friends, but felt grateful to have been part of such a magical night.

The temperature plunged overnight, and at dawn I donned my frozen, damp clothes. Annapurna II gleamed beneath morning sun. At the village entrance a kaani, an arch decorated with Sanskrit-based etchings, stood beside a long row of prayer wheels, which I spun for good luck. I encountered Simrun and Joson waiting in Telekhu for their porter to cook himself a meal. We walked together through cool pine forests that gave way to apple orchards lining the path. The outline of Lamjung Himal loomed to the west.

After a lunch of Tibetan bread with cheese, I ventured alone along cliff edges. Vertical canyon walls of the four thousand-foot Paungda Danda rock face hovered overhead. Far below, the river rushed. Bits of mountains higher than any I had ever seen loomed on the horizons and the jangle of mule bells sounded from above. I stepped across a swaying wooden suspension bridge strung beneath towering summits. Before me was the landscape I had come to see. My eyes soaked in every detail of the extraordinary scenery, for here was the essence of Nepal.

I overtook Camilla and Jonathon and PeeWee. Chhulu East rose above the others, and Pisang Peak peeked through afternoon cloud. The sun dipped below the southwestern ridge as we approached the village of Pisang, and the temperature plummeted.

Inside the lodge, travelers played cards, chess, and backgammon. Most conversations revolved around the day's walk, cresting the pass, or someone's newest symptoms. At nearly ten thousand feet, most trekkers suffered from headaches, loss of appetite, irritability, shortness of breath, or other symptoms of altitude sickness. Chris from Vancouver spent the night vomiting. Kia, a physician I trekked with for a time, attended to Chris throughout the night and at one point considered walking him down to Chame. So far I was faring well, but knew no one was immune to the effects of altitude. I decided to take a rest day to acclimatize and wait for Kathy.

For most if not all trekkers, the usual worries had slipped away. Getting from place to place, meeting basic needs, surviving day to day; these were the concerns of those in the high country.

In evening hours I strolled with Tashi, a Gurung who once was a monk in Kathmandu, though the lifestyle did not suit him. We passed a low wall covered in maani stones all hand-carved with the prayer *Om Mani Padme Hum*. Devotees repeated the chant, loosely translated as "hail to the jewel in the lotus" whenever they prostrated themselves before the Buddha. The Tibetan influence grew stronger as we moved northward, I noticed. Upon a hill overlooking the village sat a gompa, and from the small Tibetan Buddhist temple stretched prayer flags fluttering in the breeze. Whenever the flags flapped, Tashi explained, the prayers were "said."

In broken English, Tashi told the story of the Buddha. The newborn's given name was Siddhartha, and his family name Gautama. Astrologers predicted a son destined for greatness. A wise man warned that if the young prince witnessed old age, sickness, or death, he would shun all pleasures and wander the world. Fearing this prophecy, the king built high walls around his palace and surrounded his son with luxuries. In time, the young man married a princess and bore a son.

The prince's curiosity about the outside world had nevertheless been aroused. Though the king ordered every sign of suffering be cleared from his son's path, one day the prince explored beyond the palace grounds and saw a wrinkled old man. On a second excursion he saw someone dying of an incurable disease. On the third outing he saw a corpse. After seeing a wandering ascetic, nothing could deter the prince from pursuing a life of austerity.

Six years of wandering left Siddhartha no closer to enlightenment than upon leaving the palace. Realizing he must free himself from all desire, he journeyed to Bodh Gaya and there sat beneath the Bodhi Tree. Upon overcoming fear, the temptation to do what another said he must, and lust, the Buddha at last attained enlightenment.

Yet rather than remain in a state of nirvana–a mindset free of hatred, greed, and ignorance–he opted to remain in this world as a bodhisattva–one able to reach nirvana but compassionately delays doing so to help alleviate others' suffering. He spent the next forty-five years teaching others how to find their paths.

So different was his message that newfound followers asked not who he was, but what he was. "I am awake," was the Buddha's reply.

7

THORUNG LA

On the morning of departure, an escaped white yak running through dirt streets of Pisang caused a stir amongst the villagers. Someone grabbed the rope that passed through the shaggy beast's nostrils. The villager lashed him to a pole near the village well. Still heaving, the yak licked at the blood with his rough tongue and stared as I filled my water bottle.

Kathy and I climbed upwards through pine and scrub, leaving our companions behind. Pisang Peak and Tilicho Peak shimmered in the distance. At a bhatti, severed yak heads hanging from a rafter swung in the breeze. Yaks were the workhorses of the high country. Their wool was woven into blankets, their dung burned for fuel, and their milk drunk for nourishment. Since they were related to the sacred cow, their slaughter was forbidden. If one fell off the trail, however, its meat sometimes made it onto a teashop menu.

We strolled past a long maani wall of carved stones and into Hongde, where police checked our permits. Cleared to continue, we walked to Mungji, where we paused for soup and tea. Beyond lay the Sabje Khola Valley, covered beneath snow and ice and headed by Annapurna III and IV. The outpost village where we first started walking nestled eight thousand feet below; the pass of Thorung La loomed seven thousand above. When we left Pisang, the first signs of crumbly high mountain desert appeared, for the massive Annapurna massif blocked even monsoon rains. The landscape, always dazzling though often not what I expected, changed with surprising swiftness.

In the village of Manang, at over eleven thousand feet in elevation, we rested to allow our bodies a few days to adjust to the altitude. The Yak Lodge buzzed. Nepalese cooked our food. Trekkers discussed routes, acclimatization, and the day's activities. I sat with two French-Canadians, Chris and Mary. Two young Argentinean women walked in. Doctors and lawyers mixed with students and professional travelers of all ages.

One afternoon I climbed the windblown northern ridge above Manang for views of Gangapurna Glacier tumbling into a tarn. Another day Kathy and I followed a lateral moraine past fluttering prayer flags and abandoned stone buildings. The next morning I walked a section of river past grazing yaks to Braga for garlic soup and jasmine tea. Chorten monuments, painted white with mysterious symbols and reverse swastikas, stood like sentries. Maani walls were piled high with slabs of rock carved by anonymous hands. The wind-weathered formations and sculpted rocks hinted of the stark Tibetan Plateau lying ahead.

Grateful to be amidst such wonders, I contemplated the motivations that brought people to Nepal. Everyone had their reasons.

"Quit my job in Denver," Dan had told me on the trail. "Taking some time off to think about things for a while."

"What were you doing?" I asked.

"I'm a lawyer, but don't really care for it that much."

"And Ginger?"

"Social worker. She'll probably get her job back."

"Why Nepal?"

"I don't really know," he said as Ginger came from behind. "We've been talking about this for two or three years."

"There's something about the mountains," she mused. "I've always wanted to come here, it seems."

"I've always wanted to do Nepal," Kathy had told me during one late night conversation. It was a tendency of hers we on occasion laughed about. "Did this. Done that," she sometimes said. For some, Nepal was another place on the list.

One night over cribbage and gin rummy Simrun and Joson told their story. While they visited India for a double wedding, they decided to detour to Annapurna. Joson had been accepted to medical school, but he took a year of deferment.

"This is an indefinite period of self-growth," said Joson.

"Ooh," purred Kathy. "I think I'll use that."

"Mom and Dad are paying," added Simrun. "I've got 'til Christmas, and thought this sounded fun."

Later, as I lay in my sleeping bag, I contemplated my own motivations. I had come to Asia seeking a response to the heralds' question. As for Nepal, the stunning scenery, ancient culture, and Buddhist influence had certainly drawn me, yet what I sought above all was to learn something of myself. By traveling amidst exotic cultures and walking amongst the highest mountains on earth, I hoped to gain some insight about myself that I could not glean at home. I was using an experimental culture shock therapy of sorts, I thought. Whether or not my scheme would work remained to be seen.

On departure day from Manang, as we stepped onto the trail, a woman placed a white scarf around each of our necks.

"Namaste!" she said. *I salute the god within you!*

With scarves fluttering, we climbed upwards. Gangapurna's jagged séracs rose above the foothills. Meltwater from Chulu West and Gundang flowed beneath the bridges we crossed. At a ridge top shelter where we paused for tea, an old woman sitting on a step fingered a chain of prayer beads and mouthed incantations. When yak caravans approached, we stepped aside to let them pass. Goats grazed clumps of grass, but the jingle of mule trains was no more. Instead, locals traveled between villages on horseback.

We walked past barberry and rose and a few goths, huts set high upon the plateaus, until descending into Yak Kharka. Everyone had sore throats and runny noses. Dan and Ginger had stayed an extra day in Manang. Simrun took Diamox to ease acute mountain sickness symptoms. Camilla suffered for two days in her room. Three Brits in Yak Kharka had a fourth friend descend with a porter because she could not continue.

Worse, the day before we arrived in Manang, a trekker was evacuated by helicopter with altitude sickness so advanced his brain had swelled. He went too high too fast. They put him in a pressure bag to simulate sea level atmospheric pressure and flew him to a Kathmandu hospital, where he remained. Once fluid accumulated in the lungs or brain, death was unavoidable unless the symptoms were treated. And, the only effective treatment was to descend. Those remaining on the trail would be relieved to breach Thorung La pass, our most challenging goal, so we could descend to lower, safer terrain.

In the morning, everyone except Jonathon and Camilla left Yak Kharka. As Kathy and I climbed, Gangapurna dominated the skyline. At a rise we savored bowls of soup and hot tea, and then descended into a ravine before climbing to Thorung Phedi. The wind-blown lodge, at over fourteen thousand feet, stood higher than Mount Whitney, the tallest peak in the contiguous United States. We ordered lunch but hours passed before we saw all of the meal. I succumbed to a pounding headache, and lay immobile in the dormitory room.

After Kathy gave me a headache tablet, I stumbled back into the dining area. Darkness fell and with it the cold, and at seven everyone retired to the room. Rick and Barry were on Diamox and peed every hour because of it. Kathy fell asleep around midnight. Daniel did not sleep at all. At four, Rick and Barry dressed and were gone. Kathy and I lay until five, relishing the warmth of our bags, until we ventured into a star-filled night to order breakfast and await the sun.

Some of the trekkers had left as early as three, and if lucky they saw the sun rise over the pass. If unlucky, they suffered frostbite. The only others who had not left were a group of Italians. As a touch of light filled the eastern sky and the stars disappeared, we paid our bill and stepped into the frosty air.

Phedi means "foot of the hill" in Nepalese, but the track was anything but gentle. Geographically, we were hiking in the sub-tropics. Due to the altitude, the thin air remained icy cold. Heavy snow covered the northern slopes, with lesser amounts surrounding us and lying upon the trail.

The journey of a thousand miles begins with a single step, observed Taoist philosopher Lao Tzu. Thousands more comprise the path to the proverbial summit. With fingers and toes freezing, little oxygen to breathe, legs and shoulders worn, and lungs gasping, I struggled upward. I wondered whether I possessed the stamina and will to make the pass, and if not, what I would do. Left foot down, breathe, right foot, breathe again, rest, and repeat. With each stride, no matter how painful, I knew the crest lay that much closer. Ignore hurting head, heaving lungs, and pounding heart, I told myself. Focus only on that next step.

Frenchman Maurice Herzog, leader of the first expedition to climb Annapurna I and top an eight thousand meter peak, noted, "There is a third less oxygen in the air at 8,000 metres than normally. That means it takes all your willpower just to draw another breath. The whole body concentrates itself on this single task: inhale one more breath." My body heaved with the effort, struggling to bring in enough oxygen to allow me to take just one more step...then another, and one more. There were thousands yet to go—gasps and steps.

Suffering, I knew, is a central tenet of the Buddha's message. To distract myself, I thought about his teachings. After attaining enlightenment beneath the Bodhi Tree, he began a hundred mile walk towards the Indian holy city of Varanasi. A few miles from the city, at a deer park in Sarnath, he stopped. Here he spoke to his first disciples about the Four Noble Truths.

The first truth, I reminded myself, is that of dukkha, of which suffering is an aspect. As Huston Smith explains in *The World's Religions*, dukkha is the pain that shapes our existence. This is the "quiet desperation" that Thoreau observed in most peoples' lives. Dukkha is comprised of sickness, discomfort when being held to what we dislike and separated from what we love, the fear of being repulsive, dependent, unloved or regarded as a failure, the phobia of death, and physical pain. These things affect most of us at some point in our lives—for such suffering underlies the human condition.

My present suffering was alleviated for a moment when Kathy and I reached a bhatti amongst the moraines, and sun crested Chhulu East and West. We savored the warmth, grateful for the respite, although we knew true relief lay well out of sight. We nibbled on chocolate bars, chatted with climbers we passed and the Italians who overtook us, and continued upward. Gangapurna, Yak Gawa, Thorungtse, and the Annapurnas dominated the cloudless skyline and encompassed a sizeable portion of the loftiest places on earth. Black and white, rock and ice, unyielding and indifferent, the mountains' simple beauty inspired me, yet offered little solace. I had hoped they might shed light on my questions, but as I learned, I must find my answers within.

My physical suffering led me to think about tanha. Usually translated as desire, tanha comprises the Buddha's Second Noble Truth. Certain yearnings are good—a desire for liberation, for example, or the happiness of others. Coddling one's ego, however, leads to suffering. When we form attachments to ideas, people, and objects, we want what we cannot have or fear the loss of what we do have. The Buddha's Third Noble Truth follows from his second. If life's disharmony is caused by selfish cravings, then the solution is to overcome such desires.

My thoughts shifted from suffering towards home and the fact I should one day return there, out of social obligation and to see my family, if nothing else. I wondered who I would be when that day came, and whether anyone from there would be any different than when I left. I thought of Tamara and her life; my parents, both probably worried and, I sensed, not understanding my intentions; my friends and the inevitability of divergent paths; jobs that awaited me, and the fact I must move forward in that capacity though traditional careers for me rang hollow and empty.

I wondered why the customary routes through life seemed so unappealing to me. Why, I asked myself, did everyone else in my life have focused careers and growing families? They had seemingly figured out how to achieve contentment despite their obligations to family and friends. I questioned whether their lives were self-directed, or simply driven by the social values they unknowingly inherited.

My childhood was traditional, at times turbulent, but largely devoid of trauma. Over time, I had come to see that from my perspective much of what teachers, the media, advertisers, government, and religious leaders taught were mistruths. I sensed I did not fit into the culture in which I was born. Unlike those in my midst, I enjoyed exerting great amounts of energy traveling. I liked planning and executing a complicated route to a place like Pokhara, which could more readily be reached by bare bones prop plane.

I was searching for quality in the experiences I pursued, but also something more—perhaps even impossible to attain. I recalled Doris' mandate for a relationship that she had expressed back in Real de Catorce. I realized then that she was still searching after more than twenty-five years. I cringed at that thought, yet respected her resolve to find what she knew she wanted. I wondered whether I could live a life like those of my peers, and be content. If so, I had no idea how to make that happen.

Maybe the answers I need are just around the next spire, I thought. A chorten with prayer flags leading away in all directions appeared at a small rise. A few trekkers sat nearby. I wanted more than anything for this to be the pass, and for the pain in my lungs, feet, and legs to end. Surely we were not at Thorung La pass already, though. It was too soon; the pass must lay two or three hours further ahead. Yet the faces and signs around me indicated otherwise. We had indeed reached the pass! We threw down our packs and sucked at the thin air. The worst, seemingly, was over.

One did not dawdle long in the brittle air. Through the afternoon we descended five thousand feet in four hours. Knees and ankles jolted as we struggled to retard our speeds. On a grassy slope we rested. Tukuche Peak, Dhampus Peak, and Dhaulagiri filled the horizon. Kathy grew nauseous. Glenn had a migraine. We descended more, and then stopped at a tea house. I wanted to push on to the end, but the others were spent.

At last it ended. We found a room in the village of Muktinath, took lukewarm showers, and in the night played Hearts with Helga and Divy and DeeDee and Seelick and the Canadians Andrew and Kirk. We laughed and drank chhang with their porters Krishna and Nobie, and danced as they sang and played their drums. It was a fitting celebration, though strange to think the climbing of the pass was over. A kind of sadness seeped into me.

Upon learning about the challenges of climbing to Thorung La, I had directed my energies towards that singular goal. I wanted proof I could tackle whatever life threw my way. This notion became a driving force behind my sojourn around the Annapurna massif. With only a vague notion of what lay beyond the pass, getting up and over became all that mattered. In a sense, my perception of future success had boiled down to a few tiresome hours.

I had overcome tanha—my desire to reach the pass. Yet, I realized that climbing the pass had proved nothing. My belief that reaching Thorung La would translate into a life of success was an illusion. Despite my efforts, I was no closer to making any choice. Then, another realization sank in. With the pass behind me, I had no other goals in my life that I hoped to achieve.

8

SANDSTORM

Morning sun cast its first rays upon the stunning Dhaulagiri Himal massif, now visible with the pass behind us. As afternoon sun warmed the highlands, Kathy and I strolled towards the medieval-like settlement of Jharkot. Villages spoke of centuries long forgotten. Old women wove scarves on wooden looms while children played in the dirt. Chortens and gompas stood in isolated stillness. Poplars quivered on the breeze, a brook trickled past, and stone fences stretched into the distance. Swaths of desolation whipped by wind and dust and dotted with shadows of cloud reached as far as the eye could see.

Past Khingar, three Nepalese overtook us. For a moment we walked abreast, all curious about each other, yet trying to look without staring. Quick glances confirmed that they and we were from vastly different cultures. Kathy and I forked right where the path divided. Like old-world nomads, we knew not what the next night and day held or where the next shelter and food might be found.

Below a great precipice nestled Kagbeni, another medieval

village of mud and straw-roofed dwellings. Villagers loaded mules and herded ponies through narrow streets. Livestock lived on bottom floors of simple homes. If we peered through an open door or ground-floor window, a yak or cow instead of a person stared back. Women swept droppings from stone walkways while children played in backstreet courtyards. A favorite toy was a goat horn tied to a length of string, which the tykes dragged in delight.

After hot tea, momos–dumplings–and shabhale–meat stuffed into a fried flaky crust–and thenduk–Tibetan noodle soup–we slept. In the morning we found where the trail entered Kali Gandaki Gorge, the deepest in the world. Annapurna I and Dhaulagiri I both stand over twenty six thousand feet high, yet are only twenty miles apart. The Kali Gandaki flows swift and cold between them. Strong winds blasted grit and glacial silt through the gorge, and we spent the day battling sandstorms. Beyond Eklai Bhatti, the trail became a wide barren swath of gravel. We followed distant trains of mules and porters visible through clouds of dust. After the Jomsom police checkpoint the wind blew still harder. We pushed past Shyang, and after trailing behind a long mule caravan, dropped into Marpha.

Relations between Kathy and I had grown poor. We were weary from the walking, unvarying menus, constant companionship, and strain of long-term travel in strange lands. I for one needed periodic separation to recharge, and could only guess at her frustrations. Communication was not my strength, so I assumed I was part of the problem. She had mentioned already that my seeming need for isolation made me unreliable as a trekking partner. I could not deny this.

A group of Japanese showed up that evening. We had frequently run into them previously on the trek, and they had plagued us since Muktinath. There they smoked heavily at the table while we ate with the Canadians, and took forty-five minute showers while a long line of us, grimy and exhausted, waited. In Marpha, they took the dorm next to ours then broke protocol by spending the evening elsewhere. In Nepal one ate where one lodged for the rooms were exorbitantly cheap and guesthouses made their money from food and drink. At breakfast they talked and laughed coarsely. Irritated by their behavior, Kathy told them to quiet down, which they did.

In mid-morning, winds picked up and we fought the fine dirt again. Vegetation changed from dry desert to low-lying juniper to lush pine forest. I parted from Kathy and detoured through an encampment of Tibetan refugees at Chhairo via a long, rickety suspension bridge, then stopped to eat dal baht at a bhatti in Tukuche, hoping to summon the energy to catch her. As I prepared to leave she came from behind. Somehow we unknowingly crossed paths.

After Khobang and Larjung, we descended to a broad expanse of braided river and gravel bars where the Ghatta Khola met the Kali Gandaki. Kathy chose to wade across rather than use the upstream footbridge. She forded several smaller branches but the deep, swift main channel lay ahead. I crossed the bridge and from the opposite bank watched her and the porters and mule caravans cross the icy waters. I waited an hour, exasperated, and when she came around the bend neither of us had polite words to offer.

The day grew late with delays. We crossed the blue-gray waters again via suspension bridge, but realized we had veered onto a side trail. We decided to continue to Kokhethati, but when she caught up I changed my mind. We both needed rest, so I took a room.

She disappeared somewhere, I assumed to be away from me. I ordered tea and watched clouds swirl past. When she returned, smiling for the first time since Marpha, her pockets bulged with thick aromatic buds of ganga growing wild by the river. We laughed, and decided to unwind; in so many ways we needed it. I fashioned a cardboard toilet paper roll into passable paraphernalia, and let stresses and strains of the past few weeks melt away.

In a moment of silence, we peered out our window at the makeshift corral next door. A herder brought his fifty goats home from the hills, and they passed one by one through the narrow opening. He seemed to greet each as they entered, his lips moving and head nodding. I felt as though I saw the Nepalese for the first time.

After tea, soup, spring rolls, and apple pie with custard we slept easily, but morning came quickly. Powerful gusts of wind blew windows and doors wide open. Even if closed, dust and grit filtered through the cracks. The trees bent. Our gear and beds slowly disappeared beneath a growing layer of sand. At times the windows seemed as though they would shatter. Wind alone would make trekking difficult, but the sand kicked up from the Kali Gandaki would have whipped into our eyes and faces so that walking would be impossible. We sat indoors, trapped by sandstorm.

Winds calmed through the morning, but the sandstorm marked a change. After three weeks of traveling together, Kathy and I went our own ways. The parting was amicable. She could partner with the Australian couple we had met who she seemed to get along well with. I could do as I pleased and not worry about her well-being, although there had been a comfort knowing she was there should I need her.

Sun shone on Dhaulagiri and Tukuche Peak to the west. Picturesque stone houses and walls lined the track through Kalopani and Lete. I paused in Ghasa for dal baht, and then continued over landslides and a swaying suspension bridge with most floorboards missing. At a tiny lodge in the hamlet of Rupse Chhahara–Nepalese for beautiful waterfall–I rested. Three friends from the trek chanced along and stopped for a late lunch. The conversation was good, and just long enough. As shadows crept over nearby mountains, they pressed on for the village of Dana, leaving me with my thoughts and the roar of the waterfall.

While sitting there I mused about the path that had taken me from Besi Sahar to Manang and over Thorung La. With the pass breached, I focused on the future. What should my life look like? What should I choose? The Buddha had highlighted two ways of living. The first, like a fallen leaf scudding past on an autumn breeze, he called "wandering about." The second, the way of intentional living, he called the "Path."

After accepting that one's life is filled with dukkha, suffering, the Buddha's Eightfold Path provides a roadmap for overcoming tanha, desire, and the drive for private fulfillment. This Path is the fourth of the Buddha's Noble Truths. Like my path around Annapurna, the Buddha's included steep grades, dangerous curves, and rest stops, but through long and patient discipline I could emerge a different human being.

The eight steps include holding the right outlook on life, having the right intentions, using the right language, taking the right actions, choosing the right livelihood, making the right effort, maintaining the right mindfulness, and employing the right concentration. "Happiness he who seeks may win," the Buddha said, "if he practice." The Buddha's teachings made sense, but I was not certain I possessed the discipline to internalize them.

While contemplating this, dusk fell and a pleasant surprise came around the bend: PeeWee, followed by Camilla and Jonathon. PeeWee shared his hookah before we joined our Thakali hosts in the warm kitchen. The matriarch squatted by the fire and cooked vegetables and boiled potatoes while two children played. Lentils and rice waited in large pots. We sat on the dirt floor upon corn sheath mats while PeeWee translated. The women served dal baht and afterwards milk tea and chocolate cake.

A perfect full moon rose over the ridge tops, and the reflection from the white waterfall lit my way to my room. I missed Kathy's company, but relished the solitude. I lay in the dark silence, hoping my answers waited there. It was not to be.

The serenity was shattered when I sensed the ceiling of the dark room come alive. Black rats–dozens of them–scurried across the shaky bamboo ceiling a few feet overhead. I trembled in the darkness, terrified they would fall through or crawl onto me, and I lay immobile until sleep at last came.

9

SANCTUARY

At Poon Hill, rumors of civil war dangled from travelers' lips. Maoist violence was on the rise. While communism fell across Eastern Europe in the early 1990s, a coalition between the top three Nepalese political parties led to one of few times in history a communist government came to power by popular vote. The ensuing decade of broken coalitions, dissolved governments, and sacked politicians spurred the Maoists of the Communist Party of Nepal, fed up with corruption and the failure of democracy, to declare a "Nepalese People's War."

Early Maoist forces fought with ancient muskets and khukuri–traditional curved knives. Automatic weapons looted from police stations and homemade explosives upped the stakes. The army's tactics alienated locals. Land reform issues, resentment against the caste system, and lack of faith in squabbling politicians further swelled Maoist ranks. Attacks occurred in nearly every Nepalese district, and Maoists in time controlled forty percent of the nation. The Nepalese Civil War began months before I arrived, and erupted around me while I walked. Thousands of Nepalese would eventually die.

Mindful of this reality, I awoke at five to a slight rap on my door and made my way to the bottom floor of the guesthouse where a few others had gathered. Pinpricks of light snaked up Poon Hill's flanks. I followed them upward. A roundish moon lit the path. Atop the treeless knoll an international contingent waited amongst the frosty lichen-covered rocks. As the eastern horizon turned magenta, the day's first flashes of sun lit the uppermost tips of Hiunchuli and Annapurna South. Snowy peaks of Varahashikhar, Dhaulagiri, Tukuche, and the Nilgiri Himal turned from steel gray to ochre.

I lingered before making my way downslope to the police checkpoint in Sikha village. Most officials wrote requisite data into thick logbooks with complacent boredom. This one fiddled with my camera and snapped photos of the other officer. Despite the officers' pleasant dispositions, the dense forests between Ghorapani and Ghandruk had seen recent Maoist activity, armed attacks, and robberies directed at solo travelers and couples. For safety, though we were defenseless, I teamed up with three Seattleites and a Canadian couple.

We climbed past ferns and rhododendron trees to a grassy hilltop affording views of Poon Hill, Ghorapani, and the Annapurna Range. The trail followed a ridgeline of moss-covered hemlock and fir, and then descended into Deorali village and a gorge thick with epiphytes and orchids. A slow column of Germans refusing us passage on the slick, treacherous path slowed us until Banthanti, where we squeezed past and climbed again through dense jungle forests to the simple enclave of Tadapani. We followed no prescribed trek, as the rough terrain and dearth of villages attested. The others continued to Ghandruk. My ambitions lay in a different direction, beyond Chhomrong; thus we parted beneath gathering storm clouds and onset of evening.

A copper-colored cock roused me at dawn. Where cloud and darkness loomed the night prior now towered snow-covered peaks. Nothing but a vague breath of wind stirred amongst the rhododendron and hemlock until a chatter of songbirds broke the stillness. I crossed the raging Khumnu Kola on a creaking bridge with floorboards missing and holes covered by stones. Long strings of dried marigold, holdovers from the Tihar festival, hung over the waters. The track snaked past two women hand-threshing millet and a bent man prying twisted nails from timbers. I noticed rusty bottle caps in the dirt that spelled Nepal's acronym, *Never Ending Peace And Love*.

While eating dal and cabbage amidst bleeding heart, nasturtium, dahlia, and snapdragon blossoms, snow-covered Hiunchuli peeked through afternoon cloud. A jangling of bells rattled the stillness. As drivers unburdened a caravan of rice and grain, two mules escaped and tromped through the marigolds. A woman grabbed my walking staff.

"Two minute," she said, and chased after, whacking their hind quarters.

My path took me through Chuele and Garjung. At Chhomrong, I ran into Chris and Mary, old friends from Manang and back to Dhaka.

"Have a good luck," called Rhama, their guide, as the trio departed in the morning.

After crossing the Chhomrong Khola the trail climbed steeply past magnolia and rhododendron. A family of thrushes tittered in a lone eucalyptus. Two men sawed a long timber lengthwise. One sat on the ground, another stood on a log, and between them they pushed and pulled the wooden handles of a rusty blade like two woodsmen in a Shakespearian glade.

I paused at Sinuwa for vegetable soup and bread before further up and some down while walking to Bamboo Lodge for more soup. The family there watched me when they thought I did not notice. The mother of the two toddlers, perhaps eighteen years in age, wore a white scarf, gold nose ring, long brown skirt, and tight woolen tunic. She gathered cabbage from the garden outside the door and carried it into the kitchen. I sat in the dining area and soon heard loud voices. She strode in, picked up her little girl, and with dark eyes flashing rewrapped the scarf around her taut face. It seemed as though centuries separated us. I handed the empty bowl back to her and nodded. I felt her eyes boring into me as I stepped outside. What I would have given to know her thoughts.

Where avalanches and landslides had brought the trail and mountainsides into the Modi Khola, precarious constructions of bamboo and wood sticks spanned the emptiness. Mauve-colored *primula* proliferated in moist glades and along mossy waterfalls. *Pleione* orchids clung to tree limbs. By one o'clock the sky turned drizzly and chilled, and I decided to stay at the Himalayan Hotel. The groaning kerosene stove drowned the din of the Modi Khola flowing below, but all else was silent. Travelers filtered in through the afternoon, weary from the bamboo ladders and three thousand-foot climb. With no village or alleyways to explore, we sat still and fought the cold while mists swirled upon the mountains.

A tap on my foot awoke me. One trekker's watch read half past six. The elderly Australian who roused me shouldered his bag while I sipped milk tea. Still rubbing sandy eyes, I turned towards the trail. I overtook a couple and their porter on an uphill grade, and the older Aussie while he caught his breath. The moon floated above an amber snow-covered peak aflame with the first rays of sun.

I walked on and noticed, with suddenness, the trees were no more. Only low shrubs and frost-covered tufts of yellow elephant grass grew amongst lichen-covered rocks. Gangapurna's south face and Tarke Kang stood in snowy sunshine. Frost yielded to snow, and rock faces to cloud. Gandharva and Machhapuchhare still stood clear, and Annapurna III and Gangapurna nearly so. I hoped to reach Annapurna Base Camp before unsettled weather encroached.

While ascending I made way for those descending to safer ground. "Namaste! Bonjour! ¡Buenas Dias! Wie gehts!" hikers called in their native tongues. After a rest at Machhapuchhare Base Camp, I made a final climb. The toe of the jumbled glacier appeared, and a structure soon afterward. I had reached my destination! I wanted to scream in joy, but this was avalanche country. I marveled instead at Annapurna I and Annapurna South towering to the west, until dense cloud shrouded everything. I beat the weather, barely.

Nestled deep within the Annapurna Sanctuary was a four thousand-meter glacial basin surrounded by towering peaks of the Annapurna massif and only accessible via the narrow pass between Hiunchuli and Machhapuchhare that I just traversed.

In 1950, after Maurice Herzog and Louis Lachenal reached the summit of Annapurna I for the first time, they caused a worldwide sensation. During the retreat to Annapurna Base Camp, Herzog lost his gloves and an overnight bivouac in a crevasse led to severe frostbite. Due to onset of gangrene, the expedition's doctor performed field amputations without anesthetic. Both climbers lost all their toes, and Herzog most of his fingers. Annapurna I was not climbed again for twenty years.

At the base camp quarters, snow fell and kerosene heaters rattled as gathered trekkers watched the whiteness swirl past. A porter asked where I came from.

"Besi Sahar," I replied.

"Oh, many walking," he said.

Soon the roofs were covered. Afternoon dissolved into evening. We ate and joked as snow and darkness fell. Huddled together with nowhere to go, the evening hinted of Christmas Eve.

The new fallen snow gleamed at first light. Nothing stirred. Low clouds hugged the upper peaks, but white and ochre interspersed the lower flanks. I climbed towards the closest glacier as a cawing crow-like chough flew past. A sudden roar, like pounding surf in a nor'easter, erupted. An avalanche fueled by the weight of new snow crashed downward a few hundred feet away.

The Annapurna Sanctuary, home to Hindu and Buddhist deities, was sacred to the Gurung. They believed serpent-gods left their treasures there, and that the Hindu god Siva lived atop Machhapuchhare. Daily plumes of snow blowing from the mountain's apex were the smoke of his divine incense.

To the east, azure clouds drifted over Gandharva Chuli. At a chorten draped in unmoving prayer flags, I pulled from my pocket the white scarf that the woman in Manang had wrapped around my neck for good luck. On a Christmas-like morning, I tied my offering to a bough holding the tattered gifts of pilgrims past. A great crack shattered the stillness. The glacier shifted, but only clouds moved visibly.

I closed my eyes. Thank you gods, I thought, for safe passage to this sacred sanctuary in the heart of the Himalaya.

10

THE LETTER

Snow, looking and feeling like fluttering goose feathers, fell from dense clouds. Slumped porters strained upward against taut tump lines. I slipped and fell down a muddy rock-strewn swath of slick trail, but caught myself before too late, grateful for the man in base camp who sharpened the blunt tip of my trusty walking stick with his long knife.

Past Chhomrong, the trail skirted the mountainside before dropping to the valley bottom. After a rest at Khimrong I crossed the Khumnu Khola and climbed cliffs through forests of bamboo and moss-covered trees. Clouds turned midnight blue then black. A cluster of teahouses, Uri, appeared on a pass. Below lay green hillsides and golden terraces of wheat. Even with the rises, the path dropped seven thousand feet and the truly big hills loomed behind me.

Gentle Nepalese music wafted from a shack perched on a precipice edge. An old man's toothless smile accompanied a "Namaste" from his wife. Farther on, an elderly woman washing clothes at a tap waved. I expected a bhatti, but there was no signboard or teahouse, only friendly villagers. The trail led past a copse of trees, over a suspension bridge, and into the Gurung village of Ghandruk.

That night I dreamed. A band of us, wrongly accused of some crime, plotted and executed an escape. As we fled I was separated, and rounding a bend confronted a gnashing brown bear. I climbed a tree but the bruin pursued. I contemplated how to kill the bear, which at the last moment slipped away. I rejoined my companions and we were free, until in the final stretch they were recaptured. Disguised, I discussed with a guard their fates.

"They are to die," he said. "Slowly."

I stood immobilized. Soldiers and guards hovered everywhere. To attempt to free my friends would get me killed. To stand by was to watch them die.

As I pondered this dilemma I awakened. It was first light, but I could see Annapurna South perched like a huge misshapen cake smeared with extra thick vanilla icing. Machhapuchhare, Gangapurna, and Hiunchuli stretched across the horizon, silent and surreal. Redstarts and whistling thrushes, one missing a leg, flitted about. Caramel-colored butterflies danced upon indigo-red coleus and towering yellow-orange marigold growing in thick abundance. A *zebrina* grew near a chrysanthemum, leggy and listless, the last petals about to fall earthward. Purple heart and a rose clung to cracks in a stone wall, a single pink blossom sprouting from the thorny vine. Life's tenaciousness always astounded me.

A rooster crooned. Two water buffalo trekked past scarfed Gurung women in bright homespun prints preparing for a new day. Beneath eaves hung great bundles of drying corn. Racks of water buffalo horns bleached white by sun dangled from wooden posts.

Terraces brimmed with golden millet. Crouched men and women harvested the grain with long curved *karda* that they carried at their waists within wooden sheaths. The knives cut firewood, fodder, and fields. The millet lay in neat rows that villagers gathered into bundles and carried home in bamboo *doko*. Women beat the dried millet with long wooden poles.

Villagers used bamboo for everything from fences that sheltered buffalo and sheep to roofs. They made it into mats upon which millet and corn dried in the sun, and into baskets, *shu*, for carrying goat and cow milk. Other baskets transported rice, flour, and baby chickens.

A man walking past carried a thick pole over his right shoulder, from which two bamboo baskets hung like scales. He set the arrangement down and produced chilies and a rusty metal balance. A withered Gurung, pointing and gesturing, squatted on his heels. Two schoolgirls donning burgundy skirts and jumpers and carrying woolen satchels with tump lines across their foreheads watched the bartering. Another girl in violet cape stared. The men bickered, back and forth, until reaching no decision. The Gurung sent the trader away.

As evening fell, great shrouds of pink cloud like cotton candy clung to mountaintops. A prayer flag luffed; all else was still, as it was twelve hours before when the day was born and darkness turned to light. The proprietress of the lodging, Nabina, removed her scarf and smiled. She unfolded two long, luxurious braids and combed them while awaiting customers. But for the crickets, everything paused.

In the night I dreamed again. The end of the world fast approached. I joined everyone I knew at an ancient university with a strange name. While waiting for events to unfold in a field marked by a stone-carved sign I could not read, a great flood swallowed us all. Caught in the waves, I sank deeper and deeper. I fought for the surface, and with lungs bursting, broke free. Where before villages nestled within green valleys, there now swirled dark waters. I clawed my way to a high mountainside, saddened and alone, to look upon the black sea.

The gimpy thrush returned in the morning with two companions and searched for seeds until Nabina shooed them away. For them, it was another tranquil morning in the heart of the Himalaya. For me, the sky was clear but my thoughts were clouded. Snatches of my dreams returned, and with heart heavy

I descended the precipitous stone staircase. The wide, leathery feet of a shriveled woman climbed past. Children ran through flagstone alleyways carrying paper Chinese lanterns. Himalayan griffons soared overhead in lazy circles. One man cutting across a rice paddy carried a frightened chicken in a mesh bag. Another toted a wire cage filled with huddled hens upon his back. I knew I would not see them again. I rubbed my teary eyes as the village fell behind.

Above Birethanti, upon a narrow rocky shelf near a scarred eucalyptus, stood three whitewashed chorten. The only sound, but for the whir of cicada and locust, was that of the Modi Khola far below. Tied to two reeling bamboo staves hung a string of dried flowers. On the ledge lay a few sheaths of yellow wheat. Cumulus clouds above Machhapuchhare turned pink, then indigo, before finding shades of gray, then black. The scenery was timeless. Like the view before me, the clouds in my mind thickened and darkened.

In *The Snow Leopard,* naturalist George Schaller stalks rare Himalayan blue sheep across remote reaches of Nepal. Author Peter Matthiessen, a student of Zen Buddhism, accompanies Schaller while pilgrimaging to an ancient shrine. Along the way, Matthiessen hopes to glimpse the mythical snow leopard. Like him, I sought something soul-satisfying deep in the Himalaya, and I feared my search might be as elusive as his. I had hoped for a clue to the heralds' question, but my trek wound down too soon. I longed for answers, yet felt no closer to making a choice than when I landed in Bangkok. By the next evening my life would be different, though I was not ready to return to the modernized world.

Crossing the Modi River, I leaned into my load and walked along the lengthwise girders where no floorboards remained. The end of a journey often happens so quickly, I had learned. At Naya Pul, I stepped into muddy streets filled with dung and litter. Unkempt hovels cobbled together with scavenged material lined the roadsides. Iron spikes of rebar pointed upward from long-abandoned concrete foundations.

A wrinkled man near two baskets and a bamboo pole sat with eyes pinched shut. Two dirt-smeared girls warmed themselves over a fire of castoff cardboard. A woman squatting in the bushes removed her stained bra and wrapped herself in a torn sari. Naked children, ebony hair wild in the light and bellies bulging, scooped corn towards their mouths.

With no trail left to walk upon, I boarded an overfull bus and descended towards Pokhara. In the span of minutes, I reentered a motorized world the likes of which I had known all my life, but felt no longing for. Everywhere the pace of life was quickened, like a million hearts jacked on adrenaline.

As the bus driver careened downhill I noticed my beautiful walking stick had gone missing. The uselessness of my trusty stave reminded me that my month of walking had truly ended. At a stop a gnarled unintelligible man seemed intent on informing me of something vitally important. I nodded as though I understood. Satisfied, he hobbled on. As we entered Pokhara I rubbed the beard I had acquired on the trek—a reminder I had been somewhere. In doing so my glance fell to the floor, where I spotted my trusty staff.

Some aspects of Pokhara I appreciated after having been in the mountains so long—western-style toilets rather than holes in the ground, and sheets with blankets upon full size mattresses rather than a sleeping bag over bamboo mat. I also savored the ceiling fans, beer, sandwiches, and music. One day I rented a wooden skiff and paddled across crystalline blue lake waters, letting the coolness soothe my skin and tired muscles. In the evening on the rooftop with other trekkers I drank tall cans of Tuborg beer, then vodka with grape juice. We watched the sun slip behind silhouetted ridgelines while city lights flicked on one by one. The table was filled with eager talk and laughter, and we celebrated a journey's end and the joy of newfound friendships. The clouds in my mind thinned.

The time came to return to Kathmandu. I had planned to bring my faithful walking stick along, but decided the buses were too crowded. I left it at the guesthouse, hoping another trekker might find it. En route, ramshackle dwellings, trash, rubble, and odd pieces of trucks littered the roadside in a never-ending stream of debris. Polluted and dirty, Kathmandu was not the same city I visited a month before. The city was not different. My perceptions had changed.

I had arranged to receive mail before I left on my Himalayan trek. Muddy streets and brown puddles caked my boots and trousers with wet earth, for Kathmandu felt the fringes of a cyclone ravishing the Bay of Bengal. On the way to the post office I noticed a dog dying on the sidewalk. The clouds in my head thickened again.

When I reached the post office the doors were locked. A while later, I made a second attempt but this time forgot my passport. On my third try I received a handful of letters. Amidst the bundle was a notice for an express package being held across town. I negotiated puddles and raindrops to find a dark, unmarked room in the remote building where such packages awaited. Expecting urgent news, I opened the package and found inside a letter from Tamara. I tore open the envelope, eager to devour her words. I found the emotional flavors mixed—some were sweet, and others sour. I would need to swirl them around to know how I felt.

On the way back I passed the same dog that was there earlier, now with eyes vacant and paws and tongue in the mud. More than the beggars with wrinkled outstretched arms around me, I wanted to comfort this wretched mongrel. The momentary lift I had gained from receiving mail was replaced by the suffering before me. The emptiness of death, loneliness of the road, correspondence from home, and questions from Tamara all struck me in one fell swoop.

I met Kathy and Allen and Martin over beers, and then the Aussies Glenn and Kelly arrived. It was a comfort to reunite with old friends and have stories to tell and news to share. I explained my craving for solitude, which they accepted. In wee hours, Kathy and I forgave the past and renewed our friendship. Throughout the evening, I reflected upon my journey.

Trekking through Nepal had been extraordinary. I had met so many exceptional people, seen so much stunning scenery, and learned a little about Buddhism. Yet, I felt no closer to making any choice. I was not yet ready to give up on Buddhism, however. In its purest form, I thought, Buddhism must still reside in Tibet, a place I had long imagined as a spiritual mecca. I recalled my seventh Christmas when my parents gave me a Rand-McNally physical relief globe. No other bumps compared to the protruding mass of the Tibetan Plateau. Throughout my childhood, I dreamed of one day seeing the mythical landscape in person. I remembered well the Christmas at my grandmother's stone farmhouse in New Jerusalem a decade after receiving the globe when my Aunt Fay and her husband Steve returned with tales of trekking in Nepal and their attempts to cross into Tibet. Soon after college, while living in the Virgin Islands, my scuba diving partner and I pledged we would one day, together or alone, visit Tibet. I felt I had yet to fully experience practice in action, and decided Tibet should be the next destination on my itinerary.

During the evening I was also distracted by Tamara's letter. She wanted to know when I was coming home. And when that happens, she wrote, hopefully soon, could we get back together? She missed me, she wrote, and said she still loved me. I continued to swirl the obvious question around in my mind—did I love her? As the evening ended and we each went our way, I hoped I was prepared for all that lay ahead.

11

LAND OF SNOWS

Following my return from the highlands, I scanned the Kathmandu travelers' boards. Only one brief post looked interesting: *Looking for company to Tibet. Two girls. Kathmandu Guest House.* I looked them up. Meg and Emily were in their early twenties and seemingly energetic. We decided to venture together to the border–and perhaps beyond.

On the morning of departure, silence enveloped streets of the Thamel district. Touts, men selling tiger balm, tourists, and cab drivers still likely slept. At Meg and Emily's hotel, I rang the bell next to the locked gate. As I waited for them and a sleepy proprietor to traverse the courtyard, a man wishing to drive us to the bus station approached. I knew better, but agreed to his offer.

Two days prior I had found a lad who showed me where the local city buses departed. I slipped him some baksheesh, paid three rupees to the conductor, and climbed into a clapped-out bus that veered past trash and rubble to an open-air building with a row of windows headed by signs lettered in Nepalese script. I learned that buses to Kodari, on the

Nepalese border, did not depart from that location, but at another one closer to Thamel. I caught a return bus and found a man nestled in a dim cage with Sanskrit-based writing scrawled on a board behind him. I learned from him that for sixty-five rupees–less than a dollar–I could board a bus from there for the seven-hour journey to Nepal's northern border.

This time Meg and Emily and I followed the tout through darkness and mud to a tiny car. Another man sat at the wheel. As we crammed our packs into the hatch the tout explained that we needed two drivers at night for safety from thieves. Besides, he said, the driver spoke no English and did not know the depot location. We consented, and he climbed into the cramped back seat with us.

The car negotiated narrow side alleys and the morning market where all variety of produce sat in dusty streets upon thatch mats. The driver threaded his way through the maze of shoppers, bleating rickshaws, and dogs nosing mounds of refuse. We found an actual road, and then the main thoroughfare.

In thick fog and darkness, we sputtered past what appeared to be the second bus park I had visited. The tout insisted we go farther, but I disagreed and ordered him to pull the car to the curb. The girls and I piled out and we retraced our route along the road to a muddy field filled with the stench of bus fumes and sound of revving engines. We purchased tickets, and after a brisk breakfast of noodles and parsley, squeezed into a metal seat upon a Kodari-bound bus.

Morning mists lent an eerie light to sepia-colored two and three-story dwellings which lined the sprawling suburbs of Kathmandu. On city outskirts, baskets of green and yellow fruit sat by the roadsides. As we eased into the countryside, Meg and Emily read passages aloud to each other from a John Irving novel. I stared out the window at the passing scenery, thinking about Tibet.

At a nameless village we paused. The girls sought tea–Emily had caught a stomach bug–and I bought a small bag of puffed grain for one rupee. We found our seats when the engine revved, and pushed on past grimy villages and police checkpoints, climbing upwards along the rock-strewn road towards terraced hillsides. The boy next to us held a clucking hen in his arms. Yellow moths flitting about chased each other in lazy sunlight. The land appeared hard and enduring, but in places slid onto itself. Car-sized boulders and mounds of mud around most corners partially blocked the dirt track. With sleep impossible, we read or stared out the window.

A sharp hissing interrupted my thoughts. The crew replaced the flat tire, yet ten minutes farther the dusty spare was ruined. There were no more tires, so we waited. Gray clouds lent a dull glint to the hillsides, to the people, to the tired old bus. I was anxious to continue and nervous about crossing the border, but as with all travel, patience is paramount.

When another bus came from behind we abandoned the metallic carcass. Already brimming with passengers, we clambered onto the second bus's roof. With a tremendous effort the overloaded gears engaged and we clung to any available handhold while bouncing over rocks and past landslides. A half-dozen creamy white Peking ducks tied to the roof nibbled at my boots and fingers. As afternoon faded we climbed past ramshackle buildings lining a raging river.

When the driver finally cut the engine, we had reached Kodari. In gathering darkness, high above, lights of the Tibetan border town of Zhangmu twinkled. Beyond lay the city of Lhasa, roof of the world, source of Tibetan Buddhism, and ancestral home of the Dalai Lamas. I wondered about the lands lying beyond the lights, and what mysteries they might harbor. Above all else, I hoped to reach Lhasa.

I was not certain what I expected of Tibet. I was not seeking a religious experience. I knew there might be emotional pain ahead. Yet I had kept a promise to myself and now stood at a gateway, beyond which answers to my questions might lie. Perhaps I sought a place not overrun with technology that still knew something of the spiritual life my homeland seemed to have largely forgotten. Maybe, I thought, I just need something to believe in.

In early morning hours, lights of Zhangmu still winked as the girls and I stepped across a bridge spanning a thousand-foot gorge. A thin ribbon of whitewater coursed through. Low-lying clouds clung to steep mountainsides. Smashed chassis and random bits of jeeps and trucks—more mountain carcasses—lay scattered upon cliff faces. On the other side of the bridge, two uniformed Chinese officials scrutinized our passports, for their government controlled Tibet. They waved us onward. Red paint peeled from an overhead arch etched in Chinese script, and before us stretched a dirt road lined with weathered shacks and shops.

Since no public transport existed, we flagged a passing truck and crammed into the cab. Our driver negotiated the makeshift road and chain-smoked cheap Chinese cigarettes until the tail of another truck blocked the road. The driver of the other truck had struggled up a steep incline in front of us, but could not make the grade. He climbed as far as he could go, and then reversed down the hillside to clear the road. For a moment the right rear tire of the other truck slipped over the cliff edge into empty air. The driver recovered, and brought his rig back onto solid ground.

We made our own run up the steep, muddy slope. At a sharp hairpin curve our rear wheels spun, and our turn came to reverse down the hill. Men by the roadside threw rocks and sticks onto the crest and we tried again, only to spin bald tires and again negotiate the slick track in reverse. The view was breathtaking, but the white-knuckle ride a challenge. I worried about how we would make it to the border if we could not traverse this no man's land.

Our driver gunned the engine, took another puff of his cigarette, and put the shifter into gear. We climbed, slipped a bit, found new traction, gained more ground, spun, and at the last moment caught something solid. He cut the tight corner and avoided the drop into oblivion.

At the top he idled the truck and went back to help others. When loud horns sounded from above and several southbound trucks paused at the switchback, he leapt into the cab to clear the road. Our co-driver came from behind and climbed through the window of the moving truck.

At another damaged section we made it in one attempt, and after a time buildings again lined the roadside. Relieved and grateful, at the checkpoint I handed the driver rupees for the ride. Nepalese and Tibetans and uniformed Chinese officers eyed us as we approached the barrier. One guard took our passports, told us the border reopened in three hours, and directed us to a smartly dressed Chinese official who led up the hill to a government-operated travel office.

Every guide book and traveler I had encountered claimed one could not cross into Tibet as an individual traveler—that is, if not part of a tour group. Without a Tibetan Autonomous Zone permit, entry was impossible. The girls had such permits, but I did not. I did have a Chinese visa, however, which might allow me to slip over the border if serendipity favored me. A Chinese visa could not be obtained in India, Nepal, or any country near Tibet. While in Bangkok I had found the Chinese Embassy on Ratchadaphisek minutes before they locked the doors. A few hundred chattering Thai and Chinese filled the room. At a small desk sat one flustered woman.

"Ah, you come back tomorrow," she said. "Today no good. Very busy."

"I need a visa for China, please."

She sighed, but gave me a form. Slowly the room emptied. When my turn came a few hours later I asked if I could get a visa.

"Impossible. You come back tomorrow with this receipt."

Two days later I rode the number sixty, jumped off too soon, retraced part of the route on foot, and at Thanon Asoke threaded my way across nine lanes to wait for another bus. This time, within twenty minutes, I left the embassy with a Chinese visa.

Now, on the edge of Tibet, and feeling anxious about the idea of being turned away from the border, I clutched my passport and settled into a metal chair next to Meg and Emily. The Chinese official relaxed behind his desk. Meg and Emily produced their permits, and I nervously presented my visa.

"Technically," the official said, "you shouldn't be here at all. However, with a travel permit, vehicle, and driver, I will grant you entry. All this will cost one hundred fifty dollars—per person."

Our jaws dropped. He smiled as we suggested other more affordable options. "In a few days this office closes for the winter and no travelers at all are allowed across the border," he said. "The choice is yours."

Unsure what to do, Meg and Emily and I walked across the street for tea and vegetable thukpa. After returning to the checkpoint we tried to talk to an immigration officer, but he would not speak to us without the government official present. We trudged back up the hill.

"You may walk back down to Kodari if you please," the government officer said. "Without my approval and a travel permit, the border guards will not speak to you, much less grant you entry." With no other choice, over the course of another hour we secured permits, visa stamps, driver, and vehicle. I gritted my teeth and wondered how much of our money went into the official's pocket.

While loading gear into the rear of the rented Land Cruiser, a Tibetan who spoke no English got behind the wheel. He indicated that his name was Dorje. His eyes were kind and he smiled as we crawled inside. After a Chinese passenger joined us, we climbed upwards through Zhangmu. Tibetan women and some of the men we saw wore long braids pinned atop their heads. Tibetans never cut their hair, though that tradition was for a time repressed by the Maoists. One shirtless man, bathing at a waterfall with long hair unbraided, watched us open-mouthed as though he had never seen a vehicle in all his life. On one stretch, where tents with smoke pouring through the roofs lined the roadsides, children stared after us.

There remains some debate as from where Tibetans derive. Some say they migrated from India, and are of the Sakya race; others claim they came from the Malay Peninsula. One theory holds that before the Yellow Emperor of China entered the

Central Plains he established a capital at Kunlun, and during the course of his journey, a contingent was left behind, which evolved into the Tibetans of today.

Tibetans themselves, though, have no doubts as to their origins. Scholar Tiley Chodag documents much Tibetan lore in his work *Tibet the land and the people*. Avalokiteśvara, the Lord of Mercy and Bodhisattva of Compassion, lives upon Mount Potala. As Chodag relates, the goddess long ago ordained a monkey as her disciple and ordered him to travel to the Land of Snows. There the monkey focused his mind on the merciful nature of the bodhisattva, as commanded. While deep in meditation, an ogress appeared.

"Let us be united!" she urged. The monkey demurred, for he would be breaking his religious vows should he marry.

"If you refuse to marry me," the ogress persisted, "my fate will bind me to become the wife of an ogre in the future. If this comes to pass I will be the cause of thousands of deaths, and will also give birth to countless ogre children and grandchildren."

The monkey contemplated this paradox. To refuse her request would be to commit a great sin. He turned a somersault and made his way to Mount Potala.

"This is a good omen," the goddess decided. "If you unite with the ogress, mankind will multiply in the Land of Snows."

The monkey did as commanded, married the ogress, and bore six monkey offspring who he took to the forest to live on their own, nourished by the ample fruit growing there.

Three years later the monkey visited the forest, and saw that his descendants had increased to five hundred. The fruits had dwindled, and his offspring were on the verge of starvation.

"What will we eat? How will we survive?" asked the young monkeys with paws outstretched. The father monkey returned to Avalokiteśvara.

"I will feed your descendants," she promised. The monkey came back to the forest with five kinds of wild grain seeds, which the monkeys came to use to sustain themselves. Over time their tails grew shorter, their tongues grew used to human speech, and they became people. These were the ancestors of the inhabitants of the Land of Snows.

The road climbed up and out of the valley along lush tree-covered slopes and past waterfalls cascading at every turn. The vegetation thinned as we ascended and hints of snow-covered peaks appeared on the horizon. Green rolling hills turned brown as we climbed higher. Patchy snow covered the starkness. Besides a few trucks kicking up clouds of dust, the spaces stood empty.

A collection of buildings, Nyalam, appeared. Two *dzopkyo*, a cross between a yak and Tibetan cow, battled in the street and one pinned the other to the ground. We waited until someone prodded them to the side with a stick. After refueling, we continued into the desert, still climbing upwards, as afternoon deepened with the cold.

At a brisk wind-blown crest named Lalung La, we stopped at dusk at a mass of prayer flags. Other than the occasional pair of headlights probing the darkness, the only signs of humanity were occasional clusters of earthen whitewashed dwellings set amongst the emptiness. Royal blue trim decorated the windows, and painted onto the whitewash were red, white, and blue stripes–wisps of color against the ubiquitous browns and grays of the land. Flat roofs held dry brush, firewood, piles of yak dung, maybe some grain.

Stone fences lined courtyards and fields holding two-wheel tractors and herds of *dzopkyo*. Woolly sheep and goats with long curving horns roamed the road and hillsides. Far from artificial lights, the misty Milky Way gleamed with mind-numbing clarity. An upside down Big Dipper rose and a falling star caught my eye. On occasion, men on horseback wearing fur hats and yak skin boots appeared from shadows.

Without warning, Dorje pulled the Land Cruiser into a courtyard and motioned that driving for the day was finished. We had reached Tingri. Inside the doorway, covered only by a heavy blanket, comely Tibetans sat around a table. One girl fed juniper scrub into the stove. They pointed and giggled at our fair skin and hair. Though not hungry due to the nearly fourteen thousand foot altitude, we ate thukpa and momos and drank hot butter tea. Dorje was handed a bowl of ground barley flour. He added butter tea and kneaded the concoction into a thick white paste. Laughing all the while, he rolled out balls from the tsampa and plunked them into his mouth.

With stomachs bursting, we settled back and learned how to say "thank you" and also "hello"–*tashi dele*. When the others filed outside, we followed beneath a clear night sky. Inside our frigid, unheated rooms we huddled beneath heavy blankets. The girls had felt odd at dinner–sluggish, light-headed, and dizzy–and I suspected a long night. I heard wild dogs howl in the distance. We were warned to carry stout sticks to drive them off, and I wished I had not left my walking staff in Pokhara. Through the thin wall, I heard Emily mumbling. Moments later she rushed to the door and puked a long trail of butter tea and thukpa onto the frozen ground.

Before sunrise a knock awakened me, but the girls barely stirred. The wrinkled proprietor brought eggs and chapati, an unleavened flatbread. Clouds moved in so we hustled against the chill. We climbed into the Land Cruiser and soon Dorje lurched down the dirt track. Slivers of sunshine mottled the brown plains and barren hillsides. Beyond frosted windows, the surreal scenery resembled a snow-covered moonscape.

Dorje broke my trance. "Chomolungma! Chomolungma!" he yelled while gesturing wildly.

I followed the direction of his pointing finger. There on the southern horizon the highest mountain in the world brooded over the Tibetan Plateau. We stared dumbfounded upon the peak known in the west as Mount Everest.

According to legend as related in *Tibet the land and the people*, the Tibetan plateau and roof of the world was once a massive, boundless sea. Foaming waves crashed onto beaches covered in hemlocks and palms. Above the forests, mountains rose into the sky one upon the other. Exotic flowers and grasses grew in the forests; herds of antelope and rhinoceroses roaming the forests came to the water's edge to drink. Cuckoos, thrushes, and larks flitted from treetop to treetop.

One day the tranquility was shattered by a giant five-headed poisonous dragon, which rose from the depths of the sea. The monster threw up waves that destroyed the flowers and trees. The birds, deer, monkeys, and hares thought the end had come. With no hope left, there appeared over the sea a five-colored cloud which transformed itself into the Five Sister Dakinis. These had supernatural powers which they used to defeat the dragon. The great sea was again calm.

"Wait!" cried the birds and animals as the Dakinis prepared to leave. "Please stay and favor us with your presence!"

Out of compassion, the Dakinis remained and ordered the sea to retreat. Dense forest grew in the east. The west turned into an endless expanse of fertile soil. The south became a land of flourishing flowers and grasses, and the north changed into boundless grassland. Then the Dakinis transformed themselves into the five main peaks of the Himalaya that tower at the southwestern border of Tibet. The main peak became known to Tibetans as Chomolungma.

As Chomolungma fell behind us, a barren landscape unfolded. We shivered despite glimpses of sun, yet locals walked, galloped on horseback, or rode in the backs of open-air trucks. After a steep ascent we came upon a mass of prayer flags and stones marking sixteen thousand foot Lagpa-la pass. Below the pass we followed the holy Brahmaputra River, which wound like a silvery dragon from the flanks of sacred Mount Kailash to the Bay of Bengal in Bangladesh. Sometimes, the track was ice and water and we skidded and slid through. When a bridge was out we drove around it, always a bone-rattling affair over rock-filled washboard.

At a checkpoint near Lhatse, a mumbling woman approached. Her black hair was tied in long braids, her woolen tunic worn, her ancient eyes sunk into brown wrinkled flesh. She asked for coins, likely, but we had none to give.

In Shigatse, we stopped for lunch. Donkeys pulled two-wheel carts laden with grains and brush and earth. I entered a Chinese food stall and pointed to symbols on a paper menu tacked to the wall. A bowl of noodles with seaweed and squid appeared. Dorje and the Chinese passenger Xieqǐguāng joined me. Xieqǐguāng ordered an oversized bottle of beer. He filled my glass and kept it full. I did not protest, but marveled at his generosity. Earlier he gave each of us rice treats, the day before apples, and later on pears. Whether his generosity derived from guilt, custom, or simple kindness, I did not know.

While waiting in the sun a group of local lads surrounded me. Fascinated by the book about Tibet that I carried, they asked questions about a land they seemed to know little about—the land of their own birth and heritage.

We boarded the Land Cruiser and moved again into open countryside. Darkness fell, and in time low-rise concrete buildings appeared. These homely Chinese-built constructions were unlike the attractive, traditional Tibetan homes of the countryside. Within the urban sprawl the girls located a hotel, and I found a guesthouse. We had reached Lhasa at last.

12

ABODE OF THE GODS

Scholar Tiley Chodag relates another story from Tibet's early history. After evolving from the bodhisattva monkey, the people of the Land of Snows gathered berries, learned to hunt, and practiced a form of spirit-based animism called Bönism. One day, herdsmen spotted a youth who spoke a different dialect. Unsure what to do, elders of the tribe sent twelve wise men to ask the handsome young man where he came from. The youth pointed upward. Believing he descended from the skies, the wise men proclaimed him a heavenly son and carried him down the mountain on their shoulders. The community rushed forward, made the young man their chieftain, and named him Nyatri Tsanpo, "the chieftain seated on the throne of a neck." From that time forward, Tibetan kings were known as *tsanpos*.

The thirty-third *tsanpo*, Songtsän Gampo, consolidated his power in the mid-seventh century CE and moved his capital from Rasa, meaning goat-earth, to the site of present day Lhasa, the Abode of the Gods. Founder of the Tibetan Empire, Gampo solidified his holdings by contracting two marriages—the first to Princess Bhrikuti of Nepal, who is said to have converted him to Buddhism. The second union was to Princess Wencheng of the Chinese Tang dynasty, who also brought with her the Buddhist faith. By giving Princess Wencheng's hand in marriage the Tang emperor created an alliance, which formed the basis for the interwoven and controversial history of the Han and Tibetan cultures.

Despite this historical justification, I held a silent grudge towards the Chinese. In 1950 their government invaded Tibet. Upon my arrival in Lhasa, Chinese shops sold leathers, staples, and textiles. Chinese merchants peddled wares along the sidewalks. Chinese citizens rode bicycles and rickshaws and crowded the thoroughfares. Meanwhile, many Tibetans crouched on sidewalks and street corners with palms open. Tibetans had become a minority in their own land.

I turned into an alley, passed a few Tibetan quarters, and came upon a wide torn-up road. Lhasa's remaining remnants of Tibetan architecture were being converted to uninspiring, Chinese-built concrete block stores along dirty, rubbish-filled streets.

I found a pocket of whitewashed flat-roofed earthen buildings without galvanized garage doors or cinder blocks. I recognized this as the Barkhor district. Tibetan women bundled against the cold beneath long aprons and coats and braided red and yellow strings into their long hair, which they tied up. The men wore layers of thick homemade clothes.

The Barkhor's narrow streets had served as the spiritual heart of Lhasa for centuries. Mongols, Chinese, Muscovites, Armenians, Kashmiri, Nepalese, and Indians had traded musk, gold, medicinal plants, furs, yaks, sugar, tea, saffron, turquoise, and amber by the end of the 1600s. Chinese Muslims lived in a southern quarter. Nepalese families clustered to the north.

Even into the 1940s, local merchants catered to all tastes and imported such goods as Australian butter and British whiskey. Heinrich Harrer in *Seven Years in Tibet* describes the area as one in which "there is nothing one cannot buy, or at least order. One even finds the Elizabeth Arden specialties, and there is keen demand for them...You can order, too, sewing machines, radio sets and gramophones and hunt up Bing Crosby records."

Everything changed when Chinese bureaucrats and government troops arrived in 1950. Food rations and poorly stocked communist stores replaced the old markets. Within the past few years that too began to change as arcades and malls sprang up to cater to the Chinese masses. For the time being, Chinese and Tibetan merchants in the Barkhor still sold prayer flags, incense, prayer wheels, and other religious items.

Tibet's most popular circumambulation route, the Nangkhor, encircled Jokhang Temple and four massive incense burners of white stone that spewed clouds of incense into the air around the clock to please the gods. Along my flanks moved withered women spinning handheld prayer wheels, wild and dirty Khampas from remote reaches of the high plateaus, and monks in orange vestments holding alms bowls. All fingered strings of prayer beads and chanted *Om Mani Padme Hum*. The sights and pilgrims enthralled me. This remnant of Tibetan culture reassured me that all was not lost. I felt an uptick in my mood, yet somberly wondered how long the Barkhor and Nangkhor could endure.

Songtsän Gampo built Jokhang Temple—the most revered structure in Tibet—to house a statue of the eight-year-old Buddha that Princess Bhrikuti brought as dowry. The temple was a four-story blend of Indian, Nepalese, and Tang dynasty design with roofs covered in gilded bronze tile. Near the entrance, dozens of pilgrims prostrated themselves upon tattered blankets or cardboard. The paving stones where they knelt, then lay face first, were worn smooth by the thousands who had come before them. Some pilgrims wore rags beneath a shredded outer apron. With wooden blocks in hand they knelt and prostrated themselves, arose, moved two feet, knelt and prostrated themselves, arose, and repeated around the mile and a half circuit. Others did this for hundreds of miles along their journeys to Lhasa. A few, such as one woman with raw hands and knees, did so without any cardboard or blocks.

Such displays stunned my Western intellect. My secular mentality could not fathom the extent of such devotion. Never in my life had I encountered any cause worthy of such dedication. I wondered whether that was due to my own character, or the absence in Western culture of ideals powerful enough to warrant such ardor. I imagined the answer to be some combination of both.

Inside the temple, monks on thin mats chanted in the cold beneath long rows of butter lamps. A drum beat faster, the tempo changing with the monks' mantras. An orange-robed monk scurried past as I climbed to the roof. Below me, the maze of alleyways buzzed with activity. Vendors sold carpets, yak quarters, kitchenware, chickens, hats, and ducks. A one-eyed monk with brass bowl begged for alms. Crippled children shuffled by on their hands. An unending stream of pilgrims flowed around the temple.

Minor Chinese influences encroached on the scene, but while I peered from the rooftop, Tibetan timelessness held a while longer. No westerners were visible anywhere. Just as one did not simply show up in Lhasa, I realized, one could likewise not easily escape.

The next morning I found my way to the Potala Palace, from which the Dalai Lamas ruled the Tibetan Plateau for hundreds of years. The Dalai Lamas—monks of the Gelug school of Tibetan Buddhism—were considered incarnations of the goddess Avalokiteśvara. Their title derived from the Mongol word for ocean, *dalai*, and the Tibetan word for guru. Named for the goddess's home atop Mount Potala, the palace represented the cultural and historical base of Tibetan Buddhism, and a journey to Tibet was not complete without a visit to this sacred space.

Morning light illuminated the Potala's magnificence. Throngs gathered on the grand plaza below the palace. Beneath a red People's Republic of China flag, roaming teenage girls carried wooden trays filled with Chinese cigarettes. Tibetans in fur hats and yak skins sat upon the stones with hands extended. A Chinese man in neat suit and thin tie walked with a girl-woman in mini-skirt and ankle-length black leather coat. Nearby sat bedraggled and braided Khampas. Someone shot off fireworks while minstrels and begging children sought a few Chinese yuan.

A crowd of Tibetan pilgrims crowded around Shöl Gate at the foot of the Potala. Following the Fourteenth Dalai Lama's escape during the 1959 "liberation" of Tibet as part of the Chinese Cultural Revolution, China converted the palace into a museum. Comprised of nine hundred ninety-nine rooms and hallways, visitors only saw the few approved for viewing by the Chinese. Despite Tibetans' suppression and their leader's exile, pilgrims still traveled from afar to visit the hallowed halls. As I was about to experience, unlike most museums, the Potala Palace was very much alive—for the rooms were daily filled with hundreds of worshipping devotees.

With nervous anticipation, I ascended hundreds of steps amidst the mass of pilgrims. Beyond a courtyard lined with low yellow-walled galleries I climbed another set—the middle flight once reserved for the Dalai Lama. I entered the heart of the Red Palace. The pungent smell of burning yak butter permeated the palace. In each open room, monks dished blobs of butter into massive brass urns and pilgrims added more chunks to the kettles. Hundreds of rumple-haired, soot-faced pilgrims carrying infants, prayer beads, and meager piles of small denomination jiao filed from chapel to chapel. They bowed at each statue, recited mantras, and tossed paper money and white scarfs at the shrines.

In Sasum Namgyal the mobs became jammed. No one could exit, and guards pushed everyone into a single-file line. Even so, a man on two sticks hobbled in with a few monks. More pilgrims crowded into the room, all staring forward eagerly. A Chinese guard in olive drab uniform told me to move ahead and not queue, but I preferred to wait with the masses. When the gridlock eased, we moved past the tomb of the Seventh Dalai Lama.

The route let out on the upper western flank. I turned around, fought against the human current, and returned to the Eastern Sunshine Apartment of the White Palace. Here the Fourteenth Dalai Lama grew towards adolescence, spied on Lhasa's denizens with his telescope, and met Heinrich Harrer. Then, more than forty years ago, this palace was still the home of sacred Dalai Lamas. With the arrival of the Chinese, it would never again house another one. The old ways were dead. This truth greatly troubled me. Whatever the Chinese government's justifications, I could not accept on any grounds the destruction of a peaceful culture.

The Dalai Lamas' tenure had not been forgotten, however. In the palace study a reticent red-robed monk was my sole companion. He uttered "Dalai Lama," and turned slightly towards me. I responded, "Dalai Lama." With that his eyes closed, his eyelids fluttered, and he heaved a deep sigh.

We walked to the palace roof's edge. Rooftops of Lhasa spread to the horizons. Below lay the crumbling village of Shöl; to the east cowered the remainder of Bharkor. Everywhere else and extending for miles in all directions, were Chinese-built structures that replaced the once ubiquitous grasslands and white-washed Tibetan homes. The monk motioned for the notebook I carried. I handed it to him and watched as he wrote Tibetan script inside. I showed him a picture of the Dalai Lama that I carried. He closed his eyes and prayed to the image before taking my sleeve and leading me back to the main palace circuit.

We retraced my earlier steps. The monk pointed to golden statues of Buddha along the way, bowed his head, and encouraged me to do the same. We followed the accustomed route, unhurried, bowing to occasional monks and gesturing without words. Only the flicker of butter lamps lit some passageways. No warmth buffered the drafts that swirled in rooms and hallways.

When we exited the palace, he gestured us onward. I followed him around Chagpo Ri, the sacred hill facing Marpo Ri, site of the Potala. Together with Pongwa Ri, these three mountains composed the *Three Protectors of Tibet* and were three of the four holy mountains of central Tibet.

We climbed more stairs to Palha Lupuk, a cave temple said to be the meditation retreat of Songtsän Gampo. Inside we found trinkets, rock carvings over a thousand years old, and monks guarding butter lamps. Ragged beggars waited with hands outstretched. Pilgrims chanted. One urchin yanked my pants leg while two others grabbed my shirt. A little girl peed by my foot. Every sight and action was beyond my wildest expectation. In my naiveté, I had expected a purer vision of Tibetans in motion. Instead, I found a demoralized populace and nearly decimated culture.

At the main road the monk gestured me onward, but my energy was spent. He bowed and continued alone. I shuffled past the hundreds of golden prayer wheels encircling the Potala, spinning some as I went. One beggar with shoeless stumps asked for change. I shook my head no. Wild-haired sad-eyed men upon wooden carts sat with heads bowed. I tried to return the smiles of the nuns who greeted me, but never expected so many, or really, any beggars in Tibet.

Over a pot of tea in a second floor café, I watched nomads cluster upon the square. The uniformed Chinese guards watched too. Even in the Tibetan quarter all storefront signs followed the same format: large Chinese script atop small Tibetan writing.

Down-trodden Tibetans wandered into the restaurant, palms open. The proprietor waved them off. There seemed little doubt that should I ever return to Lhasa, the Abode of the Gods would consist of nothing more than a sprawling cityscape of Chinese noodle stalls, karaoke bars, and hair salons. So far, Tibet was not at all the spiritual enclave I had hoped.

13

TASHI DELE

After the Tibetan Empire crumbled in the fourteenth century, political power shifted away from Lhasa. The city's role as a religious center grew, however. New monasteries sprang up, especially the most influential one of the period, Drepung. I found a bus bound for the monastery, and climbed aboard. Pilgrims filled every seat. One woman wore a black yak robe. She touched her forehead with a hand of wrinkled brown skin stretched over sticks of bone. The pilgrims were jovial, and seemingly excited to see the monastery. One said something in Tibetan. Everyone aboard the bus laughed. I watched as the old woman's magenta and emerald-colored scarf fell away to reveal her one remaining tooth. My admiration at her seeming resilience was tinged with sadness by the thought of what she and so many like her stood to lose.

We rode up and into Drepung, once the world's largest monastery with over ten thousand monks. Drepung had long served as the seat of the Dalai Lamas, until the Fifth moved into the restored Potala Palace. Despite the passage of time, Drepung remained a maze of narrow alleys and stairways, multi-story white-washed residences, and gold and burgundy temples. Hundreds of gold prayer wheels surrounded the stone walls. Monks kept them well-greased, so they always spun and shouted *Om Mani Padme Hum* to the heavens.

A small group of Tibetan pilgrims eyed me—out of curiosity, I suspected. "Tashe dele," I said. *Hello.*

They stopped to gather around. I showed them my book with a picture of the Fourteenth Dalai Lama. Their eyes widened in awe, and each placed the book on his or her head out of respect. Faces beamed with happiness as they continued onward. One girl turned, put her hands together, and bowed.

In Drepung's external hall, pilgrims following a circuitous route added butter to the brass kettles and bowed their heads. Incense and the stench of burning butter lamps billowed out of the Main Hall. A monk's throaty chant filled the interior. In the cramped inner chapel, a seated monk banged a round brass drum that hung from the ceiling. He chanted non-stop while alternately clanging two metal drums between his legs. A hundred other monks draped in red robes and seated upon crimson and gold cushions chanted at their own pace and cadence. Voices loud, soft, deep, and high-pitched repeated sacred lines without pause. I listened in silent reverence.

In early afternoon I returned to downtown Lhasa. I ducked into a Chinese restaurant and ordered vegetables with fried noodles. A wizened Tibetan sat opposite. As someone placed a glass of hot water before him, he smiled. He asked where I was from, and responded with a thumbs-up when I told him. He leaned over.

"Dalai," he said in a low voice. He put his right thumb up again, and covered his smile with his left hand.

"Dalai," I said, and covered my smile also. We enjoyed our private joke amongst the crowd of Chinese patrons.

Outside, a man with bad teeth and tinted glasses stopped me. He said his name was Guan Xing and he ran an English school for Chinese and Tibetan children ages ten to fifteen. He had noticed my obvious western appearance, and asked that I speak to his students and let them ask me questions. "Non-political only," he said, smiling. "Perhaps you might teach them a song? They know already *Jingle Bells* and *Do-Re-Mi*. Maybe you know another?"

Intrigued, I walked with him to his house in a squalid concrete block neighborhood that had once housed a Tibetan community. His family smiled and offered apples. A two thousand-year-old Chinese opera played on the television. He introduced me to a lad in his class, too shy to speak. Glancing around the home, I asked why the people of Lhasa wished to speak English.

"It is better," he said, "for the people, for their future. English is the language of the world."

Upon leaving I told him I would think about his request. My headaches had recently returned, so I found a quiet bar and retreated to a dark corner. *Beer from the Roof of the World* read the bottle's label. My eyes closed as I contemplated all I had seen the past few days. I wanted to lose myself in the din around me, but could not help noticing the other foreigners nearby—the first since parting with Meg and Emily. A middle-aged Aussie recounting his life to a mildly interested French couple bragged of exploits in Afghanistan, Pakistan, Tibet, and his attempts at Bhutan. Chinese teenage girls came out one at a time, looked at my book about Tibet, asked me questions, and then disappeared behind the curtain. The Aussie claimed Lhasa was a third this size one year ago; three years ago it was a pleasant little town.

"The Chinese have ruined Lhasa!" he cried. I sipped my beer and silently agreed.

There was one more site on my list to visit. The palaces of the Thirteenth and Eighth Dalai Lamas were closed and locked, but the Norbulingka, the summer palace, remained open. Of the twenty-two parks which once surrounded Lhasa, only three were not covered by recently constructed dormitory blocks, offices, or army barracks. The Norbulingka gardens, though overgrown, untended, and forgotten, were the largest of their kind in Tibet. It was from Norbulingka that the Fourteenth Dalai Lama escaped to India in 1959 while disguised as a Tibetan soldier. After the Chinese shelled the palace during the uprising that followed, the grounds fell quiet.

A Tibetan monk, one of the staff, let me slip through when I told him I had no ticket. He suggested I tell any guards around that I dropped it. I ascended a staircase and entered the Dalai Lama's Audience Chamber, where murals depicted Tibet's history in three hundred and one scenes. Onward were his meditation chamber, a study, and his bedroom. Another monk watched over these rooms.

"I love America," the monk said.

He showed me a Philips radio from India, and an ancient phonograph with a Tibetan opera record inside, one His Holiness himself had once enjoyed. The monk asked whether I had a picture. I knew what he meant, and showed the one of the Fourteenth Dalai Lama. He looked around, in case a guard had sneaked in, and pulled from within his robe a chain hanging around his neck. At the end dangled an image of the Dalai Lama. I marveled at it.

We heard a group ascend the stairs. With pride and awe he slipped the likeness back under his robe. "Chinese," he grimaced, and balled his hand into a defiant fist.

When they entered the room, he relaxed his face and hand. He left to show them around, but turned to me, smiled, put his hands into a prayer position, and bowed. I bowed back, inspired by his defiance and all Tibetans' silent and passionate perseverance.

Downtown again, street vendors packed their wares into wooden two-wheel carts that they pushed home by hand. As daylight faded, a white crescent moon appeared over purple mountain silhouettes. Bent women donning cloth dust masks and thick robes swept streets clear with short-handled straw brooms. Monks hunched over hand-written scripts, and chanted into the night by the light of burning butter lamps.

Chinese troops standing in the back of a passing open-air military truck watched everyone mill about. A one-legged shoeshine boy called me over, but scattered with the rest of the main crowd when a policeman pushed his way through. A few sunflower seed vendors tried to wait the officer out, but also were forced to leave. After the policeman climbed back onto his motorcycle and sped off, the throngs returned to vie for my business.

A group of three nomads in thick sheepskin *tubas* and calf-high *ko-sum* boots strolled past, laughing.

"Tashi dele," they said when they saw me.

Their wild hair caught the last rays of orange sun, which reflected from their daggers swinging from wide, black sashes. Other men of the plains watched in fascination as ink poured onto the pages of my notebook. They stared at me, at the notebook, and back at me. One reached out to touch the stubble on my chin.

Later I revisited Jokhang Temple. Beggars sat in the street and lined the circuit. Old women gestured, monks chanted, deformed and legless souls crouched on the stained stones. Two children grabbed me and, crying for food or money, would not let go. I wanted to turn around but the tide was too strong, and I had no choice but to flow with the masses. The sunken eyes of an ancient woman peered up at me, cupped hand gesturing up and down. A blind toothless monk recited mantras while incense burned. A man, wife, and two crying children wearing weathered rags sat upon sacks. Their toddler urinated into the dust. The sights were overpowering. There seemed no end to the suffering around me. I could barely breathe with such a lump in my throat.

Finally I broke free and climbed to the Jokhang's roof. At the last ladder an elderly man with cane attempted to descend, and his grandson, wild-haired and toothless, helped him down. They had traveled from afar, perhaps the western plains of Amdo. After I descended, I found a corner overlooking a dark inner courtyard barely lit by butter lamps. There I stood, and let the tears fall...and fall.

I thought of these people and their land, where a westerner could visit the sacred Jokhang and Potala and remaining monasteries, though the Dalai Lama and thousands of Tibetan Buddhist exiles in other countries held little hope of ever seeing their homeland again. Of the one hundred seventy thousand residents in Lhasa, over one hundred fifty thousand were Han Chinese. The old Tibetan quarters of Barkhor and Shöl composed a fraction of the city, and those holdouts faced extinction. Lhasa had become a sprawling frontier Chinatown.

Each day, the devout bowed and prayed and recited mantras and tossed white scarves and burned butter and looked upon golden statues in wild-eyed wonder. Thousands of them daily idolized golden stupas and tombs of past kings. The unquestioning devotion, absolute subservience, and reverence for a man, a god, and a faith were evident. Yet the ragged vagabonds of the plateaus with their Buddhist notions were not a people with elevated ideals and principles. They were a poor, starving, vanquished culture on the verge of extinction. It was not the golden images or ancient temples or grand monasteries of Tibet that moved my heart, but Tibetans' commitment and willingness to sacrifice everything for their beliefs in the face of oblivion.

Buddhism in its purest form was the salve I had hoped to find in Lhasa. The Buddha's core message, based upon love, compassion, and service to others, is a powerful one. If I understood the Buddha's lessons, and was convinced that the Buddha's teachings were the right path and I tried to follow that path, then I was by definition a Buddhist. Buddhism at its core is a philosophy and way of life, not a religion. Yet the version of Tibetan Buddhism I had encountered, replete with rules, rituals, and god worship, felt to me like religion. This was not the salve I was seeking.

Disillusioned, and feeling no closer to making any choice for myself than when I started the journey, I realized that many of the tears I was shedding in the dimly lit corner of the

Jokhang were for me.

A few minutes later the elderly man and his grandson stood beside me to peer into the chapel below. I turned away to hide my tears. I wiped some from my cheeks, and then turned back. The pair prepared to leave.

"Tashi dele," I said.

The elderly man smiled.

"Tashi dele," he replied.

With a trace of pride, he hobbled onward.

14

LIGHTS OF ZHANGMU

A thin haze of incense, car exhaust, and wood smoke choked mountain-ringed Lhasa from morning until evening. Without a proper coat, heat in my room, or any source of warmth in the high altitude air, I always felt chilled. Coughing fits jarred my weak frame. Changing my clothes made me light-headed and dizzy.

The solitary road between Kathmandu and Lhasa–the only way out of Tibet to the south–soon shut, for deep snow would make the passes impassable. Since the border at Zhangmu had already closed to northbound traffic, vehicles no longer drove to the border to meet travelers and bring them to Lhasa. And, the few flights had ceased until spring.

With no public transportation and no flights, I could do nothing as nights grew colder and the snows crept closer. I struggled through my days with thick lungs, pounding muddled head, and lethargic limbs. My thoughts dwelled on whether I could manage a winter in this high country.

One day I received word that a ride was heading south. There might not be another for the rest of the year. At nine o'clock on Thanksgiving morning, I went to the unheated lobby and asked the woman to track down the driver. She called the Snowlands Hotel, and then the Yak Hotel.

"He'll be right over," she said.

The vehicle arrived after ten with a driver named Tashi and an odd, fiftyish bearded gentleman sitting in front. "I have no home," the passenger said, "though was born in India."

We circled the block to pick up a Chinese family, and with much ado, continued. After a stop for Tashi to make purchases, we stopped again. When he was ready to depart, the family wandered off. So it went. An elderly Chinese man got in, and I was further squished into the seat. We made more stops. In a concrete block neighborhood all piled out, and another Chinese family of four adults and one child crammed into the backseat with me. It seemed this was the family coming with us, and the first family had used us as a taxi. More stops. At last we made our way through outskirts of Lhasa, and then into the countryside. Hour by hour my legs grew more cramped. Breathing was toilsome with my choking lungs. The nausea made eating impossible.

At Shigatse we stopped. The bearded man demanded that Tashi take him to another part of town for business he would not discuss. Tashi left with the man, and the Chinese and I found a restaurant, where I learned that even boiled cabbage and broth were too much to keep down. Tashi brought back the bearded man, who cursed us all because he wanted more time. Tibetans sometimes approached our truck and stared, and when they did the bearded man shooed them away. When beggars came around with palms open the bearded man scolded them, rolled up the window, and turned his back.

After dusk we made Lhatse. I dragged my bag inside and asked for a single room, but the woman wanted one hundred yuan. I had only eighty, which must also include all food until I reached Nepal. She put me into a triple for forty with a warning I would have to share. The effort of walking across the room sapped my strength and made me breathless. I lay in the darkness. One of the young women knocked and told me two more would be in my room. I mumbled that I was ill. She could do nothing, she said, and closed the door.

As soon as I fell asleep, I awakened. I fell asleep again, but dreamt the same dream I just dreamt and awakened at the same place in the same dream. This continued over and over, into the night, dreaming the same dream a dozen more times and always stopping at the same point. Finally I didn't sleep at all and lay motionless. Yet the room was empty, so I had something to be thankful for on Thanksgiving after all.

Following my trekking experiences, I thought I might be immune to acute altitude sickness. But the singular rule when it comes to who succumbs is that there are no rules. Even the fittest fall prey. Few if any doctors in Lhasa spoke English, but even if they had, there was nothing they could tell me I did not already know. The only cure was to descend before it was too late. Many world-class mountaineers had died at altitudes thousands of meters lower than where we were going, because they did not get off the mountain in time.

With Tashi, we were gradually descending, but the way out of the mountains was not one continuous downgrade. It required climbing back up peaks and passes. Every few hundred feet in elevation gain, my coughs became thicker and the effects of pulmonary edema intensified. I grew weaker and less mobile while my mind became more clouded. The drive out of Tibet became a race against time. If too much fluid built up in my lungs before we topped the final pass, no rescue would be possible–and nothing could save me. The lights of Zhangmu were my only hope.

At six in the morning the bearded man yelled and pounded on my door. We squeezed into the truck. It was soon apparent the day would unfold like the one before, but worse. At Tingri, we stopped for breakfast. Unable to move, I lay on the seat. My heart beat felt irregular. Breathing was even more labored and I shivered non-stop, though the sun had risen.

Beyond Tingri we had a double pass to clear, the higher portion at almost sixteen thousand feet. We reached the first, but climbed still more. I opened my eyes a hair's width.

Massive snow-capped mountains covered the horizons. When I opened them again, everyone else piled out at a mass of prayer flags to drape white silk scarves upon the chorten. I lacked the strength to even reach for the canteen of water I had strategically positioned behind my head.

At last we fully descended. The thought occurred to me that if I was not suffering from altitude sickness and pulmonary edema but in fact some other condition that descending would not cure, then I could be in a very serious state indeed.

My head cleared a little, and I gained some strength. The sun stabbed my eyes, but a touch of hunger found me. I felt hopeful. At Nyame, I still could not walk and stayed in the vehicle. When trees and waterfalls appeared, I knew Zhangmu lay below. Tashi hurtled down the narrow street until we reached a backup of trucks. Then, half a mile before the border checkpoint, Tashi pulled over and would go no further.

Tibetans drifted our direction. The bearded man sought a porter for his luggage, and two young Tibetan women wanted the job. A struggle ensued when they both grabbed his bag. He pushed them aside, and nominated one to carry it. I shouldered my rucksack and limped to the checkpoint. Emily and Meg were there and had secured passage on the only other vehicle coming out of Lhasa that I had heard about. They too were grateful for a way out.

The bearded man wanted to share a cab to Kodari. "Fine," I said, and put my bag in the trunk.

"No!" said another man.

"I guess he's full," sneered the bearded man.

A kid asked if I wanted a lift. I climbed into the back of the truck and found a place amongst the locals and boxes and bags. The vehicle stuttered across gullies and small ditches and threw us into the air. We bounced on top of each other as the dust choked us and smothered our belongings.

Near Kodari I crawled out to find immigration and get a Nepalese visa. The bearded man had arrived at the border a short time before me, and asked if I would share an onward cab to Kathmandu. I wanted nothing more to do with him, and took a room in Kodari instead.

Before first light, the clerk knocked on my door to let me know the bus was about to leave. The little man crawled back behind his reception desk-cum-candy counter to find sleep. I stumbled downstairs and out the door. Lights of Zhangmu twinkled high on the mountainside. Nearby idled the only bus in the deserted dirt street. I hopped aboard just as it pulled away. In my seat I took the deepest breath I had in days—for I had made it to the Land of Snows, and back again.

I convalesced at the Kathmandu Guest House, a Rana-era mansion converted into an upscale accommodation. My small room cost four dollars, though others paid upwards of thirty. For a time I could not travel beyond the fragrant gardens. The only moments I managed full breaths were when I inhaled steam from the scalding showers I often indulged in. Suspecting that bronchitis or pneumonia had complicated the pulmonary edema, I took the partial course of antibiotics a friend in Alaska had given me some time ago, and rested in the wood-paneled lobby while watching cricket with the Brits.

Struggling for motivation, I considered packing it in and heading home. I missed my family. Tamara's letter still plagued my thoughts. If I summoned the energy, I might still find a flight and reach my grandmother's stone farmhouse in order to be with my family for Christmas.

I switched to a noisier, cheaper hotel. At this point even four dollars per night was a financial burden. This one had no lobby, but did have a rooftop. One evening, Canadians with bottles of juice and vodka poured me a strong one. The drinks flowed as dusk settled and a red-orange moon crested the snow-capped peaks. More travelers joined our full moon party.

For days before the party I had debated my options. Tibetan Buddhism was not my answer, it seemed. Perhaps India, I mused. The ancient land was suffused with and had been influenced by every major historical religion on the planet. On reputation alone, it was a spiritual mecca. I recalled the Christmases at my grandmother's stone farmhouse when Aunt Fay and Steve spoke of the many months they spent traveling around the Indian subcontinent.

"If I were asked," noted scholar and Indian philosopher Max Müller, "under what sky the human mind…has most deeply pondered over the greatest problems of life, and has found solutions to some of them which well deserve the attention even of those who have studied Plato and Kant–I should point to India."

Perhaps what I sought waited there. The familiar anticipation that stirred inside me was tempered by the fact I had heard that India was overwhelming and exhausting even for the ambitious and healthy.

The Indian embassy, which I dragged my ailing body to, required seven to fourteen working days to telex my government before issuing a six-month visa. I had left one hundred dollars and my passport there in the event my strength returned and I found the ambition to continue. The day after the full moon party, I received word that my papers were ready. I debated what to do.

One afternoon I ventured out. A shoe shiner found me on a sunny corner. I had been waiting for the right one. He highlighted weak spots of the rough, faded leather needing attention, and added rubber where the thin soles had worn down. A small crowd gathered to watch. With the restoration, at least my trusty boots were up for the challenge.

The day came to decide whether to head home to family I had not seen for so long, or undertake a new phase of the journey. I drank San Miguel beers, ate yak cheese, and watched British football. Zola scored a goal, and the teams tied. No one won, but the two teams would one day have their chance to play again. On some days a draw is the best you can muster. Unlike football, however, life does not always offer a rematch. Sometimes, I thought, you only get one shot.

PART II

Each man's life represents a road towards himself, an attempt at such a road, the intimation of a path…It was wrong to desire new gods, completely wrong to want to provide the world with something. An enlightened man had but one duty—to seek the way to himself, to reach inner certainty, to grope his way forward, no matter where it led.

- Hermann Hesse, *Demian*

15

INTO INDIA

All through the night, a loose window funneled frigid Himalayan air through the unheated bus. With teeth chattering I reached up every few minutes to latch the broken pane. When the conductor yelled "Sunauli" the twelve-hour journey ended in the Nepalese border outpost of dilapidated shacks and corrugated tin. Stepping into crisp night air, I savored the aroma of incense and steamed dumplings.

I huddled in a nearby teahouse until dawn broke, and then swallowed the last sip of tepid tea, shouldered my faded rucksack, and walked the dusty road southward. The listless bureaucrat inside the weathered hut of thatch-covered concrete stamped my worn passport twice then waved me onward. A fading hand-painted sign welcomed visitors via English, Nepalese, and Hindi.

As I prepared to step into India, a hazy orange hue filled the eastern sky above Uttar Pradesh, the most populous and one of the poorest of India's states. Beyond ramshackle street-side dwellings lay fallow fields shrouded in early morning mist. Endless grumbling trucks each with half a dozen wiry men inside hauled timber, vegetables, and livestock. Cycle-rickshaws—three-wheel bicycles with doublewide seat behind straining driver—crowded the unpaved streets. At the Indian customs office the agent studied my visa, added a flourish, and returned to his newspaper.

Multitudes of oddly garbed people streamed over the border. A barefoot toothless man smiled through blackened gums. He set his infant daughter, clad only in a navel-length teal smock, onto the dirt. One lad raked debris onto a smoldering mound of rubbish while a white-bearded elder in tattered wraps paused to warm his hands over the flame. Mange-infested furless mutts nosed rotting garbage. The fruit vendor shooed them away then returned to his wooden cart laden with brown apples and overripe bananas. A woman in crimson shawl, wide brown eyes gleaming beneath red bindi upon her forehead, contemplated his wares.

Out of misty darkness a rickshaw-wallah cling-clanged past carrying a groom and his Muslim bride, her face shrouded beneath black veil. In Hindi, the all-encompassing language of the north, "wallah" meant "man" and could be added to near anything. Thus a dhobi-wallah washed clothes, a paan-wallah sold intoxicating betel nut concoctions, and a taxi-wallah drove, what else, but a taxi.

I found a seat aboard a bus bound for Varanasi two hundred more kilometers to the southeast. A Hindu holy man, a sadhu, boarded to bless passengers for the upcoming journey by marking holy ash upon each forehead. Many sadhus wandering the countryside half-naked with matted hair and flowing beard used the ploy to make a few rupees, while others followed genuine spiritual quests. This one expected a few coins. Even in India, it seemed, religion could be a commodity.

Thirty minutes stretched into one hour beyond the scheduled departure time, with still no sign of activity. The sadhu left, and another boarded. As in the rest of South Asia transport ran tardy, rarely leaving until filled to capacity, and once underway buses and trains often stopped for inexplicable reasons.

The rickety bus at last moved onto mist-shrouded countryside segmented centuries ago into fields and cultivated plots. Medieval scenes slipped past dirt-smeared windows while bleary-eyed passengers bounced as one beneath a milky white sky. Water buffalo and oxen yoked to wooden harnesses pulled crude plows across fallow pastures. Distant figures hunched over fledgling crops. Sparse trees dotted the landscape amid great mounds of hay drying in early morning sun. Goats and cattle wandered dusty streets amongst villages of wood and stone. The road passed ponds and rivers, swaths of green meadows, and thick stands of woodland.

The sacred Ganges River flowed through this flatland, dropping a few hundred feet along this portion of her fifteen hundred mile course. Each year India shrinks as the subcontinent drives slowly into Eurasia and pushes the Himalaya higher. To the northeast, India curved almost entirely around Bangladesh. The Arabian Sea lay along the country's southeast boundary, and the Indian Ocean lapped at her southwestern shores.

The plains of northern India ran evenly to the horizon without an undulation in sight, as British novelist E. M. Forster describes in *A Passage to India*. "No mountains infringe on the curve," he writes. "League after league the earth lies flat, heaves a little, is flat again. Only in the south, where a group of fists and fingers are thrust up through the soil, is the endless expanse interrupted."

Though much of India lay flat like a pancake, a few bumps such as Ooty and Mahabaleshwar once served as British hill station retreats and later provided cool respites for tourists seeking relief from the suffocating heat and humidity of Indian summer.

My plan entailed encircling the whole of India. The largest democracy in the world maintained a caste system and was home to the world's largest film industry and oldest religions. India possessed nuclear bombs while ranking among the poorest nations on earth. To breach her border, I knew, was to only scratch the surface of such contrasts.

We passed through Gorakhpur and a dozen smaller villages, pausing sometimes for food and other times for no seeming reason. Women walked the roadsides wearing brilliant saris of every conceivable color. Saris consisted of a single length of material wrapped about the body and held without any fastenings over a short blouse known as a choli. The final length was draped over the shoulder. Saris were exotic and emphatically Indian.

Vendors peddled cabbages, carrots, radishes, and onions. Tidy young men wearing colorful scarves and baggy, pajama-like trousers strolled the roadsides. Bicycles plied every road and village and even the dirt fields. Auto-rickshaws clogged the narrow arteries and filled the streets of almost every city. These noisy door-less canvas-topped three-wheel motorized transports with a front seat for the driver and one behind for two or three passengers were the perfect height for gulping copious amounts of bus and truck fumes.

We stopped by the roadside near one nameless village. A man served chai—sickly sweet Indian tea—in disposable funnel-shaped clay vessels that patrons smashed into the dirt when finished. Slivers and shards of pottery littered the roadside. Another sold samosas, fried dough holding curried vegetables, and served them upon small hand-woven reed plates. At other stops vendors sold fried banana and vegetable thukpa.

Darkness gradually overtook the light as the bus made its way through the landscape. Isolated flickers of fire or lantern sometimes appeared through distant gloom, but even medium-sized villages lacked artificial light. Around some islands of flame, men sold the day's remaining wares; at others family members warmed their hands over burning refuse or cow dung.

When we found white light instead of orange, the city of Varanasi lay before us. The bus negotiated narrowing streets before turning onto a still more slender debris-strewn alley, whereupon a mob of screaming men descended. They were touts of northern India, dreaded for their haranguing attempts to lead or ride one to a "cheap hotel" that paid a handsome commission. Any other guesthouse was "full," "booked-up" or "closed." As the engine stalled, the second twelve-hour journey in a day ended. A growing nub of fear crowded the corners of my mind. I cringed. The chaos beyond the windows and uncertainty about what lay ahead must be what a soldier feels at the edge of battle, I thought.

An Englishman took a breath and peered through the window. Every member of the mob gestured wildly. "Bloody hell," he muttered, and then leapt into the mass.

A French-Canadian named Isabel I had met at one of the rest stops crammed into an auto-rickshaw with me. We directed the driver to a restaurant we had heard of, pretending friends awaited us there. The driver negotiated a buzz of motorcycles, taxis, and buses along over-crowded highways. Cool air streamed through the open-air three-wheeler as we avoided near collisions and scurrying pedestrians.

We piled out near the Ganges River and found rooms amongst the twisted, bustling side streets where sacred cows wandered at will.

"You like beer, sir? Cheap and good," a Hindu whispered coarsely into my ear as I stood in the hotel's reception hall. Without turning, I ordered two oversize bottles. Though forbidden in Varanasi, apparently there were ways. Isabel met me on the hotel rooftop, blue eyes flashing. She had exchanged khaki trousers for a flowing dress and silk lavender scarf.

Legend held that the city was founded by the Hindu god Siva five thousand years ago. Varanasi was one of the longest continuously inhabited cities on earth. It was also the holiest Hindu city in the world. Even in the Buddha's day Varanasi was a religious and artistic center known as Kasi, the luminous one. All that happened in the ethereal city was ancient, beyond time, unlike anything in the New World.

We sipped our beers and relaxed beneath a reddish-yellow moon. Firecrackers exploded in streets below. Sounds of the city drifted upward.

"This city," Isabel breathed, "is amazing!"

16

GANGA MA

I awakened before the dawn. Unintelligible voices echoed from alleyways. A chant sounded from afar. Clanging bells rang nonstop somewhere in the distance as someone sang. Within that soothing realm I gazed onto sacred banks of the Ganges, backed by mosques and towering fortress walls sinking slowly into swirling sediments. Ancient steps called ghats led down the banks to mist-covered waters that flowed towards Bangladesh. Upon those waters ragged bands of children offered rupee rides in weathered wooden dories.

Lengthwise the Ganges is not one of the world's exceptional rivers. The Nile, Amazon, and Mississippi are all more than two and a half times as long. The Niger, Danube, Brahmaputra, and many others exceed her length, yet the Ganges is without doubt one of the world's exceptional rivers. Eric Newby, who journeyed nearly her entire extent, in *Slowly down the Ganges* claims the Ganges is great,

> ...because, to millions of Hindus, it is the most sacred, most venerated river on earth. For them it is

Ganga Ma–Mother Ganges. To bathe in it is to wash away guilt. To drink the water, having bathed in it, and to carry it away in bottles for those who have not had the good fortune to make the pilgrimage to it is meritorious. To be cremated on its banks, having died there, and to have one's ashes cast on its waters, is the wish of every Hindu. Even to ejaculate 'Ganga, Ganga', at the distance of 100 leagues from the river may atone for the sins committed during three previous lives.

Ganga Ma has no less than 108 names, extolling such qualities as ancient, holy, pure, swift-flowing, and eternal. She is considered a protector of the sick and suffering who come to her for refuge. She is *Ajnana-timira-bhanu*, a light amid the darkness of ignorance. Her seventieth name is *Svarga-sopana-sarani*–flowing like a staircase to Heaven.

Watching life unfold along the Ganges made clear how she underlay foundations of the religion followed by eight-tenths of India's billion-strong population. Hundreds of sagging women bathed in muddy waters. Robust men wearing white loincloths performed ritual ablutions. Brown-backed dhobi-wallahs pounded garments thin upon smooth stones using stout round sticks as saris dried upon sunbaked mud. Saffron-robed sadhus sang and clapped while encircling miniature temples of Siva. Upon platforms beyond the shoreline bare-breasted devotees of both genders chanted and prayed to the morning sun. Despite, or perhaps due to, no known founder, no fixed doctrines, and no common worship of thousands of gods, Hinduism overcame five millennia of invasion and reformation.

A frail-looking lad offered me a ride upon the river. He pointed to his craft, a wide flat-bottomed dory of creaking wood and broad-bladed oars. I crawled aboard and sat upon damp boards as he cast off. Morning mist covered horizons and dilapidated buildings stretching into unseen distances. We floated downstream past bathers washing themselves as they did each morning. A long dorsal fin atop a blubbery gray back knifed the water's edge. The boy spread his hands wide and pointed into the water. Sometimes, he motioned, the long-nosed freshwater dolphins exceeded the length of the twenty-foot dinghy.

A few other boats, dark silhouettes against white mist, also plied the waters. Above the eastern bank a brilliant orange orb appeared—sunrise upon the holy Ganges.

Near a half-sunken hull listing to starboard the boy turned his craft around to row against the current. Along the water's edge a small band of robed holy men beat two-sided drums and blew horns to welcome the dawn. Devout Hindus stripped to the waist crowded the stone steps and devoted themselves to their gods by praying to the Seven Sacred Rivers.

"Oh Holy Mother Ganges!" they recited. "Oh Yamuna! Oh Godavari! Oh Saraswati! Oh Narmada! Sindhu! Kaveri! May you all be pleased to be manifest in these waters with which I shall purify myself!"

At Dasaswamedh Ghat I left my oarsman behind. Throngs crowded the ghat. Men offered shaves for ten rupees, or massages for fifteen—about twenty-five cents. If refused, the clever masseuse said "okay friend" and extended his right hand in friendship. When the unsuspecting victim shook hands he received a massage of his left hand, arm, and shoulder while the masseuse held the right hand in a vise-like grip. Soon I walked with hands thrust deep into my pockets saying "no massage, no massage."

The sun turned from blood-orange to yellow and finally into searing whiteness. A few lads played pick-up cricket. Red paper kites guided by unseen hands twirled overhead. Boats glided past as supple half-naked forms bathed in morning light.

At Manikarnika Ghat a bent man motioned me away from water's edge. Non-Hindus were forbidden from walking any farther. He pointed towards a hollow two-story structure overlooking the Ganges. I stepped inside and climbed a steep stone stairwell. Overwhelmed, I tried to make sense of the scenes below.

I had read that the sprawling literature, complicated rituals, vibrant art, pantheon of gods, and lengthy history of the world's oldest religion embraced vegetarianism, internal meditation, philosophy, asceticism, cults, and human sacrifice. Yet, three practices remain consistent amongst all forms of the religion.

First, one can never be converted into the religion, for at birth the steadfast rules of caste dictate one's lifelong status. Lower castes undergo countless rebirths in pursuit of moksha–the liberation from anger, death, and one's body–and an end to samsara, the cycle of rebirth.

Second, to achieve liberation–or moksha–one surrenders to a particular deity and performs acts of worship–called puja–as a means towards salvation. Karma, the law of cause and effect, determines whether a rebirth will be favorable or not. Believers must live as closely as possible to the dharma, a moral standard and way of life appropriate to each individual.

Hinduism's mythology began with King Bharat. In old age the king retired to the forest to prepare for death and his release from samsara. In so doing he adopted an orphaned deer, which he grew to love so dearly that at death instead of being liberated he entered instead the body of a deer. In time he was reincarnated as a human. To avoid any attachment to people, he pretended to be dumb. By shunning all human contact he gained enlightenment, and at the end of that life achieved moksha. His story embodies the essence of Indian myth–the search for a higher reality during which the soul journeys through many births to find a way out of this world.

While I contemplated this, an aged man atop the worn steps explained in slow sentences the scenes below. At Manikarnika Ghat the dead were draped in white and gold shrouds and burned to ash upon funeral pyres, one after the other, day and night, he said. Outcast chandals–part of the lowest caste–tended the ritual fires, poking a foot here, a head there into the flame with wooden poles. Burning one's dead comprises the third Hindu practice–to die in Varanasi and be cremated along the Ganges signifies instant moksha.

As the old man spoke, two brown feet dropped slowly away from one of the fires. Another body, this one draped in white, was placed upon a stack of wood. White symbolizes youth, and for a moment the face of a young man peered through the shrouds. His family gathered round while one small boy–his head shaved but for a single topknot–left the group and followed a priest to the nearby temple. The old man next to me said that inside there burned a sacred flame continuously alive for the past thousand years. The child, hand quivering, returned with wisps of straw aflame from the sacred fire. He circled the shrouded corpse five times before lighting the wood and body of his brother. All stood silent as the pyre alighted and flames flared upward.

Half a dozen boats laden with bleached driftwood sat onshore with oarsmen smoking or sleeping on gunwales. A withered man chopping timbers with a rusted axe added to dozens of cords already stacked. A boy maneuvered a wooden flat-bottom amongst the idle craft, and paused while a bearded man in orange turban clambered aboard. The man carried a white bundle tied to a flat stone which bore his infant son.

Five special Hindus never burn, because they are considered already holy. These include sadhus, who do not drink, smoke nor fornicate. Lepers are also exempt, having been burned once already by the hand of God. Pregnant women are already graced, and children are yet untainted and need no cleansing. Those smitten by cobra are considered most fortunate. These Hindus are tied to stones and dropped from boats into muddy sediments.

Lifting mists revealed barren flats of the opposite shore. During monsoon season the rivers flooded and covered the ghats, then riverbanks, next bottom floors of ancient riverside buildings. Sometimes blackened bodies, if not already scavenged by the Gangetic Dolphins, rose to the surface and floated through first floor rooms of deserted dwellings.

Eight men carried a body draped in crimson and cobalt towards water's edge. Their eerie chants forged a path through milling crowds. Another body draped in gold and black was brought to shore, submerged in holy Gangetic waters, and dragged beside a waterlogged corpse in pink and white.

The man in orange turban returned to shore empty-handed. The shaved youth still stood with head bowed next to his brother's burning corpse. Smoke and a burst of flame erupted from another pyre. The tender poked a head back into the fire, and soon no signs remained of the lucky Hindu who had broken the shackles of moksha.

I offered money for the holy man's conversation, but he refused. I left a few rupees instead at a decaying whitewashed temple that housed those with no families and little hope but to die in the streets of Varanasi. I continued to Ahilyabai Ghat. An elderly woman bathed without removing her sari, while a Brahmin priest offered silent puja. Nearby a young yogi contorted upon a stone pillar. A beggar at my feet offered to aid my ailing karma by relieving me of unneeded rupees.

A cluster of young women crouched over a small fire cooked noontime gruel. One in yellow sari with patterns of green, gold, and red held an infant son to her breast–a child bearing a child. With toes and bare feet dyed vermilion, silver anklets, brilliant saris, and gaudy nose rings, these were teenage girls long ago married.

Upon a wooden bench I sipped chai for two rupees amongst Indians speaking no English. Together we watched the sun arc through the sky as lepers sitting nearby begged for alms. A boy with no hands and clutching an empty tin between calloused stumps approached. Already oversaturated, this surreal scene inundated my senses. Each moment challenged my assumptions about what I had once believed was normal. By comparison, any North American city I had ever experienced seemed vague and lifeless.

I met a man eager to discuss his beloved Hinduism. "So many gods," I said. "Hanuman, Siva, Ganesh. Thousands maybe."

"Millions," he smiled with mouth full of paan, a red betel nut intoxicant. "Yet Everything is One. The Brahman."

"Brahman is your god?"

"No, my friend. Brahman is all, like the ocean." He spread his arms wide. "You and I are drops of sea spray separate for small moments. What you call soul we call aatman. The aatman is temporary but always part of Brahman. Aatman is Brahman and Brahman aatman."

He spat a long red trail of betel nut juice upon the ground. "All else is illusion. Only when you open your eyes…wide…may you see the Brahman and join it. Come," he mumbled. "I show you Siva temple."

"Maybe tomorrow," I told him, and after wandering away chanced upon Isabel. We walked together, and at the burning ghats climbed the stairwell of the hollow building I had visited earlier. Nearly a dozen pyres burned, and to the side a dozen more bodies awaited. Brilliant shades of gold, chartreuse, and lavender shrouded the dead. Isabel stood silent.

"Any death rite is bizarre," I said, feeling compelled for some reason to defend the sights below. "We're fascinated and frightened by death, mostly comfortable with our own traditions but disturbed by others'. These reach back five thousand years. Really, in a land of a billion souls and limited land, cremation makes good sense…"

There is no crying at the burning ghats, I noticed suddenly. Westerners such as myself, on the other hand, weep and cling to attachments and loved ones rather than accept that death is a part of life. A burst of flame erupted from one pyre. A pile of ashes marked the conclusion of another. My stomach turned at last.

17

ISABEL

As anywhere, shopping served as distraction. When a merchant waved us into his shop, Isabel and I removed our shoes and relaxed into soft pillows covering the cushioned floor. Umal waited on us and spoke lovingly of the dozens of saris he unfolded one after the other, each a new pattern of violet, mauve, and copper. Worn by every married Hindu woman on the continent, no two held the same style or hue. The finest designs were interwoven with gold-wrapped silken yarn by Varanasi's skilled weavers.

Tea was brought out, and the pace unhurried. Umal draped one sari around Isabel and led her to a mirror. Her slender physique lost beneath yards of material, we laughed at her awkwardness. With a deft flick of the wrist Umal unfolded more saris onto the floor, yet none interested Isabel. Such was the way of business.

We followed another man around a corner and up a steep flight of stairs. There a tidy man in cashmere sweater and sporting a neat black moustache unfolded scarf after silk scarf. Helpers brought more stacks from within, and a parade of color flashed past. The simplest fetched two hundred fifty rupees, around four dollars. The most elaborate hand-woven pieces cost nearly five thousand and required five months to complete. Isabel pondered which she liked as the man flipped backwards through the thick pile. She eliminated scarves one at a time until she chose two she would purchase for her father. They bartered back and forth then agreed on a price of four hundred thirty rupees—less than seven dollars.

Isabel and I lost ourselves amidst the narrow alleyways and shops filled with tika dots, powders, saris, bangles, and brass statuettes. In a dirty corner stall filled with chattering locals we drank chai and ate fried samosas before circling round to the ghats to rest upon muddy steps. Evening was approaching and a few lights began to twinkle. High in the sky dozens of kites twisted and shuddered with no visible hands guiding the thin squares of fluttering paper. Bells chimed and darkness fell. A sadhu offering puja folded his hands and bowed to the east. A young girl approached with a wicker basket of button candles, each set within a curved woven mat and filled with orange and yellow jasmine petals. Isabel and I bought several each and sent the lit candles downriver with silent prayers to our families.

En route to dinner, a traffic jam of rickshaws, bicycles, and automobiles captured Isabel and I. We peered into the mayhem from atop our cycle-rickshaw. Cattle too wandered the streets, urinating in great noisy streams and leaving piles of dung wherever they passed. No one complained, for even bovine waste was considered sacred. According to one Brahmin at Ahilyabai Ghat, if a man killed a cow he spent his life in p rison. If he killed a man he only paid twenty-five thousand rupees restitution, less than four hundred dollars. With so many lives competing upon the land, life was cheap.

Such sights spurred a discussion over dinner about the enigmatic five thousand-year-old Hindu social system. "Hindu means belonging to the Indus," said Isabel. It was from the Dravidian cities of Harappa and Mohenjo-Daro along the Indus River in present-day Pakistan that Brahminism, an early form of Hinduism, first spread. Brahmin priests rather than kings ruled this first great Indian civilization. When nomadic Aryans invaded from the north, Dravidian civilization collapsed, and many inhabitants migrated south. The Aryans cleared the great northern forests, and their hunting and herding traditions evolved into today's loose delineation between the meat-eating north and the Dravidian-influenced vegetarian south. The Aryan language, Sanskrit, underpins all classical Indian literature.

"The Vedas, written around that time, describe the universal soul, the Brahman, and the individual soul, the aatman," said Isabel. "The Brahman can't be described. The aatman is part of this indescribable Brahman. The Brahman manifests itself in many gods. The most famous are Brahma, Siva, and Visnu. Brahma created everything. Siva is both destroyer and reproducer. Those phallic-shaped lingams on the ghats? They symbolize Siva's creative side. Visnu the preserver sometimes visits Earth. Rama, Krishna, the Buddha—all are incarnations of Visnu. All other Hindu gods are some aspect of these three."

I mentioned that as Brahmin priests regained control, they absorbed Aryan nature gods into their pantheon. Determined to never lose power again, the priests developed a rigid caste system that was evident all around us.

Isabel nodded. "The priests created countless edicts about diet, travel, marriage, everything. They made themselves all-powerful."

Beneath the Brahmins were three other castes. Kshatriyas were soldiers, Vaisyas artisans, and Sudras peasants. Each was believed to have emanated from Visnu—the Brahmins from his mouth, Kshatriyas from his arms, Vaisyas from his thighs, and Sudras from his feet.

A jumbled assortment of music drew us to roof's edge. A battered flatbed truck toted a rumbling generator. Wires snaking behind led to a ragged band of parade goers carrying blinking red and white lights with dark gaps where bulbs had burned out. Men blew horns, pounded drums, or played any instrument they could find. A few sweepers followed the parade and cleared rubbish and horse dung. We watched a few moments then returned to our table. I was reminded that beneath the four castes a fifth group, once known as untouchables, held no caste and performed the most menial tasks. Mahatma Gandhi spent considerable effort elevating the status of untouchables. He renamed them Harijans, children of God, and they became known as Dalit, the downtrodden.

"I've read," I said, "that at one time if a high-caste Hindu used the same temple as an untouchable, or was touched by one, or even had an untouchable's shadow cross his, he was considered polluted and had to go through all sorts of rituals to be cleansed."

Isabel nodded. "Hindu ethics still shape who one may marry or even accept food from. It's fascinating how much influence Harappa culture had on today's Hindus. They've found statues of male three-faced gods that might be an early Siva. Black pillars are early lingams like those here on the ghats. They had an advanced drainage system, which means Hindus were compulsive about bathing even five thousand years ago!"

"Today I learned what some of the forehead tika marks mean," I remembered. "Three horizontal stripes of ash mean one is a Shaivite and follows Siva. Vertical stripes are worn by Vaishnavas who follow Visnu. The red circle in the center of a woman's forehead is called a bindi."

"Which indicates her as married."

"Right."

As we left the restaurant, another lavish Hindu marriage parade wound its way through the streets. An elephant with long ebony tusks led a procession of musicians, dancers, and a boisterous band with little regard for rhythm or melody. Women wearing long flowing saris followed. The proceedings were illuminated by men carrying fluorescent light tubes connected by a wild array of wires leading to a mobile generator aboard a rickshaw. Fireworks shot into the sky and burst overhead. Bicyclists rode past unconcerned. We watched warily, unsure whether the homemade devices would fizzle or hurl shrapnel into the air.

Earlier we had seen the groom parade alone through the streets on horseback wearing a traditional *sehra* garland. Now he and his bride sat high upon a wheeled chariot at the end of the parade. Not until the bride placed a *jaimala* of white jasmine and orange marigold about her husband's neck as a sign of respect and good luck could they consummate their union.

A man pulled me into a wild frenzy of dancing men and boys. Isabel too was pushed into the melee. I slipped out beneath dragging wires to find Isabel. She had been groped and grabbed, but not robbed nor hurt, though her flagging perception of Indian men plummeted still further.

Morning had not yet arrived when I descended the stairs of my hotel. I slipped past slight men sleeping in the shabby lobby under thin cotton blankets. Outside, midnight blue sky still covered the land, and vendors lay beneath the stars asleep in their stalls. The steady pounding of clothes against river stones echoed from nearby walls. In the gloom men pulled twisted timbers from a rusted steel scale and tossed them onto the riverbank. A woman dragged sopping garments from the river and hung them to dry on a sagging line. Thick smoke poured from a pyre just lit, and a scattering of goats, dogs, and cattle scavenged the ashes. As a half-moon faded the sky turned hazy white, and another day unfolded on the Ganges.

I met Isabel at the Bread of Life bakery in the center of Varanasi. The proprietor joked with us as a corpse swathed in yellow and pink shrouds flashed past on the roof of a speeding auto-rickshaw. Another tied to bamboo poles passed on the shoulders of six singing men. I could not help but think I was there to buy the bread of life in the city of death.

After breakfast we hired a rickshaw-wallah who negotiated highways jammed with bicycles, autos, and cows to reach the thousand-year-old ruins of Sarnath. We paid the sweating driver and wandered amongst scattered stones.

In the second millennium BCE, as the Aryans consolidated

their power, they faced an invasion by the Macedonian king Alexander the Great. His armies marched east in a long series of battles that brought them to the cradle of Indian civilization. After crossing the Indus River, Alexander's infantries fought Prince Porus' war elephants at the battle of Hydaspes. After killing twenty thousand soldiers, Alexander's men refused to continue, and he wept, as Plutarch wrote, because "there were no more worlds to conquer." Alexander turned towards home without entering the heart of India, and left a vacuum which enabled the spread of Buddhism.

"The way of Buddha," related the young red-robed monk sitting by our side at Sarnath, "is not religion, but philosophy and way of being." The monk, Songten, studied in Dharamsala to the north, where His Holiness the Dalai Lama had resided and taught since exiled by the Chinese. "After the Buddha find enlightenment," Songten said, "he come here to teach first sermon, about Middle Path. He reject god worship, caste, the aatman. He say being reborn many times not necessary. We can reach nirvana in one lifetime.

"This is where it all begin," murmured Songten as we stood before Dhamekh Stupa, the shrine marking the spot of this first historic sermon about Buddhism.

After a century of war, northern India had coalesced into a single kingdom, Magadha. During his long march to the Indus, Alexander met a young adventurer named Chandragupta Maurya. When Alexander turned his armies towards home, Chandragupta seized the Magadha throne and filled the power gap. Chandragupta's empire spread across north India, and reached its peak under Ashoka, Chandragupta's grandson. Ashoka converted to Buddhism and declared it the state religion. He built stupas and monasteries, erected pillars and rock-carved edicts, controlled more of India than any ruler except the Mughals and British, and sent missionaries abroad bearing Buddha's message. Emperor Ashoka contributed to the rise and popularity of Buddhism more than anyone beyond the Buddha.

"All life is suffering," said Songten. "All suffering come

from greed. Suffering only end when greed end. To stop suffering and find enlightenment, follow Eightfold path. These are the four noble truths."

We stood by a carved eight-wheel chakra wheel near foundations of the main shrine. "This wheel symbolize Eightfold path," he said. "He who follow the path, find nirvana." He held up eight fingers and ticked off the essential milestones. "Right understanding. Right thoughts. Right speech. Right action. Right way to make money. Right effort. Right mindfulness. Right concentration." He smiled. "Simple!"

Following Ashoka's death, however, his empire collapsed. Though Buddhism faded in India as Hinduism revived and reinvented itself, Buddhism had grown too popular to be forgotten. Hindus incorporated Buddha as the ninth of Visnu's incarnations, and again Hinduism absorbed a competitor. With Ashoka's missions already spreading Buddha's message to the rest of Asia, the seeds had been planted for a new world religion.

On a certain level Songten was right. The Buddha's original message is simple. As I had learned, practice and integration into my daily life were the challenges. After traveling in Tibet, I had also seen how his message could be convoluted from a path of self-actualization into a form of god-worship. Nevertheless, original Buddhism does carry a powerful message, and humanity is far better, I knew, for the myriad gifts the Buddha's insights have provided.

A few days later, somehow the promise of "maybe later" became "now" as I followed a gaunt man through twisting alleyways towards his cousin's silk factory in the Godaulia district. Three times he had pestered, and each time I refused.

"It cannot hurt to look," he said, and finally I agreed after growing weary of the game. To be fair, a part of me was curious to see what passed for manufacturing in this city.

In his cousin's factory, half-finished works of brilliance sat upon wooden looms as weavers moved pedals and manipulated silk fibers into saris, scarves, and brocades. He led into the cushioned showroom surrounded by stacks of silks. "I come only to look and wish to buy nothing," I warned. It seemed clear that the bearded man there had heard such words thousands of times before. Mouth filled with bright red paan spittle, he barely paused while executing his spiel.

"Seven generations have been producing these fine silk garments upon hundreds of looms!" he said, and he would show me his merchandise if only I promised to not allow others the opportunity to copy his grandfather's original designs.

"You *must* promise. To not buy, okay. But to steal design," he said with hands over his breast, "will break my heart." I promised.

He unfurled dozens of silks, one after the other. He tried every trick to separate me from my rupees. "In one hour, five hundred silks will be exported to Bombay for ten dollars apiece. But, I will sell you whichever you like for seven and a half each!" I congratulated him for his wisdom in selling all to the Bombay merchant for the better price.

"Ah, that money I will not see for three months," he said.

"Perhaps I will come back later," I said, "when I have rested."

"In one hour there will be none left."

He emphasized that he knew many merchants in America very willing to buy silks, and had many friends there. He pressed the point that I might make a healthy profit through his contacts and my ingenuity. He claimed an American in the other room just purchased four hundred dollars' worth of silks for that exact purpose. I explained again I agreed only to look.

"Fine!" he said loudly, "never return here! I have opened over a hundred silks and still you will not buy."

"I never asked to see saris," I said, "and never promised to buy."

"If you buy one," he said, "I will not be rich or you poor. Buy just one and I will be happy."

"I'm sorry, I just don't need one today." He cursed me and

spat into the air. As I donned my shoes, the American he had mentioned peered at us through a slit in the curtain.

I left the showroom and to avoid the dark thin tout I wandered along the river. There I saw the man from the day before who I had spoken with about Hinduism.

"Come," he mumbled with mouth full of paan. "We visit Siva temple." This time, I agreed to visit the temple. As we walked, he explained the abundance of silk merchants and factories in Varanasi. When we stepped into inevitable cushioned room, a man in stockings sat upon the floor folding silks. Immediately I thanked all and retreated, backwards, into the street.

Within a dark restaurant corner above the din of street sounds and classic chords of the sitar, smells of curry and incense wafted upwards. Saris of a hundred colors drifted past in gathering darkness. Muslims and Hindus mingled while rickshaws careened over puddles of piss and paan.

A familiar face caught my eye. Out of countless choices for fare, Isabel had chosen mine. We were happy to see each other again, though unsurprised–for amidst the magic of India coincidences and strange happenings seemed almost commonplace.

As we wandered to Harishchandra Ghat we chattered like old friends about what we had seen. Darkness had descended by the time we arrived. Tall flames reached into the sky and sparks shot upward. The outline of a body lay on the river bank in orange silhouette. Indians stood silent and pensive, watching flames lick at timber and flesh.

A sadhu on a platform upon the water twisted and turned a candelabrum that held dozens of burning candles. Horns and bells sounded. A drum beat faster. Ganga Ma's one hundred and sixth name, *Ramya*, rang true. She was delightful and beautiful.

Isabel and I took leave of each other upon the ghats, she in the morning to the railway station and I towards an uncertain future. I realized that I perhaps needed the comfort of Isabel's companionship. She was the only thread of familiarity I had in this exotic land. Her conversation and friendship had softened the harshness of India's cultural edge. I turned for one last look, but she was lost to the crowd. I had thought she might help me find some of the answers I sought, but now it seemed that would never be.

My time in India never failed to overwhelm me. Falling sick, being suckered, or getting robbed may await the unsuspecting traveler. Loneliness, too, was a risk. I found that every moment in a northern Indian city brimmed with wonder and change.

Amidst a whirlwind of sight and sound, thousands streamed past: caste-conscious Hindus, ascetic sadhus, fez-donning Muslims, troupes of monkeys swinging across rooftops, untouchables performing demeaning labors, faceless Moslem women draped head to toe in black cloth burkhas, Hindu women wearing brilliant saris, the wide staring eyes of a million Indian men, throngs of limbless beggars and lepers slowly dying, pungent odors of excrement and urine, relentless touts and rip-off artists, countless cattle wandering busy highways and narrow alleys, pushing, shoving, desperation, the daily struggle for sustenance, and the clamor of a billion souls in perpetual maddening motion. I staggered like a drunkard. Ah, India, I thought. You are indeed all that you promised.

18

AGRA EXPRESS

Along a bustling thoroughfare, three of five Indians that I queried about Allahabad pointed to a sad-looking mostly full green bus. The engine revved as more locals hopped aboard behind me. Inside I kicked up clouds of yellow dust while cramming my rucksack under the rusted metal seat. The bus lurched ahead and with horn blaring nonstop, the driver swerved past rickshaws and galloping cattle then loosened the throttle and barreled down the crowded highway. Distorted countryside rolled past beyond a splintered spider web of window. Every bump and bounce threw more of the choking yellow dust into the air.

When the bus shuddered and died somewhere in Allahabad, an impatient mass of gasping travelers lunged at the narrow doorway. With a glance through the grimy window, the hungry rickshaw-wallahs pegged me as a Westerner. Soon every one of them yelled and gestured at me. Whereas train stations provided some means of orientation, buses stopped on random corners and unmarked side streets and put me at a disadvantage.

I named a hotel near the train station that someone had mentioned, and one rickshaw-wallah offered a ride for five rupees. I hopped aboard and we moved with the throngs into congested chaos past open-air stalls and street side vendors. Soon all traffic came to a standstill, and even my nimble cycle-rickshaw driver could not move.

In Allahabad, the mythical Saraswati River joins the Ganges and Yamuna Rivers at the *sangam*, a mystical convergence with great soul-cleansing powers. It was in Allahabad where Mahatma Gandhi announced his plan to achieve an independent India through nonviolence. Myth holds that eons ago the gods and demons battled over possession of a coveted *kumbh*, for whoever drank the contents of the pitcher would be ensured immortality. Hindu gods won and drank the nectar, but in their haste four drops spilled onto the earth, one each at four cities, including Allahabad.

Every three years a festival, or *mela*, commemorates the holiness of the four cities. The *mela* rotates among the four, thus each site hosts a festival every twelve years. The holiest Kumbh Mela, at Allahabad, draws millions of Hindus who bathe in the *sangam* to escape samsara and be cleansed of sin. Three years hence, in 2001, an unprecedented sixty million would attend, making Allahabad the most highly attended pilgrimage destination in the world.

Even in non-festival years, humanity jammed the city. My rickshaw-wallah inched through traffic. "Hotel Milan, Hotel Milan..." he repeated.

"No, Prayag," I said. "I told you Hotel Prayag!"

"Milan," he said, and pointed forward. This, I knew, was the rickshaw-wallah game. Draw the fare in by agreeing to whatever destination he chooses, then take him instead to whichever hotel pays a handsome commission. When my driver stopped at Hotel Milan and refused to go further, there was little choice but to get out.

I shouldered my bag and handed the rickshaw-wallah a ten rupee note. Unsatisfied, the wallah followed alongside as I walked the boulevard toward my chosen destination. He suggested other hotels.

"No thanks," I called. One I stopped at looked appealing so I stepped inside. There were no vacancies, as apparently was the case with all other reasonable accommodations. It seemed pointless to spend a week in crowded Allahabad before catching a westbound train, so I decided to walk to the train station and check timetables for an earlier departure. Thousands streaming into the city clogged the roadsides, filled the gullies, and blocked the way. I paused for samosas at a roadside stall to wait. Somehow my obsessive driver found me after managing to negotiate the tangled snarl with his rickshaw. I begged him to leave me alone.

"Two rupees to Hotel Prayag, sahib," he said.

"Train station," I countered.

"Five rupees."

"Okay."

We hummed over quieter back avenues and passed the bus stop where we started. He strained over an arched bridge, rounded a corner, and made the Prayag. "Twenty rupees," he said. When I gave him ten his face contorted, indicating the bridge and long distance covered. I explained, slowly, that had he brought me to Prayag originally, as I asked and he agreed, he would have avoided the superfluous ride downtown. Furthermore, I had paid him ten rupees earlier and ten now, so we were in fact even.

Across the street from Hotel Prayag loomed the Allahabad Junction Railway Station. I stepped inside the yawning hall and faced a disconcerting scene involving dozens of endless queues, ragged people upon filthy blankets, incomprehensible signboards lettered in Hindi, and a seeming lack of central organization. Indian Railways, the world's largest employer, kept a million and a half on the payroll. The system was fourth largest in the world, each day running over seven thousand passenger trains, carrying eleven million passengers, and connecting over seven thousand stations.

Behind a window headed *Enquiries* sat a nonchalant heavyset man in tailored coat and white scarf who eyed with disdain the Indians elbowing their way in and shouting questions at him in Hindi. Learning nothing from him I found a room headed *Reservation/Cancellation* with its own set of meandering queues. Isabel had advised me to have a properly filled form ready, or I could spend an hour or two in line and then have the clerk send me away when I finally reached him. I found a form for the second class sleeper car, filled it in, and joined a line. Men persistently jumped to the front.

At the head of the stretching line at last, two men pushed ahead of me but the clerk waved them off and took my form. "To Agra," I had written. "No train to Agra tonight," he said, "but you may go to Tundla, arriving at two in the morning, and there await a train to Agra." I must visit a window in the first room next to the original *Enquiries* counter to purchase such a ticket.

At the *Enquiries* counter the heavyset man directed me two windows over. There I waited. The man behind the window could not help me, and sent me back to the *Enquiries* window. I fought my way in, only to be sent to the window next door a second time. I waited, but he repeated he could not help me. I protested. "I have been told to come here twice!" He glanced at my form again. "No second class here," he said. "Only second class AC." It seemed all sleepers had air conditioning. I changed the form. "Wait," he told me, and disappeared.

Nearby, the heavyset man in white scarf settled back, ignored the queries a bit, and then answered a question or two before waving them off. Others crowded behind me.

The clerk reappeared after fifteen minutes and shuffled a few papers. He disappeared again, returned, and donned his eyeglasses, but removed them for inspection. He found a cloth and slowly rubbed the lenses before putting them on. Still not right. He wiped them again in slow circular movements, and then leafed through a thick stack of papers until finding the sheet he wanted. A few of the Indians shoved their forms through the hole in the glass. He sent them away for various reasons. When my turn came he scribbled something and mumbled "seven-thirty."

"The train leaves at 7:30? Fine, how much?"

He shook his head. "Seven thirty rupees," he said, "for second class AC." Seven hundred thirty rupees!

I gave up on the unaffordable sleeper car berth and decided instead on a second-class reserved seat, with no bed. That meant going to a different window. I looked around but only saw more long lines extending from small windows headed by Hindi script that might say anything. I imagined the signs read *No Foreigners*, or *All Tickets <u>but</u> Agra-bound*. After three-quarters of an hour I reached the window and flashed my inked form. The clerk pointed to the *Reservations* hall and took the next man in line. I cursed silently then trudged over there. When almost to the front a closed sign dropped before the hole. I stood in silent rage.

I moved to another line. When the men stared, I glared back. They laughed, spit phlegm near my feet, shoved and pushed me aside, ignored any decorum, and treated life and people with little respect. I imagined pounding some paan-chewing lout into the dirt.

After the hour wait my turn arrived, whereupon I learned no second class reserved seats remained to Agra, Tundla, or anywhere else. The price for a second class AC berth to Agra had even increased—now it cost seven hundred fifty-five for a ticket the next day. I trudged into darkening streets where half a dozen rickshaw-wallahs called out.

"You won't take me where I wish," I replied, "so why bother?"

"Okay," one said, "five rupees."

After finding a room at the Hotel Prayag I returned to the station to try the unreserved line. While there an affable man with a thick Hindi accent bent my ear. He found it strange I traveled alone, and that I had no girlfriend along. Most foreigners he encountered traveled with a partner if not group. He asked my opinions on the Kashmir dilemma, my government's position on India's recent nuclear tests, my country's angle on international terrorism, and about the Taliban and its policies.

Nearby, two men exchanged harsh words. One threw down his bags and prepared for blows. A guard with heavy stick separated them and led the aggressor away. The antagonist broke free from the guard, scrambled back, pulled his scarf off, and readied to scrap.

I reached the front of the unreserved line. "You cannot buy a ticket for Agra today, sir, only tomorrow," said the clerk. My inquisitive friend pointed to a timetable and the possibility of a train at 4:30 a.m. and 12:20 p.m. He leaned forward. "There are many untrustworthy characters about," he said into my ear. "Never accept food or drink from anyone. Even street side vendors might drug and rob you. Trust no one, and watch your back at every moment." He wished me good luck, and disappeared into the crowd.

I returned to the street, where a dozen food vendors yelled to lure me through their doors. Beyond the corner, silent eyes watched from shadowed recesses of unlit streets. I had not seen a foreigner since Varanasi. Bewildered and spent, I chose the busiest establishment I could find, and scooped ghobi masala and roti bread into my mouth.

Without a soft surface to be found, the concrete walls and corridors of Hotel Prayag amplified the slightest echo. The lobby porter's endless coughs and sounds of men clearing phlegm reverberated through the night. At dawn, I slipped past the consumptive porter's wisplike form and into streets of urban India coming alive. Railway station hell beckoned, yet I came away with an unreserved ticket bound for Agra.

I steeled myself for the journey ahead with a breakfast of sweet chai, doughy sugar balls, and greasy ghobi panthati– cauliflower bread. While I sat on the sidewalk watching humanity course past, a man's inane screams and beady eyes focused on me. I looked around.

"Are you talking to me?" I asked.

He executed a jerky nod.

"Well. What do you want?"

He stood before me and spread several outdated newspapers upon my table. Even if they had been less than a week old, I held no interest in the outside world. He pointed again at the papers while yelling into my ear. I wanted to bolt from the table, yet running through the thick crowd would be impossible. The reality was I could not escape the incessant, grasping desperation that surrounded me. Wearily, I reached into my pocket for rupees to be rid of him, but the chai man chased him off.

The wretchedness of northern India tested my resolve. There was a lawless feel to the cities. Men slept in gutters, and children lived on sidewalks. Silent eyes stared. They seemed full of malice, though it was probably no more than wide-eyed curiosity. In India one could push, shove, defecate in the street, spit on the sidewalk, stare, act rude, be obnoxious, or really do whatever desired without social recrimination.

In fact, the Hindu male personality was not so much selfish as self-absorbed. Many focused not on charity or good will towards others, but the fulfillment and cleanliness of self. Scholar Huston Smith phrases Hinduism's underlying affirmation as, "you can have what you want." Hinduism encourages pleasure seeking. Hinduism knows, however, that one day–perhaps not in this lifetime but certainly in some future one–you will yearn for loftier pursuits. That is the moment, Smith observes, that Hinduism waits for.

With the newspaper hawker gone I ordered a second cup of chai, and noticed a leaning concrete electric pole with lines sprouting off in all directions like an overloaded neuron. Twenty times more wires than on a western pole looped and twisted in bent and chaotic spirals with no order or direction. I nearly laughed out loud; here was a perfect icon of India's disorder. This was not like riding a tour bus through Europe or spending a week at the beach. This was India, to be certain–desperate, frustrating, at times overwhelming, what I always hoped to experience, and in many ways more than I expected.

I was reminded of what beat poet Charles Bukowski penned in *The Shoelace*. "It's not the large things that send a man to the madhouse…no, it's the continuing series of small tragedies that send a man to the madhouse…not the death of his love but a shoelace that snaps with no time left."

As I reached for my cup of chai a rush of scenes flashed through my mind–the screaming newspaper vendor, bus and train station madness, thousands of commissioned lying rickshaw-wallahs, too many cars and not enough trains, cattle with more rights than humans, smells and piles of human and animal feces, and chaotic spiraling electric wires. There was no escape from these and a thousand other sights. I heard myself chuckle, then let out a long laugh. I realized that seeing the humor was the only way I could endure. Otherwise, one more snapped bootlace might see me aboard the next homeward outbound.

On the train platform with samosas and bananas in hand, I awaited the Agra Express. "Next one," claimed a uniformed man.

Two young Indian women wearing saris smiled. "Where you go?" asked one. "Where you from?" asked the other.

As I replied, a man in blue sweater yelled something in garbled tongue, and the mass of people arose. The young women, also going to Agra, hustled. There had been a last minute platform change, it seemed. I followed them and when the train pulled in everyone climbed as one seething mass onto the overcrowded cars. With the young women lost to the crowd, I entered alone the world of Indian unreserved rail travel. Since all seats and floor space were taken, I sat on the step of the open doorway with legs dangling just above the tracks. My fingers gripped the steel bars. Maybe the shaking and rattling will bounce me into an empty field, I thought. Meanwhile, I was grateful for passage to Agra.

Fields and farms flashed past. Camels burdened beneath burlap sacks of grain trotted on dirt paths. The train accelerated and a kaleidoscope of brick homes and mud towns blurred by. Boars nosed through rubbish heaps along the tracks. Barefoot children gawked from squalid huts. Houses and roadsides lined the banks of rancid scum-covered waters. When my legs cramped I stood in the corridor. As a burgundy-colored sun set the wind turned colder and darkness fell. At Kanpur we paused, and for the few that disembarked, dozens more boarded. Conditions grew worse, yet they managed to force the doors shut. I could not move. The train whistled, and steel ground against steel. I felt an urge to scream in unison with the metallic screeching of the wheels on the rails. Instead, my eyes darted around the packed railcar in a futile effort to find relief from the crush of humanity.

One empty recess in the wall seemed just large enough to squeeze into. I climbed up, wormed my way into the recess, and looked over a sea of bodies filling the overhead luggage racks. Their eyes bore into mine and we pondered each other in muted darkness. At Tundla I slipped onto the floor among the bodies and lay beneath a maze of legs. We traveled on in cold darkness.

Inexplicable delays and frequent stops wore us down. No one knew how many hours lay ahead. Overflowing toilets and unwashed bodies festered in the stifling air. I made solemn promises—when I got home I would savor every luxury and take nothing for granted.

Hour after hour dragged by until in time the train whistled and the fog in my mind cleared enough for me to realize we had called at Agra Fort. My legs wobbled as I stepped onto the platform, still shaky from hours of disuse. Someone pursued me as I walked. He was a tout, and I had heard that touts in Agra were the worst of the breed. I gritted my teeth.

"To Taj Ganj," I said to the tout, "and the Lucky Restaurant to meet a friend."

"Twenty rupees," he said, a fair price. We rode in the chill, my breath freezing as the amiable driver asked questions and pointed out the fort. He seemed harmless, and I dreaded the thought of inevitable conflict. We zipped through narrow streets and past the Taj Mahal, mostly hidden from view behind tall stone walls. At the Lucky Restaurant I paid the driver. He thanked me, and drove off. I stared after, stunned that he did not try to steer me to an endless assortment of commission-laden shops and hotels. The restaurant proprietor ventured outside.

"I need to find a room," I told him, "then maybe food."

"Oh," he said, "we have rooms too. Sixty rupees for a single, with attached bath."

I ate masala and drank hot tea, relishing the fact that I managed to do so hours before I had dreamt possible. The kind proprietor engaged me in conversation, and bemoaned changes in Agra these past years—how business was tough though he enjoyed it; how he once traveled the country on business, except during the monsoons. I waited for some ploy to transpire. None did. And, my meal was delicious.

Even once settled comfortably in my room I awaited some disagreeable turn of events—something frustrating, disheartening, even soul-searing. And still I waited, for I had yet to learn that India was never what one expected or what one thought her to be. If she were predictable, she could never be the mythical mystery that she is. Outside the window a cricket chirped, and but for the occasional bleep of a passing auto-rickshaw, all was quiet.

19

THE MUGHAL NORTH

Darkness bathed the hotel as I stepped into morning chill. As the moon faded on its gently waning journey, the eerie song of a muezzin called devout Muslims to prayer from some distant minaret. Crows cawed, a hawk landed, and orange haziness lit the eastern sky. The muezzin's call rose, then silence filled the darkness. Before me the Taj Mahal floated like a mirage. Towering minarets hovered on clouds as cool mist of the Yamuna River swirled past the grand central dome and shrouded the four smaller ones in misty whiteness.

The apparition took form, white against white. I set my shoes near the entryway. Inside the mausoleum, a hanging latticed lamp cast soft light onto false tombs resting within screens of fine cut marble. Other-worldly sounds emanated from high above.

An elderly Moslem entered. He pointed to Quran verses inscribed in black Arabic script and semi-precious stones inlaid over decades upon every wall through an art form known as *pietra dura*. When he called "hullo" his voice echoed a dozen times from the curved ceiling and marble walls.

The Mughal emperor Shah Jahan ordered construction of the massive tomb of white marble for his beloved wife, but the origins of India's most famous monument began a thousand years prior in Mecca with the birth of Muhammad–the Apostle and Prophet of God and Seal of the Prophets. Soon after Muhammad received his first revelations, he fled with his followers to avoid persecution. This migration marks the start of the Muslim calendar. When he returned triumphant to Mecca he began teaching his new religion, Islam, meaning "submission to the will of God." Muhammad taught his people, known as Muslims, to stop worshipping idols and instead submit to Allah, the one true God. Followers believe that God spoke through Muhammad, that the Quran is His word, and that no other prophets will follow Muhammad.

Arab armies carried Muhammad's message as far west as Spain and to the east penetrated present-day Afghanistan. Islamic influence through Muslim rule became widespread in the sixteenth and seventeenth centuries. In India, Islamic rulers became known as Mughals. Unlike prior invaders, Mughals retained their Muslim identities. Even after eight hundred years of Muslim domination, less than a quarter of India's population had converted to Islam.

The Mughal emperor Akbar, for example, knew he could not subjugate so many Hindus, and instead integrated them as generals and advisors. Akbar's strategy fostered a golden age of Islamic-Hindu integration. The Mughal School of Miniature Painting, a synthesis of Persian and Rajput traditions, flourished. Architectural styles reflected both religions.

Shah Jahan succeeded Emperor Akbar. After waiting five years to marry on a date ordained by court astrologers as most auspicious for a happy union, Jahan named his bride "Mumtaz Mahal, Chosen One of the Palace." Poets extolled her beauty, grace, and compassion. He married two other wives and sired a child with each, but according to court chronicler Motamid Khan "the intimacy, deep affection, attention and favor which His Majesty had for the Cradle of Excellence exceeded by a thousand times what he felt for any other."

Mumtaz served as Jahan's trusted confidante, and despite frequent pregnancies, travelled with his entourage. When she died on a military campaign while giving birth to their fourteenth child, the emperor went into a yearlong secluded mourning and began planning a mausoleum that took twenty-two years to complete. The grandeur surrounding me was inspired by one man's love for a woman. I wondered whether I was capable of the level of devotion that Jahan seemingly felt.

At nearby Agra Fort, a sea of vendors along Amar Singh Gate sold souvenirs, food, guide services, and rickshaw rides. Rose-ringed parakeets trailing long feathered tails glided from high sandstone walls towards an algae-covered moat and overgrown gardens where princes and queens once reposed. Hundreds of rooms, most stripped by nineteenth-century Jat invaders, invited wandering. Under Shah Jahan, Agra Fort evolved into a regal palace. Built of white marble, it once housed the ruler's sapphire, ruby, emerald, and pearl-encrusted Peacock Throne.

Jahan intended to build as his own tomb a black marbled negative image opposite the Taj Mahal. Prior to construction his son deposed him, in part to halt such extravagance. Jahan was confined to an octagonal tower Jahan had built for Mumtaz Mahal. There Jahan spent the remaining seven years of his life looking upon the Yamuna River and his wife's white marble sarcophagus–the Taj Mahal–in which he too would be entombed.

From atop the hotel rooftop I watched the Taj reflect the day's last rays. Hundreds of Indian tourists waited in long snaking lines to gain entry, and many more milled inside. Four Israelis found my refuge. Two of the men hoped to find Enfield motorcycles for touring around India. A third read from his Hebrew guidebook, moving his eyes back to front and right to left. The young brunette asked how I entertained myself since I carried no music, watched no television, and had seen no recent movies. "By observing people and exploring new lands," I told her. She seemed disappointed. I shrugged and turned towards the Taj, mesmerized by its timeless beauty.

Downstairs, an Indian fellow cornered me with endless questions. Aswal said he traveled on business from the northeast, and spoke of his charity work with the less fortunate and downtrodden. Some of the indigenous tribal folk earned only ten rupees per day. "They will still give to a hungry street person," he said. "Most of the rich, however, give nothing."

After dinner we strolled through the old city of Taj Ganj. "The landscape changes so much from east to west and north to south," Aswal noted. The cuisine differed too. "No word for soup exists in Hindi," the language of the north, he said. "Northern food would be considered inedible in the south! Cooks in central provinces use no spices." Beyond food, hundreds of languages canvassed the country. Clothing styles varied across the landscape. Only the banner Republic of India bonded so much disparity.

Late night we drank Indian rum cut with water, and listened to flute and santoor ragas play upon his mini-cassette recorder.

"Such music may arouse multitudes of emotion," mused Aswal. "Melancholy, happiness, a burning heart, memories of lost love, romance, even anger. Such an artist devotes much time to his craft, and thus puts his heart into his passions. His goal is to evoke emotion, whatever it might be."

He told me this is the way of the guru—not interested in money, power, or prestige, married instead to whatever purpose or personal endeavor he follows. "If he finds recognition, fine. But this is not his chief aim. Those in the western world seek money and recognition for accomplishments. This is merely satisfaction of the ego." Many Indians regard Americans as arrogant for this reason, he added.

"The answers are always there in front of you, whether here or at home, and lie in seeing properly, in knowing how to look." Aswal turned towards me. "You wear blinders, as many do, and miss what needs to be seen. You must look into the music, food, souls, hearts and silent eyes of these people to understand." I contemplated his words as I headed to my room. I wondered how much I had already missed. I resolved to pay closer attention, and look past the physical discomforts so common in India.

Over breakfast, Aswal noted that every day brings a fresh start and new beginning. "We have every morning the ability to begin another perspective," he said, "yet so often stick to old patterns. Real change thus happens so rarely."

I looked outside while considering Aswal's words. Thick winter mists of the Yamuna River obscured distant buildings and swirled through the streets. Passersby donned shawls and woolen wraps for huddled walks. Every face seemed friendly, the streets clean, each individual's story one I felt I wanted to hear. A wave of optimism washed over me, and a refreshing sentiment hung in the air. The irresistible nature of this East Indian who helped the deaf, blind, and lepers seemed to be inspiring a fundamental change in me as well.

I left Aswal and Agra via bus on the Great Northern Trunk, a corridor dating to Emperor Ashoka's day. Upon that ribbon of road belching trucks and overcrowded buses roared towards Delhi at breakneck speeds. I shut my eyes for a brief nap and opened them as we passed an overturned semi-truck and the crushed, twisted remains of a jeep's chassis. Four khaki-uniformed policemen surrounded two inert white-shrouded bodies lying on the bloodstained pavement. How quickly everything changed; only minutes before, I surmised, the men had probably discussed wives, children, politics.

Near the Old Delhi bus station below Kashmir Gate, I battled the crowds to find a rickshaw-wallah for the ride downtown. The rickshaw driver suggested we stop at a government information office to locate a hotel, and I agreed since it was Sunday and most businesses closed. The office's overeager help and a lack of sterile inefficiency made me suspicious. I quickly ducked back outside. The driver followed and tried to steer me towards a guesthouse of his choosing. I turned down a side alley where the rickshaw could not follow, but found myself lost amidst streets labeled in indecipherable Hindi script.

Two Sikhs sporting massive moustaches and wearing bright blue turbans pointed me towards another "government" tourist office. "Only for a minute, sir," said one.

Dozens more questionable travel agencies with official sounding names lined the street. All purported to be government offices or tourist information centers, but in reality were fake agencies that depended on commissioned touts for business. At every corner, men stepped in front of tourists to guide them into their shops to sell tickets and tours at inflated prices.

"Hullo, 'scuze me, where you from? Where you go?" touts pestered at every turn. Rickshaw drivers puttering past tried to take me places I had no wish to go.

Pains had wracked my gut since I stepped off the bus, and now they returned with more urgency. There were no facilities in sight on the open street. I knew I was suffering from "Delhi Belly," derived no doubt from suspect food. Most stores were closed, but at one restaurant waiters wearing black vests and bow ties ushered me to a table. I dropped my backpack and rattled the locked bathroom door. The maître d' noticed my plight and—just in time—pushed the stuck door open. There was a western style toilet, which of course did not flush. I humbly returned to my table without a smidgen of hunger. Nevertheless, I ordered an overpriced lunch then returned outside to midday humidity.

At least eight ancient cities had arisen since Delhi's initial founding three thousand years ago. I strolled through the colorful bazaar called Chandni Chowk, which stood within crumbling walls of Shahjahanabad, the seventh Delhi. Souvenirs lined vaulted arcade walls where the royal household once purchased gold, jewelry, and silks. Shah Jahan's construction of Shahjahanabad signaled a shift in Mughal power, though his imprisonment prevented him from entirely moving the capital from Agra to Delhi.

Through Lahore Gate stood Drum House, where musicians once heralded princely arrivals. Within the white marbled Diwan-i-Khas the emperor held private meetings upon the Peacock Throne taken from Agra Fort. Still inscribed upon the wall could be read a famous Persian couplet glorifying golden days of the Mughal Empire: "If there is a paradise on earth, it is this, it is this, it is this."

Such extravagance begat decline. Hindus sought reforms or their own empires. Sikhs and Jats revolted. Marathas removed the Diwan-i-Khas's solid silver ceiling. Persians sacked Delhi and carted the Peacock Throne to present-day Iran.

As Mughal influence faded, European interest in India grew. Portuguese landed first and captured Goa. The French followed the Danes and Dutch. The British East India Company's monopoly over all British trade with India marked a new chapter. Through wars and successions the company gained dominance over the Marathas, Nepalese, and Sikhs, and by the early nineteenth century, controlled all of India.

Laconic administration and dismissal of local rulers led to the rumor-fueled Indian Mutiny. One rumor claiming pig fat greased a new type of bullet angered Muslims, who consider pigs unclean. Another claimed the bullets were greased with cow fat, which outraged Hindus. Massacres ensued, until the British government wrested control.

I walked to Connaught Circle and the financial heart of Delhi. Colonnaded buildings devoted to shops, banks, and restaurants surrounded the double-ringed traffic circle. Half a century after intervening, the British Crown moved the capital away from Calcutta, which gave rise to New Delhi, the city's eighth and current incarnation.

My guesthouse turned out to be an abandoned pile of rubble. Passing boys pointed towards another at the end of a dead-end street. After I rang the bell a half-dozen times, a woman called from an upper floor. She directed me to the windowless room, and I never saw her again. I tossed my rucksack onto a thin mattress in the basement room of the otherwise deserted home. Overhead, a gray rat sniffed at the ceiling grate through which shafts of light slipped.

I continued to Raj Ghat, where a platform of black marble stood beside the Yamuna River. Though the First World War curbed Britain's plans for Indian independence, a young lawyer named Mohandas Gandhi afterward led a movement of passive resistance. Mohandas became known as Mahatma, the great soul. After the Second World War, Britain lacked the motivation to support an empire. Hindus dominated the independence-minded Congress Party. The Muslim minority, however, refused to live in a nation controlled by Hindus.

"I will have India divided, or India destroyed," declared the leader of the Muslim League. With so many Muslim communities surrounded by Hindus, dividing the country proved impossible.

Civil war loomed. Soon after the British viceroy announced independence, a British referee drew arbitrary borders between India and the new state of Pakistan. One thousand miles of Hindu-dominated India separated the incoherent Muslim halves of East and West Pakistan. Millions of refugees fled their homelands during one of the largest human migrations in history. Muslims sought sanctity in the Pakistani halves, while most Hindus and Sikhs remained in or migrated to India. Muslims fleeing by train were held up and shot; Hindus and Sikhs escaping east fared as well. Ten million people changed sides, and perhaps half a million died. Soon after Partition, a Hindu fanatic assassinated an anguished Gandhi.

Standing before the memorial on the banks of the Yamuna River, which marks the spot where Gandhi was cremated, I contemplated impacts of the Muslim faith on Indian history. Without Islamic influence, Partition would have seen far less bloodshed. There would also not be a Taj Mahal. Despite so many Hindu-Muslim conflicts, I felt grateful for the countless colorful cultural contributions that followers of Islam had brought to the subcontinent.

20

LAND OF KINGS

While onboard a rusty bus, as the driver prepared to depart, a half-dozen Indians asked my destination.

"Mathura," I replied.

"By bus?" they invariably asked. I answered yes to each one. We roared out of the yard and onto the freeway. When yet another man asked, "You go Mathura by bus?" I responded, "Yes, by bus!" Could they not see I sat aboard a bus?

"No train," the man replied evenly. "Only bus. But stop on highway. You catch second bus for Mathura."

The conductor came along. "Mathura bus. Direct," he said, and motioned towards the bus station now a dozen miles behind. "Leave in five minute."

I sighed. Why could someone not mention the direct bus sooner? As I was learning, Indian English differed markedly from American English, which often made communication a challenge.

After five hours, a change of buses, and dozens of near collisions a road sign indicated the turnoff. I squeezed my way past bags and bodies and tapped the conductor's shoulder.

"Mathura?" I asked. He grunted and yelled something to the driver. A moment later the bus slowed enough for me to leap out and hit the ground running.

A graybeard motioned me towards his two-wheel carriage of wood and tattered canvas, known as a tonga. I climbed in. With a flick of the old man's switch–yellowed string tied to a willow branch–the weary draft horse ambled downtown.

Youngsters watched with wide brown eyes. Some yelled and a few threw sticks or stones. We passed the Hindu temples which replaced the Ashoka-era Buddhist monasteries that comprised Mathura's original core. From my hotel I gazed across the street at the foundations of Kesava Deo Temple– the ostensible birthplace of the Hindu deity Krishna and one of the most revered sites in India. I yearned to see what inspired so many millions.

Inside the temple, pilgrims streamed into a dungeon-like room and past a worn stone slab upon which, it was said, Krishna had been born 3,500 years ago. The waves of eager pilgrims seemed never-ending.

A mosque from the Mughal era towered above the temple. Likewise, a mosque once stood atop a Hindu temple believed by many Hindus to mark the birthplace of the god Rama. Hindu fundamentalists had long demanded the mosque be demolished. The issue exploded a few years prior to my visit, when Hindus destroyed the mosque. Hundreds died in the riots that followed.

Such conflict underlay the prevailing military presence surrounding me in Mathura. Armed soldiers wielding wooden Mosin rifles patrolled the grounds and eyed milling pilgrims. An orange setting sun drifted through evening haze as I chatted with inquisitive soldiers smoking beedi cigarettes before passing through iron gates and along walls covered by swastikas and sacred verse. In one temple, prostrating Hindus prayed while a bespectacled holy man chanted, and in another, ceiling murals depicted Krishna flirting with milkmaids.

The oldest Hindu books, the four sacred Vedas, contain philosophy, hymns, myths, prayers, and instructions for reaching moksha and liberation from endless reincarnation. Contained within the Vedas are the Upanishads, which pertain to the metaphysical nature of the universe and soul.

The newer realm of Hindu literature, the *smrti*, includes the epic Hindu poems. One, the Ramayana, establishes the ideal man and hero of Indian culture and myth. Its introduction claims that "He who reads and repeats this holy life-giving Ramayana is liberated from all his sins and exalted with all his posterity to the highest heaven."

Contained within another, the Mahabharata, is the Bhagavad Gita, among the most popular of Hindu writings. In this poem, Krishna teaches that renunciation of the world does not mean abandonment of it, but rather, the surrender of selfish actions. Acting for the good of all, not oneself, allows the true self to shine forth. These are the scriptures Mahatma Gandhi followed during his campaigns of nonviolence.

Darkness descended upon Mathura and people and cattle materialized like misshapen creatures from misty gloom. Three-wheel tempos, larger versions of the noisy two-stroke auto-rickshaws, rumbled past. Bullocks pulled wooden two-wheel carts laden with silage, vegetables, and rubbish.

I watched the scene, illuminated as it was by street and building lights. A moment later everything disappeared into inky blackness. Blaring music ceased. The crowded smoky streets were gone. Every person froze in place the way an old filmstrip jams in a projector. A few candles were lit, generators grumbled, and the city took the power cut in stride.

I stood in the murky shadows shelling peanuts purchased from a sidewalk vendor and watched the faces flow past. As at Varanasi, an electric energy filled the air. This city, imbued with ancient history, also felt timeless. It mattered little whether Krishna was actually born on the worn stone slab. The thousands of pilgrims in attendance were testament enough.

At sunrise I returned to the streets. Sacred music blared from overhead speakers. My cycle-rickshaw driver stood erect on the pedals, pumping hard as he careened through busy streets towards the train station. Each pothole bounced me from the narrow metal seat, so I held tight. We passed laughing schoolchildren, and fat boars nosing mounds of soppy garbage rotting in black watery pools. A pair of monkeys paused on an apartment landing. The male's hind-end wiggled, and then the female looked at him, shrieked, and leapt into the bushes.

The rickshaw-wallah pulled to the roadside and turned part way round. "Deelee!" he exclaimed with a toothless red-gummed grin. I glanced around. Several worn buses sat in a weed-covered lot near trash-strewn railway tracks. A local train slid past, but there was no depot or waiting rail cars.

"To Bharatpur?" I called to a nearby bus conductor. He cocked his head from side to side, which in India meant yes.

"Deelee!" the rickshaw-wallah cried again, still convinced I sought Delhi.

Since there were no trains that stopped here, I settled instead for the Bharatpur-bound bus. So much for my romantic notion of entering Rajasthan—the Land of Kings—by railway. In India, you so often took whatever you could find.

Battered country roads prowled by noisy tractors and rural truckers snaked among misty pastures stretching to the horizons. At every lurch and trounce, bus passengers flew into the air and slammed onto their metal seats.

Poplars shaded farmhands resting in tidy green fields. Vine-covered stone gazebos and crumbling shrines peered from thicket edges. Bone-white egrets waded shallow ponds thick with hyacinth. At one, three bare-bottomed boys leapt from a decrepit gangplank to splash in tepid waters.

Fertile fields yielded to ramshackle buildings and city outskirts of Bharatpur, where milling townsfolk bought vegetables and spices in congested bazaars. The bus driver blasted his horn until someone budged enough to ease the gridlock. A camel towing a wooden two-wheel cart turned the corner. Adorned in necklaces, anklets, and dangling jewelry, his jaws worked steadily. The driver standing atop the cart jerked long leather reigns and yelled into the air. Together they pushed through the maze of pedestrians and rickshaws.

When the bus died, a cross-eyed lad called to me through the window. He spoke only Hindi, but I knew he wanted my business. I followed him through narrow twisting streets past lavender and carnation-colored flats, beyond Mathura Gate, and eventually into a hidden courtyard.

After negotiating a room I sought the guesthouse rooftop, where Kristopher, a young German artist-in-residence, joined me. Great bushy tufts of hair sprouting from the tops of both his ears caught rays of afternoon sun.

"In the Deutschland," Kristopher said as he peered into streets below, "unwritten mores dictate behavior, fashion, what is or is not acceptable in everyday life. Everyone dresses alike. Professionals wear identical uniforms. Jeans and track shoes comprise casual wear. Dark colors fill every wardrobe."

India follows a different rhythm, I thought. This was evident all around me. Rules were bent, trains late, and people slept midday under trees and upon rooftops. Poverty thrived, yet people were merciful. Whether by design or default, government did not crowd citizens' rights. People could do as they pleased within reason. There was a freedom here that was more palpable and real than I ever expected.

"The post-Cold War rebuilding of Berlin follows strict, sterile guidelines," commented Kristopher. "It's all glass, concrete, and steel. Bright colors are rare."

Such a contrast to India, I mused. Women wearing brilliant saris painted drab landscapes with flashes of color and personal emotion. In that sense Hindu women were freer than in Kristopher's homeland. In another sense, wearing beautiful colors was a means of defiance against the difficult lives that most Hindu women endured. After marriage a son stayed home to care for aging parents, but a daughter was a burden and when food ran scarce, she went hungry. With most marriages still arranged, a teenage daughter often found herself married to a man she had never met.

After her parents provided a handsome dowry, a young wife would move to his village to raise children, keep house, and walk miles each day for firewood, water, and fodder. Yet she had no property rights and little chance for an education. Husbands often felt it their right to beat their wives.

Small wonder Hindu women expressed themselves with bursts of silent color, within which they could hide their true emotions. They wrapped themselves in long swirls of beauty to display their perseverance and pride despite such suffering. I thought I could see the pain in some of their faces, but their world was off limits to me. I could scarcely imagine what many women endured.

Kristopher suggested I take a break from rigors of the road, and explore the nearby bird sanctuary. To my surprise conservation was not new to India. Early Buddhist, Hindu, and other scriptures taught nonviolence and respect for all life. Among Emperor Ashoka's edicts was one that forbade the slaughter of certain animals and burning of forests. At one time, Bharatpur's semi-arid temporal marshlands shriveled up after the monsoon rains ended. When the local maharaja diverted water from an irrigation canal, birds began settling in great numbers. His motives were not ecological, but a means for shooting sprees on which guests sometimes bagged four thousand birds a day. Even so, such hunting reserves maintained sustainable bird populations in a starving land.

Before dawn I peddled a rusty borrowed bicycle through damp morning fog. The bird sanctuary was deserted, but for a shawl-draped cyclist's clinking bell and dim headlights of a 1950s-style Hindustan Ambassador automobile probing the mist. I pulled my scarf tight against the chill as I made my way over narrow paths amongst woodlands and marshes.

Birds popped up everywhere, often boldly. When I paused at a canteen, magpie-robins with markings like magpies and shaped like robins, flitted about and perched upon bicycle handlebars. A hopping hoopoe searched for larvae. Chattering jungle babblers congregated in small flocks along the path. Purple moorhens waded the watery *jheels*, as did a watercock, and the sparkling blue flash of a kingfisher caught my eye. Farther along two shy peafowl slipped out of sight.

As the fog cleared more birds appeared. A cormorant dried its wings in the hazy sunshine. Ibises flew overhead. Bar-headed geese rose in great numbers from the marshes. Thousands of painted storks tended squawking chicks waiting in thick matted nests. Not all sanctuary residents bore wings. Spotted deer, called *chital*, also foraged among the thickets.

After returning to the guesthouse I met Michat and Aga, a Polish couple. We walked through streets abuzz with activity. From every shop hung silver-foiled packets of paan suspended in long strips. Men bought their favorite brand and spit red mouthfuls of betel nut juice onto the streets. Swarms of black flies covered chunks of brown unrefined sugar for sale. Pudgy shopkeepers relaxing upon thatch mats watched the world pass as cattle and swine roamed the streets.

Vendors pushed carts with pastries piled high, two rupees for one. I hesitated. They reminded me of the puffed coconut pastries sold on Bangkok street corners, so I decided to try one. Unlike the Thai treats, when this vendor broke a hole in the thin shell he put a few small pieces of potato inside. Next he ladled brew from a large steel kettle into the pastry and handed it to me. I looked at the man questioningly. He nodded. My hunger and curiosity won. I swallowed the concoction, but gagged on the foul liquid and choked down the stale shell. Later that night, wearily crouched over the pit toilet, I would be reminded that my stomach was no match for the street vendor's foul vermin-infested brew.

Meanwhile, the Poles and I walked onward as afternoon sun slanted earthward. A snaggle-toothed rickshaw-man solicited our business. We demurred. He followed along onto side streets. "No thank you," we said again. He persisted, and asked for money. "Two rupees?" he asked. "One?" Aga dug into her pockets and handed him worn notes. Still he followed.

Some men whistled at Aga; others laughed or sneered. The

women watched with sad eyes from within cotton saris. Aga ignored them all, but I glared at the ogling men. Aga's tenor seemed to slowly shift from compassion to frustration.

Near the vegetable market, away from the snaggle-toothed rickshaw-man and catcallers, we bought sweets made of paneer. Aga told her story. She was married, though not to Michat, and left her husband behind to travel six months overland with Michat across Eastern Europe, Turkey, Iran, Pakistan, and India. At thirty-one, Aga's husband was considerably older, for she was still a student.

Throughout Islamic Iran, Aga and Michat had posed as brother and sister for it was forbidden that an unmarried couple travel there together. Though India was less strict, many social mores still carried the weight of law.

"Are you married?" every male Hindu seemed to ask me. "How many girlfriend you have?" They thought it strange I traveled alone. All men, especially Americans, had a girlfriend if not several, they seemed to believe.

Even more unusual, in their eyes, was a Western woman traveling alone. Though Hindu men often treated Indian women with little respect, the typical South Asian man held an even less charitable view of Western women. To such men, with or without a travel partner and thanks in part to the abundance of bootlegged American DVDs–every Western woman was in essence a whore.

21

LA ILAHA ILLA ALLAH

The Poles and I parted company, and at the place where buses gathered I found one bound for Jaipur–the largest city in the state of Rajasthan. I huddled in back, still ill from the vendor's foul concoction, as chill winter air streamed through a broken forward window. Overcrowded buses and trucks laden with lumber, sand, and stone raced around camels toting two-wheel wooden carts.

At a nameless village, peanut vendors stirred nuts in the shell over feeble flame and maneuvered their carts towards potential customers. They wore handsome knitted sweaters, pressed trousers, and shiny shoes, and managed to make a meager living by selling full bags for only five rupees. Somehow, they supported themselves and extended families–literally and figuratively–on peanuts. In Delhi men sold combs and padlocks on commission, and male customers clustered dozens deep around sunglass salesmen to try different styles. This puzzled me, since I had never seen any Hindu wearing sunglasses. How the salesman sold enough to survive was a mystery to me.

Fog lifted and the day warmed as we came upon Jaipur, the pink city of crenellated fortress walls. Two wild-looking men approached me. While one babbled, the other offered a two rupee auto-rickshaw ride. The first countered with an offer of one rupee to anywhere. Then both laughed. A third came on the scene.

"Where you from, sir? Where you go?" he asked.

Jaipurian rickshaw-wallahs were among the worst of their ilk, known to take travelers to hotels paying thirty percent commission, refusing to go elsewhere or charging quadruple for the inconvenience, and stopping at jewelry stores along the way to earn a hundred rupee commission and cold beer whether the jeweler made a sale or not. I waved them off.

Children's kites twitched beneath auburn cloud while I walked towards the humming downtown bazaars. The warrior-astronomer Maharaja Jai Singh II founded and designed Jaipur based on an ancient Hindu architectural treatise. Chandpol Gate still stood though most of the old walls were gone. Iswari Minar Swarga Sul, the "Minaret Piercing Heaven," towered overhead.

Two well-dressed young men yelled hullo as I walked past. They ran after. "You did not stop," they accused, suggesting I did not acknowledge them properly.

"I am on my way somewhere," I said, and told them I was not interested in whatever they were selling. They hurled insults and chased again. "Stop!" they demanded. I kept walking.

In Johari Bazaar a man hustled me into his shop. "Just look, no buy," he said, and offered dozens of red garnet, purple amethyst, red tiger eye, smoky topaz, jade, and turquoise necklaces. Sensing my disinterest, he revealed his ace in the hole—tiny Stars of India. "The sacred stones will keep your chakra in harmony when properly used," he assured.

No western tourists haunted the streets. My hotel held only Indian patrons. As such, every scam artist in the city seemed to be after me. The vendors and touts were getting bolder and more desperate, it seemed. I wanted to run from all of them.

On the sidewalk, two local Muslim youths overtook me with eager questions about life at home. Their names were Nadeem and Pradeep. They said they had renounced tobacco and alcohol, but enjoyed strolling the streets rather than sit at home. They warned of other travelers' woes. A Japanese man on the train had accepted chai from strangers and blacked out. Upon awakening he found his baggage, money, and new "friends" gone. The boys also told of "silk" bed sheets costing sixty rupees to weave, offered for sale to tourists at two thousand, and sold for a supposed bargain at twelve hundred.

"Trust no one," they said.

Their conversation turned to generous women and the ample pleasures the lads seemingly enjoyed.

"Such women exist here?" I asked, doubtful. Apparently it wasn't just the fresh night air which beckoned these youths from their homes. A passing female caught their eye.

Nadeem called to her. "How much?"

"Five hundred," she said.

"Ah, we are but poor students and can afford but forty rupees," replied Pradeep. She scoffed, but agreed to fifty. "Too much," said Pradeep as he waved her away. She melted into the crowd.

"See?" smiled Nadeem. "Such women are everywhere."

They insisted we meet the next evening. "Perhaps," I said as we parted ways.

While wandering a side street, a gang of youths I had spoken with earlier approached. One warned over and over that the streets held danger. "The large black men with thick beards will slit any throat for a small commission," he insisted. All the while I wondered how the lads had found me, for I lied to all new acquaintances and claimed my residence as the distant Hotel Evergreen. He warned again of the men in black, and then was gone. My already dark mood turned further dour.

I stumbled upon the first bar I had seen in India, and drank oversize Kingfishers for a dollar each. Dark men smoking Wills cigarettes and drinking Godfather beers or Thums Up sodas took turns staring through the haze. The dusty glass chandelier cast psychedelic shadows onto the ceiling as a gaunt waiter in greasy smock and taupe bell bottom trousers wiped down tables with a brown stained rag. Two men at my table argued politics or maybe their mistresses. Both subjects seemed ubiquitous in India, so one never knew.

The common bath at Hotel Kailash had a calf-high tap draining onto moldy floor and a clogged toilet, but no sink or light. I executed a cold-water shave sans sink in the narrow bedroom, feeling like a soldier of war on leave, with tin cup borrowed from downstairs pantry, dull blade from the market, and filmy looking-glass. Refreshed, I sought breakfast, but only endless rows of shops selling jewels, silk, brass, gems, spices, tins, sweets, and shoes, one after the other, could be found along the streets.

A Rajasthani man in crimson turban and baggy trousers crouched at the curb to urinate into the gutter, as men often did. I recalled two Canadian women debating amongst themselves. One claimed Hindu men to be great lovers, with their Tantric practices, mystic teachings, and openness regarding bodily functions. The other shook her head. "These self-absorbed men know nothing of womanly pleasures," she said. "Or if they know," she mused, "they seem not to care." In the end neither agreed though both continued to ponder.

A motorcycle pulled to the curb. Nadeem had waited at Hotel Evergreen an hour because, he said, I "promised" to meet up with him. I had made no such guarantee and wondered how he found me. I climbed onto the rear of his Yamaha anyway, and we roared into streets bustling with orange and red turbaned men. An elephant lumbered past beneath a load of sugarcane, the driver on top holding tight. Indian transportation included airplanes, buses, trains, ferries, taxis, private automobiles, auto-rickshaws, cycle-rickshaws, human-rickshaws, three-wheel tempos, two-wheel horse-drawn tongas, bicycles, horse-drawn victorias, motorcycles, mopeds, scooters, camels, horses—and even pachyderms.

"There is no God but Allah," said Nadeem as we strolled among ancient corridors of Hawa Mahal, Jaipur's most distinctive landmark. Also known as Palace of the Winds, honeycombed semi-octagonal windows of pink-hued sandstone highlighted the brilliance of local artistry.

"Muhammad is his prophet. Muhammad was born into a world of great inequality and much corruption. Female babies were buried alive. People worshipped many gods."

On the roof, remains of once intricate rooms stood empty. We looked upon the awakening city as ladies of the royal court once did.

"All people are children of God," said Nadeem. "And all prophets are men. Jesus and Muhammad are not gods, only messengers."

We descended and walked to Jai Singh's ancient observatory. A curious collection of sculptures measured positions of the stars, altitudes, azimuths, and eclipses. We paused before a massive sundial with thirty-meter high gnomon whose shadow moved up to four meters per hour.

"What is the essence of Islam?" I asked.

"There are five basic actions," said Nadeem. "A Muslim must first believe in the one true god. He must pray five times each day—at dawn, in the early and late afternoon, just after sunset, and again after night has fallen. He must always pray towards Mecca. He must fast, especially during Ramadan. He must also give to the poor."

"And the fifth action?"

"He must try to make *hajj*, at least once."

"Pilgrimage?"

"Yes. To Mecca."

"How does one become a Muslim?"

He turned. "You must repeat: *La ilaha illa Allah; Muhammadar Rasul Allah.*"

"There is no God but Allah," I said, "and Muhammad is his prophet."

"Yes," he said. "But you must believe it so."

I nodded, but said nothing. Nadeem smiled. "May you find

your path," he said, "and the peace you seek."

A few minutes later, he dropped me at an unmarked corner. I shook his hand and wished him success before walking alone amongst the teeming throngs. Buses and scooters flowed around lumbering bulls like muddy currents past stubborn stones. Parakeets perched upon minarets, and monkeys scurried along roof ledges with stolen morsels. Shop windows glowed one after the other.

Mischievous lads lit firecrackers in the streets, and I raced past before they exploded beneath my feet. Young men yelled from across the street, old men insisted I enter their shops, boys shouted "hullo." One man ran up from behind as I crossed an intersection.

"Why is this?" he asked. "You are our guest and you won't speak with me."

Sometimes the effort to wave them off was too much. "Please. I don't wish to buy anything."

"But I sell nothing."

"Not now, perhaps. But really, what is it you sell? Gems, silks?"

"No, no. Only silver. Very high quality. You visit shop. No buy." I ignored his pleas.

Minarets stood in silhouette against the darkening backdrop as a muezzin called his followers from afar. Twilight faded, a few stars twinkled, and today slid into yesterday. A small girl watched me pass, her brown eyes wide in wonder. The sight of me rendered her speechless. Some reactions to my presence would mimic my expression should alien beings descend from the heavens. Such shocked faces reminded me how I felt every day on the road of India—awed, bewildered, and humbled.

22

SHEKHAWATI

I crammed myself onto a bus bound for the downtown stand. A few locals crawled through a window. More hung from the doorway. The tilting bus rumbled on with men hanging from both sides. I fought my way towards daylight as we approached my stop.

I changed buses and on one bound for the city of Fatehpur, women holding wide-eyed children came one after the other with arms outstretched and palms open. Men peddled food wrapped within smeared newspaper. Boys selling comb-pen-watch combinations in clear plastic pockets yelled Hindi into our ears. When the driver climbed through his sagging door and the motor roared to life, beggars and hawkers scattered.

Green fields gave way to sepia-colored grasses and gnarled acacia trees of the Thar Desert. We continued into a dusty region known as the Shekhawati. The bus passed scatterings of villages that Muslim clans settled in the fourteenth century. These had grown into trading posts along the caravan routes between north India and ports of Gujarat. Fading architectural gems, havelis, still filled the villages. The grandest mansions, all built by Muslim traders, had four courtyards and reached six stories high. Gods, erotic images, royalty, historic scenes, and everyday moments painted by long-dead artisans still adorned inner courtyard walls.

At Fatehpur the bus shuddered to a stop. Here two-wheel tonga carriages drawn by plumed horses in bright harnesses plied the sandy streets. I asked around and a man led me to the wrought iron gates of a courtyard overhung by a metal signboard etched in Hindi script. He led to a windowless concrete room with a prickly thatch mat and candle nub. The man tossed a grimy blanket into the room and motioned me into the family's quarters. I signed the register—assorted grades of paper bound by bits of frayed string—and paid him a dollar.

As usual, after checking in I went exploring. One lad I met in the sandy street claimed two hundred havelis dotted Fatehpur. The rich merchant owners of the near-deserted havelis lived in Bombay, Agra, and Delhi, so thin men wearing long turbans and loincloths lived in the crumbling mansions in their stead. I paid a few rupees to one of them, a reticent soul, which earned me an unguided peek. Another aged man upon the balcony of a chartreuse haveli waved me inside. The hobbling caretaker pointed to murals of Siva's marriage, Queen Victoria and King George, men flying Wright Brothers-era aircraft, and hundreds of others.

In the sandy street, a gaunt vendor sold apples and overripe brown bananas from a cart with flat, twisted tires. Two girls sold pencils and bric-a-brac from a tattered blanket, every couple minutes saying "hullo" to show me something new. One crouched to the side and urinated into the dust. As darkness fell, music played in the streets. An orange-robed sadhu with blanket in hand stood at my shoulder while devotees passed beneath a towering mulberry tree to worship figurines of Ganesh, Siva, and a sacred cow inside a miniature Hindu temple. Each visitor rang a brass bell at the entrance. I watched the worshipers in silent reverence.

As on most winter mornings in India, the fog settled thick and damp. Christmas, only a few day away, would surely be a strange one, I thought. I huddled upon woolen blankets and sipped hot chai, waiting for the world to come alive. The bus I awaited was soon due. The stall proprietor near me sat with legs crossed. He faced the main street and every few minutes turned part way round to ask me a new question. Our conversation veered towards cricket, the national pastime. A small family gathered to watch us.

My bus arrived, but the engine died. Four young men pushed the bus and rocked it back and forth until the driver found enough momentum to shove the gearshift into second and release the clutch for a makeshift jumpstart. The young men ran alongside and then leapt through the open door. Twisted barren trees loomed through chill fog. Married women walking the roadside wore crimson saris and gold two-inch nose rings.

Upon arriving in Mandawa, I longed for a warm place to eat. A shop vendor named Singh directed me to a place down serpentine alleys where an iron kettle bubbled over orange flame. An Indian moved to my side and bought me chai despite my feeble protests. He offered to show me havelis, but after downing the last of my tea I instead wandered in silence.

I found myself back at the market, where a tout gained my attention with a luxurious though affordable room offer. Leery, yet tired and hoping the offer was true, I followed Aneesh to a palatial haveli with king size wooden beds, cathedral ceilings, western sit-down toilet, and even toilet paper. The simple, unadorned room he showed me, however, lay in the dank, windowless basement. I wondered why I had thought it might be a good idea to spend Christmas in India. I turned to leave.

"But wait, sir!" Aneesh called. "I call boss for better price."

While he did so, I climbed to the flat rooftop for a view of the ancient village. The boss did not answer his phone, so Aneesh and I walked to the man's house, a partly restored haveli. Upon entering we pondered paintings of Krishna and his bride commingling with Rama, two men riding elephant-back when viewed from the right but riding bullock-back when viewed from the left, two camels copulating, on and on.

In another room an elderly man wearing a white dhoti, open-toed chappals, and four-day salt and pepper beard sat near his aged wife draped in sunglow sari. Two young girls stared at me in wide-eyed wonder. The boss, a sturdy fellow, appeared and spoke privately with Aneesh.

The elderly man offered me chai, and the woman disappeared to brew a batch. When the sweet tea arrived, my paranoia surged. Warnings that Nadeem and Pradeep in Jaipur had spoken of surfaced in my mind. Might these strangers try to dupe or drug me? I caught myself. This kindly family did not seem malicious. I relaxed, settled onto the thatch seat, smiled at the young staring tykes, and chatted with the gentle folk.

"A room is available," Aneesh said, "though not the one you want." He confided that price depended upon mode of transport. Travelers arriving on foot or via local bus paid far less than couples driving automobiles. We agreed on a fair rate. It looked like it would be Christmas in Mandawa, then.

Later, I wandered desert outskirts that seemed devoid of life. Then, a peacock leapt from a wall. Hoopoes fluttered over a fence. I passed two elderly men sitting on the stone steps of a forgotten Hindu temple. They smiled when I greeted them. Now and then women wearing saris shuffled past carrying water urns or firewood atop their heads.

Abandoned stone wells and cisterns dotted a landscape of mostly barren sands. Their steep walls plunged into darkness, too smooth for climbing. No gates or chains prevented me from tumbling into murky depths a hundred feet below. Worn wooden pulleys dangled from weathered pillars. At one time, heavy buckets tied to stout ropes were dropped, filled, and pulled to the surface by an oxen driver and his harnessed team.

A young woman in reddish-brown sari hid behind a domed Mughal kiosk. She peered around a pillar with shy, curious eyes. I nodded to her in greeting. A gulf deeper than the bottomless wells separated us. Two children climbed the steps, and all three giggled and chatted in brisk Hindi.

I walked back towards the village, past camels and turbaned Rajasthani, sometimes joining men and boys who warmed their feet and hands over smoldering embers of white and black ash to ward off the chill.

In the main bazaar I passed a familiar shop, and Singh spotted me. I had not seen him since I stepped off the bus. He motioned me to his shop, suggesting we discuss religion.

"Five hundred years ago," Singh said, "Guru Nanak at age thirty underwent a mystical experience." Nanak was Hindu, but admired the Islamic faith. While bathing in the Bein River, Nanak saw an apparition which inspired him to follow God's path and lead a new faith that blended both traditions. He kept Hindu beliefs about reincarnation and karma but rejected nonviolence, and accepted Muslims' devotion to one God. Nanak was the first of nine successive gurus, Singh explained, who made contributions to the growing movement.

"Guru Nanak started Sikhism. The fifth guru founded the village of Kartarpur," said Singh, "my home!" The fifth guru also compiled a Sikh bible of poems and prayers. The ninth guru, Gobind Singh, moved Sikhism in a militaristic direction due to persecution they were then enduring. Sikhs were charged with wearing the five *kakkars*: the *kesh*, long uncut hair on one's head and chin; the *kangha*, a comb; the *kaccha*, short pants; the *kara*, a steel bracelet; and the *kirpan*, a dagger. In 1708, the ninth guru declared he would be the last.

I appreciated Singh's passion for Sikhism, but knew this was not my calling. I shifted our conversation towards the village. Singh spoke of merchants who owned the havelis, and how Europeans were robbed by the few overpriced hotels. We entered his shop, where he offered handicrafts at exorbitant prices. Next door, the man who earlier bought me chai asked me to tour his shop of miniature paintings, which I did.

After returning to my room I visited the rooftop. An orange sun disappeared behind distant trees. Parakeets twittered overhead, a peacock called, and children's kites rippled. A sadhu's eerie song floated atop the muffled din of a village in motion. As Moslems bowed eastward, the constellation Pegasus emerged from inky heavens, and the silver crescent of a waning moon slid past the zenith.

Over the town's loudspeakers at dawn a voice sang in swirling tongues. Soon the chatter of sparrows outside my window replaced the faded intonations.

On a frigid sandy street an old man boiled milk and sugar. He pulled the tin kettle from flame before it boiled over, and then sieved the concoction into a soapy glass. The warmth seemed to melt ice in my veins. I watched the lean face of a young boy staring at me transform into a wide grin before he ran off to show friends the fifty paisa—less than a cent—that I slipped him.

Nearby a barber lathered a patron with thick foamy cream. He pulled the long razor downwards in swift motions, applied lotion and powder, then poked two naked wires into an outlet to turn on a hot water urn for the next patron's shave. Like the many chai men, he was an artist in his trade.

Mists lingered past midday. I day-tripped to Jhunjhunu, where vegetarian all-you-can-eat *thali* stands lining the street offered endless portions of dal, potato, and chapati flatbread for fifteen rupees. Little boys shouted "hullo," children chased after me, and young women's haunting eyes watched from within their saris.

At a crumbling Moslem palace, a wizened man in white dhoti and burgundy scarf greeted me. The roof, reached by narrow stone stairwells, offered views of the city and an abandoned fort. Near the gate lay a dozen half-empty fragrance bottles and the man's red woolen blanket. He asked in broken English that I sign the voluminous register, empty but for a few inked entries. He delighted in the addition.

Upon returning to Mandawa's main bazaar, townsfolk greeted me as though I had lived there much of my life. The chai man nodded and smiled. The beer seller shook my hand and voiced commands to an assistant without my asking anything. The clean-shaven young man from the barbershop asked me to his shop. He and his brother wore smart beige sport jackets like professional high-end merchants. Though the bottled perfumes for sale, along with imitation jewelry, white toy dog, and cheap gold-plated picture frames evoked pitiableness, the proud men earned my respect.

I found the omelet man, and without a word he prepared my dinner. A small crowd gathered to watch. I spoke with a Muslim while standing in the candle-lit street. The fasting holiday of Ramadan started two days ago, he explained, forbidding food, tobacco, and alcohol between sunrise and sunset every day for one month to express one's love and devotion to Allah. The gentle twenty-four-year-old spoke of home life and his three children, the eldest already celebrating his sixth birthday. The crowd hung on every word.

The prior evening I had craved a sit-down restaurant, but finding none, settled for evening omelets. On this night I returned to feast in the street with thirty new friends. When a boy patted his stomach I gave him my toast, and he helped himself to a corner of the omelet. I ordered more omelets to share with the crowd.

Christmas Eve arrived. I sat on the rooftop with an oversize Kingfisher beer. Here and there on neighboring roofs a man or woman watched the day fade. Now and then someone joined me to ask questions or discuss Hindu life.

As I descended towards my room past garlands of orange marigolds, replaced daily as tokens to the gods, two young Canadians bartered for a room. I waited as they agreed on a price, then invited Lana and Stephanie into town.

We strolled to the maharaja's long ago converted former castle. Raj-era portraits and antiques hung in the anteroom. From the turrets spread views over the city. Steps and corridors led to a grand inner courtyard illuminated by torches and burning lamps. Fog swirled at our feet. A host seated us in the main garden near a towering Christmas tree. Blue jackets, white dhotis, and orange and red turbans adorned handlebar-mustachioed waiters floating about the room. Women wearing brilliant dresses danced past as musicians played. One man breathed fire, and a woman danced with bowls stacked atop her head while her partner added more until a dozen piled high. Another placed a python around Stephanie's neck. We laughed and ate and drank and celebrated, and after the musicians' grand finale, took tea by the fire. Lana wandered off so Stephanie and I explored hallways, courtyards, and rooms en route to the roof and turrets.

We found our way to our hotel. In their room we shared our hopes, dreams, where we had been, and where we hoped to go. I remembered how quickly bonds form on the road.

The courtyard clock struck twice, and the chime transported me to my grandmother's 1820 stone farmhouse, where every Christmas my parents, sister, cousins, aunts, and uncles gathered. I remembered the aroma of basting turkey, creamy made-from-scratch gravy, homemade potato filling, and homegrown sticky sweet potatoes, green beans, buttery yellow corn, lima beans, and nutty dried corn that melted all thoughts of snow-drifted fields and frozen cornhusks outside.

Scratch desserts always waited in the unheated shanty. My favorite was hickory nut cake. My mom craved the fruit salad; my father and sister preferred the "CMP" dessert but also tried the apple pie and sand tarts and Melt-In-Your-Mouth cookies.

After dinner we gathered in the oversize living room as my aunts tossed gifts from the pile to my cousins and me. We played while the men drank cans of Yuengling beer and spoke in quiet tones and the women smoked Lucky Strikes and adjusted their beehives and sipped peach schnapps slushies.

"Ach yungie," one would call out in Pennsylvania Dutch when one of us said something we shouldn't. "Shrets net so dume." *Hey youngster. Don't talk so dumb.*

By evening most families drifted home one by one. My parents and sister remained though, and we brought out the leftovers and chatted with my grandmother and lingerers until the grandfather clock chimed and we knew it was time for bed.

In the morning my mother brewed the first pot of coffee,

then dashed outside to the cellar to pull out of the freezer homemade scrapple or hand-cured bacon from one of my uncles. She scrambled eggs with white American cheese as we sat in the kitchen and visiting cousins and neighbors dropped by and caught us up on local news. I never wanted to leave my grandmother's stone farmhouse.

On Christmas morning in India, I awoke to find tied to my outside door handle a small bag holding red rose petals, an unsharpened pencil with "Canada" painted in red block letters, a plastic sharpener, and a postcard with a snake charmer coaxing a python. Written on the back were words of gratitude and encouragement from Lana and Stephanie. With gifts where none should be, tears fell.

I ordered a large pot of tea to be delivered when Lana and Stephanie awoke, then took final leave of my room. For the first time in weeks no morning fog shrouded the land. I said good-bye to my chai man after a farewell glass, and waited on the edge of town for a Delhi-to-Bikaner through-bus.

In Bikaner, a family of beggars barricaded my path. Pedestrians squeezed by racks of wares as scooters, buses, autos, rickshaws, and cyclists streamed past in an unbroken procession of fenders and blaring horns. I threaded a jagged path among the speeding vehicles to a rundown side alley hotel with cement walls. I took a cheap room, then wondered if it was worth it after finding a single dangling fluorescent bulb, metal bed frame with paper thin foam pad, grubby threadbare blanket, and dingy, stained pillow. There was also a cramped smelly bathroom with leaking taps and layer of brown cloudy water. Pigeon droppings covered the sill of the lone window. I left the shutters closed.

At a bar on Sadul Circle I settled into a nook. With no companion but my thoughts, I kept the booth's smoke-stained curtains parted. It felt luxurious to order paneer masala dosa and milk tea from a menu rather than subsist on omelets in the streets. But, I realized, I greatly missed my Shekhawati friends.

23

GOLDEN CITY

At the bus station, each man I spoke to held a different answer regarding departures to the village of Jaisalmer. The *Enquiries* counter said ten o'clock. The ticket window claimed none until one in the afternoon.

Two men conversed near the feces-strewn urinal as a stray calf wandered past. When I joined them, the elder of the two said he was divorced and never remarried. I said he was free. Both of the men laughed. Divorce, though legal, was rare in India. If a marriage failed a cloud hung over the husband, but a life of ostracism awaited the wife.

The divorcé said a bus soon left for Pokran, from where I might find one bound for Jaisalmer. He was right. Aboard the bus I watched sparse scraggly trees of the Shekhawati yield to pockets of shrub and low scrub. Sun burned the flesh and covered the land in a white blinding sear. After hours of riding someone tapped me and motioned. Someone else then pointed to a full bus, which I boarded for the onward journey.

When we arrived in Jaisalmer, fifty miles from the border of Pakistan, a tout led me to a cheap room. As I registered he tried to sell a three-day camel safari package—unsuccessfully. Boys pitched handicrafts and carpets. Another man decided he had become my good friend within three minutes of seeing me, then offered opium or whatever I wished. Failing that, he insisted we meet the next day for morning tea.

Every structure in the complacent golden-hued town was built of yellow sandstone. Camels hauled rough blocks from far-off quarries and dropped them at depositories. Workmen, I learned, spent lifetimes hand-chiseling the stones into smooth rectangular blocks. These were used to repair nine-hundred-year-old walls surrounding Jaisalmer Fort, as well as tightly packed houses and shops of the old city.

The majority of Jaisalmer inhabitants were Bhati Rajputs that descended from a warrior who lived a millennium ago. In those days clans fought for waterholes, mud forts, and caravan staging posts that connected central Asia to Gujarati ports and distant shores of Persia, Arabia, and Egypt. For a thousand years Bhati Rajputs fought competing clans for control of the forts and palaces that princes built for protection and prestige.

Rajput translates as "son of a king." Warriors valued bravery and independence above all, and fought until every hope of victory was lost. If defeat appeared imminent, clan leaders declared *jauhar*, in which women and children immolated themselves upon a massive funeral pyre rather than surrender. Men, wearing saffron robes, rode out on horseback to meet the enemy and their own demise. Following the independence of India the Rajput kingdoms joined together as the modern state of Rajasthan, the Land of Kings.

At Jaisalmer Fort, singing voices filtered upward from beneath the ramparts, while a brass bell chimed somewhere far off. Like all elements in this outlying Rajasthani outpost, the singing voices harmonized perfectly. Here in Jaisalmer I found a secluded pocket of one of India's oldest religions—Jainism. Like Hinduism, it has no single founder. The faith was revealed to a number of leaders, *tirthankaras*, of whom Mahavira in the sixth century BCE was the most recent of twenty-four such teachers. Born into the warrior class near the Ganges, at age thirty Mahavira became a wandering ascetic and after twelve years attained enlightenment. His twelve disciples spread his teachings across India. Like Buddhism, which developed around the same time and holds a similar origin story, Jainism began as a reform movement against caste and Brahmin rituals.

Monks and nuns memorized early scriptures, forbidden as they were from owning possessions such as books. Some of Mahavira's words were lost in the fourth century BCE when many monks succumbed to famine. As with other eastern religions, Jains believe that life is a series of deaths and rebirths, and that karma influences how a person will be reborn. Jainism's spin is that the karma a person attracts is a physical substance, which attaches to the soul. To break free from the endless cycle of reincarnation, Jains undergo purification as described in the teachings of the *tirthankaras*.

Jains follow the path of the Three Jewels—right knowledge, right faith, and right conduct. Monks and nuns on the path of renunciation add asceticism, a fourth Jewel. All Jains take vows that guide them along the proper moral path, and which grow more restrictive depending how ascetic one chooses to live.

One belief that sets Jains apart is that of *ahimsa*, or nonviolence. To them earth, air, and metal are living things, and can be hurt by human activity. Not only are Jains vegetarian, but regard for the welfare of plants and animals is mandatory. Sawing a timber causes injury to trees; cultivation harms the soil. Therefore, occupations such as carpentry and farming are forbidden. Monks carry a small brush to sweep insects from their path, strain drinking water to avoid swallowing microscopic organisms, and avoid lamps so moths are not drawn into the flame. It was the Jain teacher Raychandbhai Mehta who helped Mahatma Gandhi embrace the value of nonviolence, which underpinned Nationalist resistance to British rule and eventual Indian independence.

In the fourth century BCE a rift split the Jains. One camp argued that all possessions, including clothes, posed barriers to liberation. Even washing clothes in the river risks killing living creatures, they reasoned. Remaining Jains held that purity had more to do with the mind than with clothing. The latter sect still occupied a few Rajasthani outposts, such as this one at Jaisalmer.

Some of the same elements that had attracted me to Buddhism could also be found within Jainism. I liked that the religion originated as a reform movement, that an individual could attain enlightenment in a single lifetime, and that nonviolence was a cornerstone of the teachings. Accepting that life was a series of deaths and rebirths should also in theory alleviate my anxiety about needing to accomplish as much as I could in my single, short lifetime. Nevertheless, for me the essence of Jainism still fell short. Undergoing purification from a *tirthankara* felt too ritualistic and hierarchical. I struggled with the notion that others should judge what comprised the right path for me—and what was moral or immoral. I decided that Jainism was not my calling.

Movement upon the landscape ebbed and flowed the way currents surge and recede in shallow tidewater. Girls swept stone-paved streets clean of dung and rubbish after cows ambled through and fouled them. Goats skittered past, someone scolded a heifer, and piglets scurried down roadways. Skinks slithered through cracks in stones near women squatting in cotton and silk saris. Shadows grew, and a slight breeze roused some inhabitants from the apathy of noontide slumber.

A sense of déjà vu enveloped me. As at Varanasi, I had the sensation of passing through Europe five hundred years ago. Cattle and calves bawled, goats whinnied, dogs barked and scrapped. People tossed trash and sewage through windows and into the streets. Little boys with pants at their ankles crouched over open sewers. Mules and cattle lived on bottom floors of homes, but roamed freely. Foot power remained the primary mode of human transport, while bullock carts and horse-drawn tonga carriages ferried wares. Lavish palaces and golden forts protected the privileged few. Tents, shacks, and simple dwellings housed the rest. This is the closest I will ever come to time travel, I told myself.

The sun turned deep orange. A teenager with babe in her arms asked for chocolate. I offered a sweet leftover from Mandawa. She wanted a second for her baby, and I gave my last. Another girl running towards us cried for chocolate, and then a third. When the misunderstanding cleared and they understood I was not a candy man with unlimited samples, only a sliver of sun remained. A shallow layer of lavender dust hovered upon the horizon. Pigeons burst into flight as twilight descended, then surrounded a pearl white half-moon.

In the midnight hours mosquitoes buzzed my ears, and I feared the ills they might harbor. Other recent visitors to Jaisalmer had reputedly come down with deadly dengue fever. Early morning darkness found the mosquitoes replaced by flies in my mouth and eyes. Unlike the Jains, I swatted any I could.

They were not the cause, though, when soon afterward I found myself down the hall with my nose inches from the toilet—merely a stinking hole in the lavatory floor. It was the first of many such gut-wrenching trips from my room along courtyard walls and through winding dark corridors. Upon each return I curled into a ball on my bed and clutched a pillow, wondering what I had eaten to cause such daggers to slice my stomach. With nothing to numb the pain, I could only dream of better days.

24

THE PATH TO DHARMA

The better days I dreamt of while ill in Jaisalmer were only partially fulfilled upon my arrival to the city of Jodhpur. Men and women lay one after the other in neat rows upon city sidewalks. Black blankets once white, white sidewalks now black, lives once hopeful now but blank, they slept each night along Nai Sarak.

One man with no hands and blackened gums awaited spare change. Another on one twisted leg and a broken crutch limped past a balding torso, who in hand-cranked wheelchair, rimmed into traffic. Unshaven men in shabby wraps slept in locked doorways and stained streets. Beggar children, faces more brown from filth than race, nipped at my heels. I soon learned that to give to one meant a dozen hiding in shadows would spring forth.

"Why do you come here?" asked the men.

"I am tourist."

"No. Why do you *come* here?"

Two youngsters with blackened sticks for legs stood before me. I looked up into unwashed hair, ears, and faces. They offered me the last bits of whatever snack they feasted upon. It was as Aswal had said—the poor understood compassion, knew the value of sharing. I dug deep, and gave what I had. They wanted more.

Someone's grandmother sat upright, licked her swollen gums, and stared at no one through cracked trifocals. She lay back upon her cardboard mattress for another chill night, perhaps her last. I trudged to my barren roach-infested room. Upon my initial arrival my annoyance peaked when I had to plunk precious rupees on the counter for the overpriced, paper-thin, bedbug-filled mattress. My mood shifted to gratitude when I returned, later, thankful for a roof and modicum of privacy.

I pushed my rented bicycle uphill through bustling markets and winding neighborhoods to massive Mehrangarh Fort. Handprints known as *sati* marks adorned the high wooden gates. These were all that remained of the former maharaja's widows who threw themselves upon his funeral pyre. From the lofty ramparts spread the lavender-hued homes of the five hundred-year-old "Blue City." A child's cry, a hammer, an irregular drum beat, the bleat of a rickshaw—these sounds combined with thousands of others into one collective din.

In evening's damp chill I rode a rickshaw into the countryside. It was New Year's Eve. The bar I had found beforehand was like every other—dark, thick with smoke, occupied by pairs or small groups of men, never a woman. Gaudy green and yellow tinsel hanging from the ceiling did nothing to lift my mood.

The rickshaw left me at an upscale country club. On the lawn, groups of chairs surrounded kettle fires. A band on the makeshift stage sang Hindi songs. The holiday feast began with tomato soup in Styrofoam cups. Celebrants grazed from the buffet as the night grew colder and hour later. When the band rested, I danced to *Kuch Kuch* and *Macarena* tunes with a pair of Israelis, the only other non-Indians amongst the gathering of local well-to-do Marwari people.

There was no shortage of eager male dancers for the many traditional competitions. When frequent power cuts froze the action, guests stood in darkness until recorded tunes picked up where they had stopped. As midnight approached the emcee took the stage. The judges had made their contest decisions. Lights suddenly failed, and all groaned good-naturedly as stars and a nearly full moon emerged overhead.

Then, loud explosions startled the crowd. Fireworks erupted feet away and shot into the night sky. We laughed, for they had fooled us. The lights returned and scores of revelers took to the stage at the stroke of midnight to dance to *The New Year Song*. They ripped down streamers and balloons, tore the stage apart, and sang their way into a new year.

I found a ride home with a wealthy Indian couple. They dropped me near my seedy hotel, and then disappeared in the bustling streets. I stood outside my locked hotel gate, ringing the buzzer at three in the morning, and wondered whether I would be sleeping on the stained stoop.

A young fellow walking by asked why I stayed there. "This isn't a nice place," he said.

In my country, relatively speaking, I was not much better off than him. "I am poor too," I replied.

He smiled. "Happy New Year, then," he said, and trotted down the alley. The old man arrived and unlocked the gate. I lay in my bed with the bed bugs and roaches and listened to blaring music until daybreak.

The next day, a little-used rural road took me through the Thar Desert towards the city of Pushkar. The bus paused at remote villages to take on turbaned farmers and bangle-clad women. Midday sun scorched the land. At one stop uniformed boys gathered round as I bought water. At another an old woman in plaid orange-brown shawl puked mottled green splatter through her window.

Tree branches smacked the windows when we passed occasional trucks on the narrow single lane road. As everywhere in India, immobilized vehicles and broken-down semis were often abandoned in the middle of the road. With not enough room to squeeze around them, we drove onto the sands to pass. When a fleet of trucks barreled towards us we bounced sideways over rocks and sand to skirt disaster. The daughter of the young mother next to me, her face shrouded behind yellow sari, got sick and wretched upon the floor.

When we made Pushkar the touts converged. I followed one to his newer, charmless concrete block hotel, and then wandered instead to the lake where a hand-painted sign led to someone's lakeside home. Asmu, the owner, had a sparse room with high, plain, white-washed walls, thin pad upon the floor, alcoves for candles and incense, and no window, light, or bed—exactly as I imagined a room in India should be.

This room in the heart of Pushkar sat next to a sacred lake surrounded by bathing steps called ghats. In Sanskrit, Pushkar means blue lotus flower. Hindus believe the gods released a swan with a lotus in its beak. Brahma, creator of the world, intended to perform a grand ritual offering where the petals fell to earth. That spot, Hindus believe, is Pushkar. The sacred lake was said to have been created by Brahma, and was therefore a place of pilgrimage.

A family preparing to bathe upon the ghats removed outer wraps and prayed a dozen feet from my door. Sitar music drifted over the lake as holy men scattered flower petals onto sparkling waters and offered puja—prayers—to pilgrims. The family redressed while a cow ambled past. This first day of the last year of the twentieth century, I thought, likely differed little from the last day of the first year of the fifteenth.

My thin mattress offered scant comfort. Before dawn an ethereal voice rose atop soothing background sitars that filled my dreams, and I drifted between sleep and semi-consciousness. As it had for thousands of years, light washed over the valley. I heard a Brahmin clang a tarnished bell hanging outside my door. He intoned a deep "Om" and chanted until the bell fell silent. It was clear that every facet of the residents' lives revolved around their gods. For them, God was everywhere.

Hundreds of shrines filled the city. Some were no larger than a closet, and others such as Brahma Temple held great significance. God's presence permeated the profusion of marigold and jasmine garlands, pilgrims bathing upon the ghats, monkeys, pigs, cows, holy waters, chiming bells, temple spires, praying Hindus, omnipresent bare feet, puja-offering sadhus, devotees feeding pigeons, the pigeons themselves, and a thousand other manifestations.

Asmu, the young female Brahmin whose family ran the temple guesthouse where I stayed, asked my caste.

"I have none."

"What is your father's name?" she laughed, "for this is your caste."

I had not considered Asmu's observation before. Wealth, ethnicity, and gender did stratify the west, though not in the same way that caste divided India. The Indian system maintained effective control, and brought with it rampant social injustice. Even those in power were not necessarily free, however. Asmu spoke with subtle ambivalence of her impending marriage. She wore attire of her choosing, but once betrothed would wear traditional sari, nose rings, bangles, finger and toe rings, and anklets befitting a proper upper caste Brahmin wife. Tradition and customs die slow deaths.

Asmu and her brothers gently guided my behavior in their home, pointing to my feet when I trod where I should not and my shoes when they rested where they should not. My continual mistakes reminded me I was not of their land, nor of their religion. They were patient with me, for which I was grateful. Slowly I learned the nuances of their customs.

From my guesthouse I watched old women bathe in sacred waters, then slowly rewrap saris around brown sagging breasts. For hours, flashes of yellow and orange descended and ascended the ghats. A confident, tranquil air pervaded the village. Hindus live for God. The devout know their purpose in life and why they are here. They know they will one day get what they want, for their souls live forever. They do not fear death; to them death is not an end, but an opportunity to climb a higher rung on the cycle of samsara along the path to liberation. For them, there is no need to hurry or feel daily anxiety.

I studied the pilgrims as they arose one by one from their worship upon the ghats. How satisfied their souls must be, I thought. There were no bathing ghats and sacred lakes in my life. Even poverty-stricken Hindus I had met seemed to pity the likes of me—a westerner—for in some way they seemingly knew how terrified I was of the brevity and harshness of life. For months I had watched broken bodies hobble through trash-filled streets, lie on dirt floors, and die of starvation. Rather than inspire me, such sights had humbled and frightened me. Unlike the Hindus, I lived life by rushing headlong towards somewhere, trying to accomplish all I could before my brief, singular life ended.

Thin, orange dagger-like streaks pointed at the temple of Brahma then widened into broad pink bands. The sun slipped behind a bank of cloud but reappeared at the last moment as a brilliant ball. Bells chimed and drummers on the shore marked the sun's movement. As the sky turned violet, a full moon rose brilliant white. Incense burned, sitars and tambours sounded, and a sadhu sang.

A cheerful man approached from behind as I walked. "My name is Bhamin," he said. "Where do you go?"

"Around this lake."

"Ah!" he said, touching his stomach. "Have fun! I go take sheet."

I chuckled as he wandered into the woods. For many, happiness proves elusive. Yet Hinduism knows that life eternal, boundless knowledge, and infinite joy are what humans really desire. Hindus would claim that all three are within our reach.

For most Hindus, the journey of life is a pilgrimage along a well-worn, understood path. For others, the path is unclear. It has been written that one who longs to leave home is unhappy.

As Hermann Hesse advises, we must each grope forward along our own path and seek inner certainty, as best we can, no matter where that journey leads. My own doorstep was thousands of miles away; in fact it was not even mine anymore, for I had vacated my apartment. Even now, on the banks of a distant sacred lake, I was not certain whether I agreed with the Hindus' path.

On a practical level, Hinduism was not the right solution for me. I had not been born into the religion, and I could not convert to Hinduism. From my perspective, there were too many gods, rituals, and traditions, not to mention excessive dogma and hierarchy. There was a reason, I thought, that Buddhism and Jainism emerged as reformations against Hinduism.

However, in some respects it is as the Hindus claim—to be happy we must each find dharma, our true path. While wandering Pushkar lost in my thoughts, I realized that though Hinduism as a whole was not my answer, perhaps the path to dharma had something to teach. It was up to me to find that path.

25

THE COFFEE GRINDER

I purchased a bus ticket for the city of Udaipur. The travel agent told me to report to his office at eleven o'clock the next morning. When I arrived on time, the agent could not be found. A neighboring storekeeper looked in and said he would try to locate the agent. On one wall of the cramped office a poster read *Travel teaches toleration*. After ten minutes I looked next door to find the storekeeper still drinking chai and chatting with another man. I glanced again at the poster.

A curvaceous blonde wearing a snug sleeveless top and clingy cotton capris stopped by. Sandy sought the same man I did, as she too was going to Udaipur. She offered to lead me to the area where her tourist bus had arrived, unlike the local run, which had dropped me as usual on an anonymous side street.

We paused at her hotel to retrieve baggage. In contrast to my threadbare ghat-side temple room without amenities, hers with wicker chairs, tables, and wide windows cost no more rupees than mine. Her room came with a hidden cost, however—westerners crowded the gardens and restaurant.

At the staging area we waited. She had been traveling and

teaching abroad for two years. Her East Coast homeland lay near mine and we spoke of familiar places, foods, and expressions even other travelers might not know. As the first American I had met in India, we conversed like old friends.

In mid-afternoon a battered bus arrived. Some windows were covered by plywood, one nearly shredded tire had a mammoth gash in the sidewall, and smoke poured from the exhaust. When the driver tumbled out a heated argument ensued. We stared stupidly as the driver and another man screamed at each other and nearly came to blows. The driver leapt aboard and tore away in a cloud of dust. The Udaipur bus, we realized, had come and gone. A third man came round with refunds. We trudged back to town, and then parted.

I strolled around Pushkar's lake once more and enjoyed a curd lassi—an Indian yogurt drink—at a lakeside garden. As the full moon rose, I met Sandy for dinner. In early evening we returned to the bus area for a second try, and this time managed to get on board. We reached the city of Ajmer, and after two hours, caught an onward bus.

Still, we wondered whether we would escape this remote corner of Rajasthan. The horrendous road bounced us from our seats. Barreling trucks without headlights sometimes drove us from the narrow highway onto desert sands. Once, lightless tankers with "HIGHLY INFLAMMBLY" painted on the sides—Indian-English for "Flammable"—nearly forced us into a concrete bridge. Our driver slammed on the brakes and came to a stop. Four inches to the right and we would have joined the crushed ranks of buses and trucks abandoned by the roadside. After the wailing trucks screamed past, our driver restarted the stalled engine and climbed back onto the road.

At four in the morning someone yelled and another man motioned. With that the harrowing ride ended. What was planned as a five-hour journey had stretched into fifteen. I drank a glass of chai while Sandy flagged a passing rickshaw. She found one and beckoned me to climb in. As I stepped in I remembered it was my birthday.

Winding narrow streets lay empty in the still of night. We

found a place along Lal Ghat. I rang the bell, and while we waited Sandy asked how old I was. A sleepy woman unlocked the iron gate, rubbed her eyes, and peered into me. On the way to our room we paused at an overhanging niche that looked out over a lake. Domed cenotaphs and arched windows of whitewashed sixteenth-century dwellings lined the nearby ghats. The Lake Palace Hotel, a gleaming gem of Moghul extravagance, sat upon an island in the lake center. The moon cast its face upon silent waters. Tinkling chimes underscored ethereal chants of a morning muezzin echoing across the obsidian-colored lake. Speaking in hushed tones, we awaited the dawn.

Sleep would not come so we found breakfast, rounded the lake, sat upon the ghats, and listened to the whomping sound of dhobi-wallahs pounding clothes clean. In late afternoon we lit candles and incense and relaxed in the room with a few bottles of beer. The beers picked us up and we took turns slipping downstairs to the hotel fridge for more. The notion of dinner on the town slipped away.

When Sandy's turn came again to fetch beer, she disappeared an extra-long time but returned with a heaping plate of masala, rice, chapati flatbread, two beers, and a slice of chocolate cake with lit candle. Somehow she had convinced the restaurant across the way that carry out did indeed exist.

Despite forty hours without sleep, we felt awake as ever. Earlier, Sandy seemed surprised when I told her I had turned twenty-nine. She wondered what I had done with my years. My heart lurched a moment and I began justifying my life and accomplishments. My life was worthy, I claimed, and full of successes. At last she shushed me, and my mind strayed from the travails that torment a traveler lost on the road of India.

We later laughed and talked, and remembered our past few days in the city once called "Venice of the East." We had spent hours together in a window nook of the Queen's Palace overlooking lake waters, strolling rose gardens at the city park, lying in the sun watching paper kites flutter overhead, and indulging in long conversations with curious locals who crowded around us. We shared a laugh each time we passed the man who sold sweets and paan from within a tiny niched recess of wall and always called out "small shop, many things!"

A rickshaw man drove us to the abandoned Monsoon Palace as the sun sank. While our driver waited outside, we stood together atop the steep hill where winds blew and hawks glided past. Valleys green and fallow stretched into the distance; cool mountains fringed the horizon. Within the ancient palace chattering sparrows built nests in empty rooms and ghosts haunted narrow darkened stairwells. Our driver returned us to town, and we descended in neutral as a wild smile filled his young face.

When the road called, men gathered around to watch us play rummy while we awaited our southbound bus. One rushed up to tell us the bus had arrived. Sandy flipped another card, for no buses were in sight. He bordered on frantic.

"The bus waits for you!" he cried. We arose, and around the corner men pointed to an idling bus.

Desert gave way to palms and farms and countryside of Gujarat where the plague had recently returned, as it sometimes did. Road warriors drove in the middle of byways barely wide enough for two vehicles to pass. They swerved to the left with seconds to spare and passed each other with a chorus of horns. I watched the little men huddle inside the truck cabs as they passed by inches away.

In the trees, a body in dirty shroud lay next to a truck with cab smashed. A few meters beyond, another truck lay on its side with cargo scattered across the road. Men gathered bags of rice under the eye of a khaki-uniformed officer. It has been said a girl becomes a woman when she gives birth, and a boy a man when he accepts death. By this standard, I was no man.

Bouncing in our seats upon the rough road, Sandy and I played a game of pretending we may have anything we wish by willing it. Feeling hungry, I told her we would stop shortly.

"Too soon," she said, looking at her watch. Five minutes

later the bus pulled into a noisy truck stop. We fed like mad cows on palak paneer and aloo mutter. When we roared off she looked at me quizzically.

"Make these bumps stop."

"They will."

"When?"

"Oh, forty minutes or so," I said jokingly.

Thirty minutes later we rumbled to a stop by the roadside. Trucks grumbled past with headlamps turned off and horns blaring. Men wrestled in the dirt beneath our bus with tools and tires while we napped without any jostling.

In fleeting pre-dawn hours we reached outskirts of Mumbai. Hovels of rubble seemingly ready to collapse at any moment perched atop rocky trash-strewn hillsides. Slums and decrepit street-side shacks surrounded outdoor bathers and vendors selling brown vegetables. Worn forty-story buildings rose around the slums like bombed-out relics of war. A lavender-orange glow lit the blockish horizon.

"It's beautiful," murmured Sandy. On some troubling level, it was.

The taxi-wallah wanted two hundred rupees to the Colaba district, but I told him I would rather walk. We agreed on sixty each. Sandy and I breakfasted at an open-air cafe with high ceilings, tall columns, and dark-complexioned waiters wearing white shirts and black pants. The two of us took turns going into the streets to check hotels. We settled upon an overpriced double with a bath and half-window for five hundred rupees.

Blocks away along shores of the sparkling Arabian Sea, Indians walked a narrow promenade. Waves crashed upon jagged rocks; moored sailboats and ketches rolled on quiet harbor waters. Wooden dories painted bright red and blue puttered dockside. Indian tourists strolled beneath the Gateway of India, an arch commemorating the fact that until the advent of flight, most visitors arrived to the subcontinent aboard ships bound for Mumbai.

Roaming children and a man with pet monkey begged for handouts. A brown torso sitting upon plaza stones with an aluminum bowl on his lap awaited spare change. This limbless boy, with four brown stumps projecting subtly from a T-shirt and shorts, haunted my dreams for weeks to come.

The Taj Mahal Hotel on water's edge, where rooms ran to eight hundred dollars per night, exemplified the disparity of wealth that ranked among Mumbai's most striking traits. Though extravagant buildings lined bustling streets and well-heeled businessmen scurried to and fro, the city also drew impoverished villagers that its infrastructure could not support. Many of India's wealthiest lived amongst Asia's worst slums.

I kept my eyes open for any passing pedestrians wearing a *sadra* and *kasti*, a sacred shirt and thread. Such people represent a much less visible aspect of Mumbai–the few tens of thousands of followers of one of the world's oldest religions, Zoroastrianism. The prophet Zarathustra, known to the Greeks as Zoroaster, late in the second millennium BCE spoke of one invisible, all-powerful God who created all things and is the source of all goodness.

Zoroastrianism attracted few followers until the sixth century BCE when the founder of the Persian Empire sent his royal priests, the Magi, on diplomatic missions throughout Asia. The Magi carried with them news of Zoroastrianism. In the second century BCE the Parthians overtook Persia, and gathered Zarathustra's teachings into a holy book.

With Islam's rise in the seventh century CE, Zoroastrians found themselves a persecuted minority. Many migrated to India, where they became known as Parsis–the people from Persia. At one time the religion stretched from India to the Mediterranean. In the modern era, adherents survive in small populations such as this one in Mumbai.

Zarathustra preached that good and evil are in constant battle. Despite these two forces there is only one just and supreme god. Thus, Zoroastrianism is monotheistic. Parsis believe God intends for people to join him in the struggle between good and evil, and so gave humans free will. With this gift humans make moral choices that differentiate between good and bad. At death and at the Last Judgment, individuals will be punished for moral failings with a stint in Hell. Once corrected in the afterlife, the sinner joins God in heaven. Every individual through each action wields an opportunity to make the world better, and has a responsibility to do so.

In Mumbai there are large circular structures called "Towers of Silence." They ring a central pit with walls several stories high and often more than a hundred feet across. To avoid polluting the earth, Parsis do not burn or bury their dead. Instead, they leave bodies atop tall platforms where birds of prey pick the corpses clean–leaving behind piles of bones that get swept into the pits. Only Parsi eyes can view the sacred sights, but on occasion, one might if fortunate spot a Parsi wearing the sacred shirt and thread.

At a funky bar playing European tunes, Sandy and I downed a dozen beers and talked into the night. London-like double-decker buses and shiny black Ambassador taxis plied city streets. Sandy's talkative nature at times sapped my energy, until she uttered something inspirational and I remembered how fortunate I was that we had come together. If she caught me dwelling on the past or worrying about the future, for example, she reminded me to enjoy this present moment, for now is really all we have.

She talked often of life at home. She had a long-standing penchant for antiques but her ex-husband, Henry, had never allowed any in their modern-decor condominium. When Sandy's parents divorced, they rid themselves of the many antiques they had collected over the years. Sandy at least wanted to keep her mother's old-fashioned hand-crank coffee grinder, but Henry refused.

"My mom has one of those," I said. "She uses it all the time."

"Oh! Will *you* buy me an antique coffee grinder?"

I smiled. "Maybe!" I admired how the afternoon sun played across her tan cheeks and golden hair. I brushed a strand from her forehead. "But, whoever buys that coffee grinder, is the one I think you're meant to be with."

She smiled at this idea. We ordered another round and gazed upon silky waters of the Arabian Sea. Later in the evening, after we wandered home, Sandy read a quote from her meditation book.

"Patience is acceptance of events uncontrollable in the external world," she read. "Accepting what you cannot change and finding humor in it, rather than living grudgingly and unhappily because events do not go as you wish."

So much—broken buses, no trains, monsoon floods, falling in love—was not controllable. I often felt like a bottle bobbing on the sea. I felt adrift and wanted to reach shore. Yet I also felt increasingly less anxious about where I landed. Perhaps I was learning something about patience, and tolerance too, on the path to dharma.

26

SHANTI, SHANTI

We found a night bus bound for the province of Goa. Potholes, rattling broken seats, roadside stops, mechanics' tinkling tools, and delays while negotiating overcrowded Mumbai slums thwarted any hope of restful sleep. After twelve hours, a red dawn rose over green cashew fields, slender coconut palms, and rolling mist-shrouded horizons of Goa.

Bus passengers stirred as the shaded town of Mapusa emerged from jungle thickets. Sandy and I rejuvenated with a few glasses of chai, and then took breakfast in a small street-side dosa shop with low prices and questionable food. Neither felt whole, and each made a mad dash across the street where one rupee bought a spot in the filthy bus station head.

In Siolim, a battered blue-gray river ferry took on passengers. Enfield and Rajdoot motorcycles crowded the upper deck, for they outnumbered autos on Goa's narrow rural roads. The ferry's sputtering diesels strained against loose tappets and worn gears. On the leeward shore, a gang of fishermen mended nets. Goans standing upright in the shallow sterns of their wooden dugouts paddled past. Rebar poked above workers puttering beneath the unfinished column of a bridge. One day it would carry vehicles across the river and relegate the rusting ferries to dry docks. At Chopdem, the motorcycles zoomed past while we boarded a waiting bus.

Throughout India's lengthy history, many rulers have claimed Goa as theirs. During Portugal's four-hundred-fifty-year reign, Jesuit missionaries converted many locals to Christianity. Though Hindus still predominated, Goa brimmed with dark-skinned Catholics, church steeples, and white crosses set amongst bougainvillea and hibiscus. Christian women were less timid than Hindus, and men more eager to lend quotes or compliments. I noticed one Christian girl on the bus holding a bouquet of fading raspberry-colored Chrysanthemums in the lap of her teal dress. Men onboard had a small Christian cross tattooed on their right hands in that fleshy place between index fingers and thumbs. As I later learned, this served as a promise that he would raise his future children as Christian.

Palm trees thick with coconuts crowded the roadsides, until a blue swath of Arabian Sea appeared beyond the swaying palms. Near a small cluster of faded buildings, fishermen's wives sold fresh-caught mako shark and albacore tuna. Sandy and I walked towards Arambol, a collection of worn shacks and shabby restaurants lining a dirt path. The room we found near the squalid beach was not quite what either of us envisioned as paradise, but was passable.

"Goa is paradise, yes?" said a British man sitting next to us, indicating the beers, flying fish sandwiches, sand, and sun.

I nodded. "There are worse places indeed." He smiled.

A petite Russian woman sat by his side. "She speaks no English," he said. "But it is no matter. We have communicated these past four days," he winked, "via the language of love."

In evening hours Sandy and I dined on the beach, dug our toes into cool sand, and watched surf crash a dozen yards away. A three-legged dog haunting our restaurant sought handouts. With the electric power off, a common occurrence, we ate tandoori-grilled mako shark by candlelight beneath the stars, drank feni—a local cashew-flavored liqueur—and washed the meal down with sweet ruby port.

Two long-haired men sat nearby. One, gaunt and shirtless, sat asleep at his table. The younger one tried to rouse him, failed, and left. For a moment the gaunt one sat upright. His hollow eyes stared at nothing before his head slumped onto the table beside his untouched glass of whiskey.

Similarly, a bearded Frenchman who frequented our guesthouse restaurant twitched and jerked whenever he walked past. "He seemed normal once," the restaurateur commented, "but after an especially intense beach party a few years ago, something changed."

As writer Gita Mehta describes in *Karma Cola*, over the decades a lexicon of Eastern terminology permeated Western culture—incense, the Tantric scriptures, yoga, chai, sitar, Ravi Shankar, mysticism, spices, enlightenment, Nirvana. The West adored the exotic eastern imports. The hippies discovered Goa, Varanasi, Nepal, opium, hash, freedom, and cheap living in the early 1960s, and used the drugs to fund endless wanderings. Most diehards had moved on from Goa, though a few remained at Arambol and other beaches. In so doing, the hippies had opened India to tourism.

Young people such as myself were drawn, then as now, to see what it is all about. Myths and stories from books and old travelers describe strange smells and sights, Moghul and British Raj palaces, and a romanticized poverty. By the time I arrived, a new generation of fashionable hipsters had replaced the old set. Even so, the icons of India remained, and still bespoke of a mystical place where weird and wonderful things happen. Gurus, ashrams, Hindu gods, and jasmine garlands were still part of India, but as I discovered, so too were techno music, busloads of German tourists, and European resorts.

I adored Europeans when I traveled in their homelands, for their progressive lifestyles and taste for food, drink, and politics. I did not care so much for their influences on modern India. Industrial tourism had done few parts of the world any favors, and many individual travelers seemed oblivious to local custom. In my opinion, Indian culture was best left alone.

Change was inevitable, however, and in fact Europeans had introduced many innovations to the subcontinent. European influence, I conceded, was simply another aspect of India's ongoing evolution.

The following morning the three-legged dog found me. He limped behind during my beach walk as surf rolled in and morning sun cast shadows from fishing boats. A woman strolling past sold yellow bananas from the thatch basket atop her head. Four boys working a net into shore snared small silver fish within the tangles. Two fishermen carried samples of the morning's catch for sale at beachside restaurants. The young girls began their rounds, selling sandalwood necklaces, lungi, and hand-stitched shoulder bags. Men hawking handmade drums pulled hypnotic sounds from stretched skins.

"Shanti, shanti," said the Indians. *Slowly, slowly.* The sun rose high overhead, and the beach simmered. We had chai near the water as flat seas rolled in from African shores, and then worked on omelets and cinnamon rolls. A chisel-faced man with vacant gaze lit another cigarette.

I asked Sandy to channel his thoughts.

"He is thinking," she said, "what am I doing here?"

We walked along the beach, letting waters swirl about our feet, and lay upon sarongs in the shade of an evergreen. A bare-chested local climbed one of the palms, long curved knife in hand, and dropped a dozen coconuts onto sands far below. When we sweltered, Sandy swam in the ocean.

Later while Sandy strolled the sands, I sat at a restaurant along the beach. A group of four from Sri Lanka, the war-torn island nation off India's southeast coast, prepared to leave. One man asked whether or not I liked India.

"I love India," I replied.

"India is no good," he said. "Only Goa. And Goa is not India."

"Goa is India," I said. "It's another piece in the puzzle."

"No. Goa is of the Portuguese, and not India."

"What is your religion?" I asked.

"We are Roman Catholic," he replied, revealing the tattooed cross on his right hand.

"Have you been to other parts of India?"

"No. Only Goa. We are told since childhood that India is bad. Goa good."

"And why have you come here?"

"Ahh," said the man, hands spread wide. "This is Goa! With her beaches and beauty."

I watched them gather their things. To say this was not India, I thought, was to say India was not part of Asia. India was a collage of culture and humanity, and Goa another fragment of the geographical patchwork.

"You should travel around a bit by bus," I suggested, "so you may see India for yourself."

They laughed. "India is dirty, her people rude and obnoxious," the man said. "We've no wish to go there."

Life was different in Goa, to be sure. Mechanical music emanated from the jungle and beaches long into the night. European women sunbathed topless and men swam naked or in thongs, despite signs requesting otherwise. Drugs were plentiful despite local laws. Goa was not my Shangri-La, but after nearly two months in the country, I was grateful nevertheless to be firmly rooted in India's essence.

Sandy and I retraced our steps to the main road where a grumbling bus took us to Mapusa, then Vagator. No breeze moved through and the air was hot and stale. Sweat rolled along every brow. There was nothing we could do but sit in silence and suffer with the Goans. Bougainvillea and hibiscus bloomed on the roadsides, and wrought iron fences surrounded overgrown gardens fronting red-roofed stucco villas. Eucalyptus and acacia crowding narrow roads prompted memories of my days spent living in the Caribbean.

Greater Vagator Beach seemed shabby and uninteresting, but a wrong turn brought us to a fabulous guesthouse and quiet cove near Little Vagator. Every pocket along the coast of Goa engendered a different feeling. Sometimes you must employ a little trial and error to find your slice of paradise.

We settled into Le Bluebird guesthouse, and at dusk dined upon peppered kingfish sautéed in lime butter. Palm fronds and white hibiscus graced gardens surrounding the guesthouse's open-air dining area. Exotic birds and jungle fauna sounded from the darkness; no traffic, people, or mechanical music intruded.

"I am the explorer!" exclaimed Sandy, and she reflected enthusiastically upon her thirst for new adventure after another fine day lying in the sun, reading, tossing a Frisbee, feasting on flying fish sandwiches, and celebrating our willingness to take risks, which in the comfort of Le Bluebird seemed to far outweigh benefits of security.

We drank Fanta sodas and local feni in our room beneath the whirring ceiling fan. We talked of destiny and purpose, until I suggested the possibility that both were illusions. Sandy replied that she would lack the courage to go on if that were the case, and demanded we speak of it no more. Even explorers who have encircled the globe sometimes have horizons yet to reach, I thought.

At sunset a topless and deeply tanned Frenchwoman played Frisbee on the beach before a gallery of gawking male and female Indians. Goa was to the Indian what Varanasi was to the European. There, Hindus bathed on the ghats and burned upon pyres under the gaze of German tourists. Here, busloads of dark-skinned men from Tamil Nadu and Karnataka state arrived daily to ogle near-naked Western women.

One morning, Sandy and I awakened ill. Our blame lay with the very restaurant feeding us the best food we had yet eaten in India. "It's possible," Sandy mentioned, "for a bug to lie dormant weeks or even months without manifesting itself." Not until the subconscious feels safe, she explained, does sickness come on, and is thus the reason many travelers fall ill after returning home. I still suspected Le Bluebird.

We day-tripped to Anjuna anyway. In late morning hours,

all beachside cafes remained abandoned except one. Beneath shady palms we discussed our tentative plans, neither sure what would happen next. I mentioned returning home in a few months. She opposed the idea, insisting I travel abroad another year rather than become mired in routines of everyday life.

The sun grew hotter. Nude people flitted about. We walked to Little Vagator as waves rolled gently shoreward and a light breeze wafted across the sands. Sandy wished to hike over the headland towards Greater Vagator. Soon I would travel south despite Sandy's subtle protests. Already the explorer in each of us had grown restless.

Twice Sandy commented that it would be nice to travel the rest of India together. "But I know you need some time to yourself," she added for the second time.

"Soon you'll get that coffee grinder," I said. "You deserve it."

On our last evening we drank port and spoke further of our plans. She was unsure about hers, she said, perhaps because having too many options complicates decisions. So many people spend their lives seeking something to which they desperately want to surrender their freedoms, she mused. She was right, of course. As humans, we seem compelled to attach ourselves to people, ideas, and objects. For the moment, we celebrated the freedoms we did have. Drunk on port and life, we toasted India, each other, and whatever life next offered.

27

JEW TOWN

Sandy said nothing as she waited with me at the main road. When a bus approached, she smiled half-heartedly. We hugged and then I stepped aboard. I waved as the bus churned forward, but my head felt light and my stomach heavy. I knew I would miss her.

Portuguese Catholic churches slid past beneath overhanging palms. At Mapusa I caught another bus, and at Panaji another. It felt suddenly strange to be alone, and I wondered whether I was doing the right thing. I loved her company. Yet she was not ready to leave Goa, she had said, and did not know when she would be. On the other hand, I felt an urgency to continue south. The heralds' question beckoned me forward.

From Margao, an overfull bus rode through coconut palm forests and thick humidity past nude hilltops exposing the same red soil that stained my worn boots. Humid haze obscured blue-green hills. Vultures and kites soared overhead in lazy circles. When darkness descended the town of Karwar, in Karnataka state, came alive. Men sold mangoes, bananas, grapes, and coconuts in the streets. I wolfed down a dosa, masala, and rava–a grain pudding–and later lemon soda and butterscotch ice cream, and wandered fat like a pig.

Under a cornflower blue morning sky, a khaki-donning coin box-wielding man directed me towards a Mangalore-bound bus. The only passenger aboard indicated he headed to Vasco.

"And by the way," he asked, "will you give me your watch as a present?" Shaking my head no I marked the seat with my scarf and dashed into the terminal for bread, dal, and chai. He followed, and then returned to the bus when I did. As the engine rumbled to life he sat next to me.

"Mangalore?" I asked the sleepy driver. "Does this bus go to Mangalore?"

The ambivalent head-shake left me wondering, so I asked the man beside me. "Yes, Mangalore," the man said, and motioned for a drink of water. I drank one last swig and handed him my bottle. He took a swallow, poured the rest onto the floor, and handed the empty container back. Perplexed, I stared at him.

"Vasco!" yelled the conductor as the bus leapt forward.

I had no wish to go to Vasco. "This bus. Does it go to Mangalore?" I asked the man beside me yet again, thinking perhaps he misheard me.

"No, only Vasco. Mangalore…" His words trailed off as he pointed towards the bus stand. I called to the driver, and hopped off. A few feet away sat the waiting Mangalore bus.

In Karnataka state, the pace of life was slower and the frenzy to snare tourist customers nonexistent compared with northern India. The Arabian Sea stretched to the horizon. Wooden fishing boats sat upon deserted white sand beaches. The road descended into jungle and wound past thatch and mud huts surrounded by groves of banana and eucalyptus. Men in wooden dugouts paddled unhurriedly along palm-lined shores, for heat canvassed the land. While my bus paused at the villages of Ankola, Honavar, Coondapoor, and Udipi the passengers grew hot and restless.

Karnataka locals spoke Kannada, a Dravidian language tracing to the sixth century BCE. Round, looping swirls had replaced rigid Hindi script upon street and storefront signs. The conductor's voice and beggar children sounded similar to the croaking of frogs on summer evenings.

After Mangalore the coast fell behind. We ascended jungle-canopied mountainsides, curving round and round, barely missing tanker trucks turning wide on steep descents. Though vehicles traveled in the left lane per English tradition, most drove on the right or at best center of the road. On blind uphill grades drivers casually drifted into the left lane, assuming enough seconds remained to swerve back before any buses or trucks hurtled around the bend. All trucks lying wrecked by the roadside had been stripped of any usable parts by thrifty men. A few squatting by mud and thatch huts along the road watched us grumble past. We descended into darkness as the crescent sliver of a waxing moon hung gently in the sky.

In Hassan, a bustling indifferent city, a shabby hotel near the bus station had a room with worn beds, crumbling plaster walls, dusty wooden chair and table, and rusted iron bars over the windows. The fan's whirring barely stirred the stuffiness. I lay back, watching blades beat the stale air.

I missed Sandy, although I relished the silence. Within the stillness were all the answers I sought. The bleating of a bus announcing its arrival disturbed my thoughts. I heard someone cough in the hall. I noticed a sullen wife clanging *katori* dishes in the roofed courtyard. I remembered, with a pang of remorse, that in India there was never silence. I missed Sandy all the more.

In the morning, battered red and white snub-nosed buses roared in from all corners of Karnataka. One nearly ran down a dozen people as it swung round and reversed into an open slot. Tires and undersides caked in red dust, most lacked taillights, and all were labeled only in round Kannada flourishes. These conveyances were how the masses negotiated bumpy rural outreaches. Hand sown fields of banana, cashew, groundnut, sugarcane, and cucumber rolled past my dirt-smeared window as brown gangly legs of malnourished men worked the fields.

At Halebid, throngs of Indian tourists strolled through Hoysaleswara Temple, covered inside and out with hand-chiseled deities, sages, animals, birds, and scenes of life and war during the Hoysala reign of the twelfth century. A man explained their significance in choppy English and Kannada. Another sold old Indian coins, mostly anna and half anna from the late nineteenth century.

In Belur, a man sold slices of watermelon for one rupee each near a cricket match that played out upon a dirt field and was cheered on by a few hundred male spectators. After pausing in the shade of a snack stand for dosa and Thums Up soda, I found the Channekeshava Temple with sculptures similar to those at Halebid.

I stowed my bag under the seat of a weathered Mysore-bound bus before hopping off to find tea. While looking over the two English newspapers, I heard a rumble. Though all the red buses looked alike, the one holding my few belongings seemed suddenly missing. I panicked at the thought of losing my rucksack. I tossed a five rupee note at the man and ran.

I loped behind the accelerating bus, found a smooth stride, and slowly caught up. A ladder leading to the roof rack was attached to the rear of the bus. I considered grabbing it. As my fingers stretched towards the ladder the driver took his foot off the gas pedal to avoid running down a pedestrian. In that second I gained half a step, and pounded the rear panel twice. The driver did not stop, of course, but tapped the brake enough for me to leap through the rear door, to the amusement of the chuckling conductor.

Villagers looked up as we plowed past with horn blaring. Women draped in shawls crouched over vegetables. Men wandered streets and rice fields with hands folded behind bent backs, scarves wrapped around their heads.

I found a hotel room in Mysore, where yellow and blue

two-wheel covered tonga carriages drawn by plumed horses plied streets lined with remnants of European-era architecture. Devaraja Market bustled with tangerines, bananas, coconuts, kale, and radishes for sale. Sacred cattle painted yellow, pink, and blue wandered amongst scurrying inhabitants and whining rickshaws. One bovine, black and pink with red horns, eyed me with disdain.

During the night, I dreamed that I rode upon a rural bus. We encountered scattered pieces of cow littering the road. The driver smiled.

"Meat!" he said.

I turned my head to look around, and saw what remained of the cow we had just demolished. To my chagrin, the severed head stared back at me.

More stops; more waiting. At one depot I waited hours for a supposed six o' clock departure to Cochin, only to finally learn what the clerk had neglected to tell me. All deluxe buses were fully booked. This meant I would have to stand through the night on a crowded local run. While wandering about I discovered a bus heading to the city of Ernakulam. Every bench seat was filled, but eager to be moving toward somewhere, I chose to sit on the steps.

The driver climbed aboard, and at that moment the rarest kind of bus, one with individual cloth seats, roared up next to us. My hopes rose. They fell again as dozens of men crowded around the door.

"Reservations only!" yelled the conductor. A man saw my disappointment and told me to wait. "Seat thirty-four," the conductor said minutes later. Somehow, I had a spot.

"This is Ernakulam," said a man at first light. I pulled my bag off. "No, that city is another hour farther," said another. I climbed back on.

I asked a Hindi speaker whether the conductor spoke Kannada. The man said he had no idea. In a country with hundreds of spoken languages, villagers sometimes could not communicate with other locals only a few villages away.

Though the conductor mistakenly thought I sought Thiruvanthapuram, I found my stop in Ernakulam near the ferry dock where worn wooden boats departed for Cochin and various islands. My wiry helmsman cast off and the ferry puttered past gargantuan tankers. At a bare spot of earth I leapt from the vessel, and wandered past decaying waterfront, pastel-painted homes, shuttered windows, and dark-skinned men.

At Cochin, fishermen manipulated wooden Chinese cantilevered fishing nets with weighted stones and ropes. Beach vendors sold fish fries–fast-food local style–to Indian tourists. On a steamy Sunday afternoon along river's edge thousands of Indian tourists walked the waterfront and picnicked on the sandy shoreline. Brilliant saris flashed by, and massive merchant ships churned their way to other ports.

"No reason," said one young woman when I asked why they came. "Only to enjoy the water."

The evening's performance of Kathakali dancing began as dusk settled over the outdoor theater in Cochin that I visited. During the tight performances musicians accompanied mimes with drums, cymbals, voice, and harmony. The beaten bark of certain trees, dyed with fruit and spices, composed wigs. Colorful paints and black eye shadow were based in coconut oil. Eggplant flowers tucked under eyelids turned whites of the eyes deep red. Actors and musicians demonstrated words and phrases using facial expressions and eye, hand, and body movements. A full-length traditional performance lasted nine hours; this one fortunately only lasted one.

As unusual as Kathakali dancing might be, the voices emanating from St. Francis Church the next morning seemed wholly out of place. India's oldest European church, around the corner from my hotel, dated to the arrival of Portuguese Franciscan friars in 1503.

Even more out of place than the congregation singing

Christian hymns was the small district near my hotel called Jew Town. Judaism, I recalled, is one of the oldest monotheistic religions and traces its roots to Abraham. Jews wandered the wilderness until Moses received the tablets of law atop Mount Sinai, which initiated the Jews' covenant with their God.

Some believe that after Babylon conquered the Jewish kingdom of Judah, a few Jewish exiles made their way to India. It is thought these immigrants settled in Cochin. A twelfth-century Jewish traveler, Benjamin of Tudela, noted that here on the Malabar Coast "the inhabitants are all black, and the Jews also. The latter are good and benevolent."

Muslims later attacked the Jews, based in part on their dominance of the lucrative pepper trade. The Portuguese Empire too persecuted them. The last Jewish prince was forced to swim to Cochin with his wife on his back.

Upon my arrival, only five Jewish families remained on the Cochin Peninsula. Cochin Synagogue, oldest in the British Commonwealth, was destroyed in the seventeenth century but rebuilt in a corner of Jew Town. I sat inside and contemplated the silver oil lamps, chandeliers imported from Belgium, and thousand hand-painted Chinese willow-pattern floor tiles.

While reposing in the deserted synagogue, I reflected on the nature of Judaism. I knew the faith was not my path, for many of the same reasons that Christianity is not. As scholar Huston Smith explains in *The World's Religions*, the early "Jewish quest for meaning was rooted in their understanding of God." Though other cultures of their time had many gods, early Jews focused their energies on the idea of a single, supreme, nature-transcending deity. This concept conflicts with the view of transcendentalists–which I supported–that nature transcends God. I did not believe that one all-powerful God–in human form–had created the universe and would one day judge my fate based on arbitrary rules about how I should have lived my life. These tenets seemed archaic and outdated to me. I knew that a different model, more in line with my experience and beliefs, was what I needed.

Onward, I thought.

28

THE TURN NORTH

Monsoon rains loomed. At least travel was still possible, unlike at the height of rainy season when roads, fields, and towns often lay beneath muddied floodwaters.

To the south, Alappuzha bustled. A cemetery within stone walls held rows of etched iron crosses. Church bells pealed. In the corner, wreaths made of newspaper and colored paper-mâché covered a Styrofoam box. A young stern-faced woman entered the graveyard, and set half a dozen white lilies on a fresh grave.

Many of India's twenty million Christians lived here, in the state of Kerala. The first local converts likely followed the teachings of Thomas Didymus, one of Christ's twelve apostles. According to tradition, Doubting Thomas reached India in the year 52 CE and the descendants of those he baptized became known as Saint Thomas Christians. After his death by spear, he was martyred and became India's patron saint.

No roads went south from Alappuzha, but I arranged transport by boat through the Kerala backwaters along palm-lined canals paralleling the Arabian Sea. Narrow slivers of land separated the waterways from inland stretches of rice and open water. Upon the spits, sometimes only a few meters wide, clustered coconut palm groves, wooden shacks, cattle, banana trees, and those calling the backwaters home.

The day burned hot. Placid fishermen in wooden dugouts drifted past. Thin dark men wielding long poles helmed flat-bottomed coconut, brick, and sand-filled hulls with gunwales inches above water's surface. Naked brown boys swimming in tepid waters called out. Women hand washing clothes paused to watch. A wee lad wearing no trousers burst from his parents' shack. Schoolchildren dressed in white shirts and blue shorts and standing along a narrow shore hollered and waved as though they had never before seen people from beyond the backwaters.

"One pen. One pen!" yelled young boys racing over jagged stones and crumbling dikes before splashing towards us when someone tossed one overboard.

At lunchtime the boat paused in the shade of a thatched roof overhang. Dhoti-donning men placed a bright green banana leaf plate and dal, curry, pile of rice, and grilled fish before each passenger. All one could eat, followed by fresh pineapple for dessert. When the captain tooted his horn, the break ended.

My days on the backwaters glided past like dugouts slicing serene waters–seemingly gone in moments. The canal widened. Afternoon sun glinted upon blue-green waters. Claw-like arms of cantilevered Chinese fishing nets stood like sentinels. Northern breezes pushed faded patchwork sails and Kollam-bound fishermen homeward. The sun dropped into the Arabian Sea as terns skimmed the surface.

When the diesels slackened we drifted to shore. I booked a room right away. Earlier I had chatted with a young woman named Bettina, an impatient New York photographer. She vacillated about whether to book a room or take the last bus to Varkala. Sure enough, she missed the bus and within five minutes all rooms were taken.

Bettina struggled with the notion of people in no hurry,

drinking chai on street corners, or doing nothing. "That never happens in Manhattan," she said with a sardonic tone. I had struggled with the same conflict when I first arrived, though felt less strongly as I grew used to India's pace. When her agitation peaked, I offered my extra bed. She accepted gratefully. After masala dosas for dinner, eight hours of sun, and evening chitchat, we fell into deep slumber. By daybreak, she was gone to Varkala.

I soon caught a dilapidated bus to Thiruvananthapuram and stood with the throngs. By the roadside, scores of men and women hammered at towering blocks of blue-gray granite. The gravel crushers spent their lives breaking rock into walnut-sized pebbles, one swing at a time. On the outskirts of Thiruvananthapuram, traffic stopped. We sweltered together while creeping forward with the rickshaws.

A second bus led to the trash-cluttered beach at Kovalam. A sickly haze covered the land. Beached fishing boats awaited cooler hours. Even the touts were lethargic, though napping vendors sold sunglasses, pineapples, lungi, and cigarettes. Powerful riptides sometimes pulled careless swimmers under. Headstrong Europeans tended to ignore the whistles, but the crisply uniformed Indian lifeguards had little intention of risking their lives for a foreigner. As the world shimmered, I listened to a Stravinsky operetta strain through my window. In such moments a bed, toilet, and operable fan brought great joy.

Waves swept in from the Lakshadweep Sea as a few hundred Indians from Thiruvananthapuram flocked to shore to watch the sun drop into Africa. Pink clouds arched across the zenith. On the southern headland, a red and white lighthouse cast its beam into gathering darkness. A line of shimmering white dots–fishermen motoring home with the evening catch–lined the horizon.

I took a seat at a small table a few feet from crashing waves. The hand-made candle fluttered as I pushed my feet into the warm sand. I savored the tranquility, until screams erupted from a rowdy band of German children. Then, a chip on the rim of my glass nearly sliced my lip. There are worse scenarios,

I remembered. I drank from the other side of the glass, and relished the delightful squeals. We have the power each moment to change our outlook. When the electric power went out and the beach turned pitch black but for the flickering candle, cries of disappointment chorused. As stars emerged, the tourists fell silent. Peace, at last.

In early morning hours, a Puccini score wafted through my window. The sky turned a shade of periwinkle. Local women walking the beach carried bananas and pineapples atop their heads, and the cigarette boys came one after the other. Europeans swarmed onto the sands, and baked in the sun like red adobe bricks. They would likely return home with tales of grilled snapper, the brilliant batik-style lungi they purchased, or the endearing British couple they met. Like them, the fury of the waves drew me to this place.

At the table where I sat, a hollow-eyed Frenchman donning worn jeans and shoulder-length curly locks sat nearby. He asked my opinion on a fair taxi fare to the airport. Next he detailed the numerous defects of Kovalam and elsewhere.

"The weather was all wrong this year. Too warm in December, and the year before too cold." All the "locals" were leaving, he said. The rave parties were no good anymore.

My dosa arrived. "Oh," he said, "the dosa here is the worst ever in three years of traveling India. I tried twice, now no more." He was leaving for Sri Lanka, though prices there were too high, he complained, and people won't barter like in India.

My dosa tasted delicious. Even in paradise while traveling through exotic lands, it is possible to be miserable. I had learned on this journey that happiness really is a state of mind. I could choose to appreciate all the beauty of the now, as Sandy had taught me. Or I could dwell on the past, the future, or what I perceived this moment to be missing. In any regard, the choice was mine.

"Bonjour," he said as he prepared to leave.

"Oui," I replied. "And good luck." He might need some.

At the bus stand, a pale-skinned Canadian bent my ear. He had been living in Madurai helping his father conduct research on the Vaigai River. His mother was in India gathering data for her doctoral thesis in psychology. Her fieldwork pertained to local beliefs that most bodily possessions involved women, and many required exorcisms to banish "demons." Such experiences can be a form of ecstasy, she theorized, and a liberation of sorts. She attributed the phenomenon to rebellion against sexual repression.

On the rough highway to Kanyakumari past signs reading *Danger Prone Zone Going Slowly* and *Take Deviation*, the Canadian prattled on about the size of rats in Madurai theaters and how loudly you must clap to scare them towards the person sitting next to you. He told of his friend recently injured in a bus accident. The Canadian fell silent as we passed an empty bus sitting idle in the road. Protruding horizontally from the open rear door was what appeared to be a corpse. We stared as our driver negotiated around the abandoned bus.

"I bet the passengers got scared and split," said the Canadian, "and left the dead guy for the police or whoever."

Once again, the prospect of imminent death on the road of India loomed before me. Questions crowded my mind. What had happened to this man? Why did his fellow passengers abandon him? What had his life been like? Would anyone remember him? What was his favorite color? Had he been loved? I realized that any of these questions could as easily apply to me, when my day came. The thought rattled me, as did life's brevity and the potential of its singularity.

Slightly shaken, after the Canadian disembarked I continued into the state of Tamil Nadu. The hazy Western Ghats loomed behind me. At Land's End, the southern tip of India, buses could go no farther. Here where the Bay of Bengal meets the Arabian Sea, the southernmost tip of the subcontinent juts into the Indian Ocean. Now, every place in India lay northward.

Land's End was a key pilgrimage site dedicated to the goddess Devi Kanya, an incarnation of Siva's wife. Long lines of devout Hindus snaked from peach-flavored sandstone temples. Ragged beggars awaited alms on stone steps above turquoise waters as pilgrims rested in pockets of shade.

Two black butterflies fluttered past several young Indian men beating two others about the head, chest, and groin. One fled to the ocean, but they got a few more kicks and slaps in before he stumbled into the water. Within half an hour another fight erupted on the edge of Asia, this one in the street. The sudden appearance of violence, an unusual sight in India, surprised and perplexed me. I wondered why this holy place provoked so many tempers.

A man sold half-frozen ice cream in orange cones, a woman vended ankle-length strings of cheap shell and coral, and others pawned postcards or coconuts. Inside a thatch-roof hut the chubby proprietor washed his face and hands after afternoon slumber. Upon a rusted grimy stove he boiled tea. Flies covered the table, my arms, and every glass rim. Accompanying two women with rolls of brown tummy spilling from within their green topas was a skinny man clad only in saffron loincloth. He ate in the corner with an obese man. The women stole glances at me and chattered with the chai-wallah.

At sunset, hundreds of Indian tourists crowded the seaside point below the temples. Some swam or bathed. Women changed their clothing on the open beach. Dozens of green, fuchsia, and cream-colored saris lay in long strips along the cluttered sands. Hindus prayed to their gods and offered puja. As the sun drifted into the Arabian Sea, a rare blue moon rose from the Bay of Bengal. Now began the turn north.

It had taken many months to get here, yet I felt this day had still come too soon. I felt no closer to the answers I sought at the start of the journey. Though I had yet to traverse the entire east coast of India to return full circle to Delhi, I had already encountered most of the world's religions. I watched the blue moon rise with a tinge of anxiety. I wondered whether my journey might be for naught.

29

I AM GANESH!

An orange moon bathed the city of Madurai, where pilgrims streamed towards the West Tower of Sri Meenakshi Temple amidst the flow of bullock carts, cycle-rickshaws, and bicycles. Men invited passersby into their garment shops to have trousers or a shirt tailored by hand. Others sold silver and gold trinkets. An elephant painted like Ganesh, the elephant-headed god of wisdom and prosperity, accepted coins from pilgrims and tapped each donor on the head with her trunk as blessing for the generosity.

A persistent tout lured me into his brother's clothing shop. When I left the store he followed to a nearby bookshop, insisting he take me to the temple in his rickshaw. "No" meant maybe to such people, and "maybe" meant yes.

"I am sadhu," said a white-bearded man in orange loincloth who cornered me with hand extended. He smiled as I dropped coins into his waiting palm.

The destitute gathered around the temples. Dark-tinted buses lined the northern wall. Pilgrims and their worldly possessions crowded sagging seats. Women with brown breasts drooping and fingers pressed to toothless gums begged among the buses. Many Indians arrived in Madurai with meager savings depleted and no way home.

At dawn the following morning, sweepers cleared streets of debris. Burlap sacks and wood crates were unloaded from bullock carts onto sidewalks littered with rag-covered bodies. Girls chalked colorful, intricate rangoli designs onto dusty streets—"for good luck," explained one man—and a new onslaught of pilgrims besieged the temple.

Inside the same corner eatery I visited the night prior, the man working the floor ushered me into a plastic chair. The moment the level of masala sauce in any tin dropped too low, he rushed to the rear and returned with more. His motives were well intentioned to be sure, but in a land without spoons, getting food into one's mouth was difficult enough without well-meaning Tamils hovering about.

I found a Tiruchirappalli-bound bus at the Anna Bus Stand. The lone remaining seat lay to the rear, behind the open doorway. Asphalt and thorny acacia whirled past as we hurtled into the heart of Tamil Nadu. The coughing man in white stained dhoti sitting next to me smoked hand-rolled beedi cigarette after cigarette. He used three or four Indian matchsticks to light each then tossed them through the open door. After getting a good drag he took four or five puffs, and crushed the butt beneath his sandal. He repeated this for hours until falling asleep a half hour outside Tiruchirappalli.

Before reaching our destination the bus stopped for a brief break at the allotted spot along a roadside. There men urinated into bushes, putrid from the legions before them. I sought water, but settled instead for mango juice and Horlicks ice cream from an enterprising vendor. After a little girl squatted in front of the bus door, everyone stepped over the muddy puddle to re-board.

As passengers settled back into their seats, a man two rows up watched me. When I met his gaze he looked away, but slyly turned back until our eyes reconnected. The Tamil are a pleasant folk, I decided, and the man a subtle reminder that the face of India changes with each passing state.

The room I rented after reaching Tiruchirappalli seemed similar to other rundown hovels on my journey. And yet, the faded pastel clapboard walls, worn wooden table, stained bed sheet, and dusty shelves held a simple romantic charm and I could almost feel the lives that had traipsed through. The doorless toilet led from the balcony, and while squatting one could contemplate golden rays of morning sun filtering through the acacia leaves. An orange and black butterfly fluttered every which way as a kingfisher alit upon a eucalyptus tree.

At a dhaba eatery, the four-foot wallah recited the full lunch menu in a language I never heard before. While waiting for my dosa, a Tamil sitting nearby volunteered his version of the story of Ganesh. After Siva and his beautiful consort Parvati had a son, Siva embarked on a long journey. Upon his return, Siva discovered a young man and Parvati together in her room. Siva lopped the lad's head off, not thinking that his own son may have grown a bit during the absence. Parvati forced Siva to bring their son back to life, but Siva could only do so by giving his son the head of the first creature he saw. Naturally, it was an elephant. With this conclusion, the Tamil settled back into his seat with a satisfied smile.

In Srirangam, around Sri Ranganathaswamy Temple, shirtless Hindus sold candles, pictures of gods, and bangles from streetside stalls. Men lighting firecrackers over and over sent rickshaws swerving and pigeons into the sky. Seven concentric walls surrounded the temple's innermost sanctum. Pilgrims lying among the pillars talked, slept, picnicked, or sat idle.

One boy with bulging eyes and toothpick legs followed me. He led into a side courtyard. On one hand-chiseled column two monkeys appeared as four; on another, two head-butting beasts were elephants or bulls, depending on the angle viewed. A man with a key took me through a locked gate to the roof. Twenty-one temples rose into the sky, each unique in color and shape.

Five men in greasy khaki coveralls peered into the exposed gearbox of my empty bus. One waved me into a seat. They replaced the metal cover and gathered together the tools strewn about. The driver cranked the engine, shifted into first, and nodded. The mechanics tossed their tools into a waiting truck, and my bus roared off.

Onboard, I recalled the full-size head atop half-formed arms, legs, and body near Sri Ranganathaswamy Temple that had slithered after shoppers in pursuit of rupees. The memory of the deformed man haunted my thoughts. It was presumptuous of me to judge this man's life. I could not know how he felt about his condition. All I knew was that in comparison to most people I had met, his quality of life seemingly suffered.

A Hindu or Jain might explain that actions he committed in a previous life had affected his karma, which prompted his rebirth in this current form. A Christian or Muslim might say that so long as he followed the word of God, he was blessed and would ascend to the gates of heaven. The Buddha may have observed that the man's physical form was irrelevant; he had the ability in this lifetime to transcend all suffering.

None of those viewpoints alleviated my anguish for the slithering man. My narrow focus centered on his condition in this present life, the only life I knew. Sights such as the slithering man forced me to consider that some fates, in fact, might even be worse than death.

As I walked homeward from the bus stand, a cycle-rickshaw driver offered a ride.

"No thanks," I replied.

"I have cheap Kerala grass," he said. I realized he was referring to inexpensive ganga grown locally in Kerala state.

No way, I thought.

Then, I stopped. What the hell, I decided, and climbed inside the cycle-rickshaw.

"I am Ganesh!" said the driver, "like the elephant." He

raised his arm as though it was an elephant's trunk. I liked the man's pleasant, disarming nature.

Ganesh cycled me through busy streets. To the east a huge murky moon rose above roadside thatch-roof huts. He stopped and disappeared into the darkness with my hundred rupees. I waited, and watched the moon rise from within his covered rickshaw.

He returned with five grams, and offered more.

"No, no," I said. "We go now."

I slipped into the shadows. Ganesh pedaled into the night.

I stood at a busy intersection next to a boy selling men's red, blue, and pink briefs from an upside-down umbrella in the dirt by the curb. Indians teemed. Buses upon narrow city streets roared by at fifty or more miles per hour. Motorcyclists and mopeds wove among cars. One motorcyclist with no headlamp passed half a dozen others plus two cars and veered straight into the path of a barreling bus. He cut left with inches between himself and the bus's front fender.

"Nice job," the grumbling bus seemed to toot.

Families of five rode on one moped. Mother sat behind father, youngest perched between the two, a fourth stood in front of father, and a fifth fit in anywhere. When couples rode together the woman always sat behind with both legs to one side and sari flowing in the wind.

Three men rode upon one Enfield motorcycle. A jeep with no head or taillights jetted past. A group of bicyclists jingled by–music in the streets. Eight schoolchildren tumbled out of a sputtering auto-rickshaw that squawked like a wounded duck.

At intersections, streams of pedestrians and vehicles crossed without signal, signs, or direction. Each assembled faction compromised on the space they wanted a little at a time–some people walked in the path of oncoming cars, a few trucks growled through. The mass of movement was a well-oiled machine that not only functioned, but operated effortlessly. Despite the volume of hurried people and mechanized contraptions churning past, I marveled that a blind man could cross the road and not be struck.

In the morning I continued northward. At breakfast I craved an omelet and masala dosa. The first place had omelets, no dosa. One had dosa, no omelets. Another had neither. A fourth had dosa after nine o'clock, and idli, a South Indian rice dumpling, but no omelet. The last had egg rava dosa and bland chai. In the south of India coffee prevails over tea, which Tamils call *thenneer*. Upon discovering this, I understood why my requests for chai, the Hindi word for tea, were often met in Tamil Nadu with blank looks.

I arrived early to the bus stand for the nine o'clock Pondicherry-bound bus.

"There is none, sahib, until ten-forty."

All timetables were scrawled in Tamil script, so I asked around. One man insisted I go to Kumbakonam, from where many buses went to Pondicherry. At quarter past ten I reached Kumbakonam. Of course, no Pondicherry-bound bus left before noon. After wandering dusty streets I returned to the stand.

"No bus until twelve-forty," said the dispatcher. "And not from here, but the other side of the depot."

On the other side of the depot, the man said no buses departed to Pondicherry. One might perhaps leave from the other side, he said, from where I just came. So it went. I gave up on Pondicherry and aimed instead for Chidambaram.

"Oh yes," he said. "Many buses from Chidambaram to Pondicherry."

"And which bus to Chidambaram?"

"Oh," he pointed, "that one just pulling out." I managed to hop aboard in time for the hour ride past green rice fields, thatched houses, and peasants asleep in the dirt. Chidambaram was a madhouse. People milled about like swarms of ants amongst the bored goats and stench of human feces. For mental stamina I took milk coffee, and slowly realized this was not Chidambaram at all but some village named Mayiladuthurai that did not exist on the map I carried.

"Bus to Pondicherry?"

"No, sir. But there goes a bus to Chidambaram."

I grabbed it, and after another hour reached Chidambaram, where a bus from there left for Pondicherry. Once in Pondicherry the only rooms I could find were a triple for one hundred eighty rupees and a rat's nest for a hundred. Through further effort I found instead a windowless single up three flights of stairs along two never-ending corridors littered with warped planks and dusty bottles. After a cold shower and shave, the laundry man took my filthy threads to the dhobi-wallahs for an overdue cleaning.

Red felt hats perched atop policemen's pates were the only remaining hint of Pondicherry's past as a French colony. As night fell a welcome breeze ran out of the east, and the brilliant moon glinted from black choppy waters. South Pacific waves thrashed the seawall and sent spray high into the air.

Indian couples laughed while they strolled the promenade, sat upon benches, and held hands. Some even kissed–the first I had seen of Indians expressing affection in public. Maybe it was something in the moon's vibrant glow–or the rhythmic pulse of the sea. Or, perhaps an undying French romanticism still surged in the hearts of Pondicherry lovers.

30

THE ROAD TO PURI

Onward I traveled, still feeling an emptiness in my soul that begged for meaning. Another bus carried me further north, to the city of Chennai. Amidst the naked begging children and determined rickshaw-men, something inside me shifted. I was no longer the same when I left Chennai behind. The unending poverty, countless broken bodies, and harsh brevity of life had decimated my spirit. I felt I could not bear one more day of the destitution around me. The sight of so many anonymous souls struggling so deeply magnified the insignificance of my own existence. I wondered how I could persevere when I already felt as though I wanted to curl into a ball inside a locked room and never emerge.

I bounced through the night upon broken roads of Andhra Pradesh, among India's poorest states. A man from the city of Hospet and his Sri Lankan companion befriended me at a meal stop. We indulged in omelets and bananas. They suggested the train as a more comfortable alternative to rough buses.

"Perhaps," I responded. With no seatmate on the bus I could lie down with legs folded, making snatches of sleep possible despite truck jams and decrepit highways. "After riding unreserved on the train," I added, "this bus isn't so bad."

Dawn brought red sun over misty fields and rural villages. As the bus rolled through the landscape I watched passing scenes through my window. By the roadside, in bushes, along the riverbanks, and in open fields countless men squatted and emptied their bowels. Others walked to or from their choice spot with a tin of water in hand. We passed naked brown behinds for miles.

In the villages, overflowing gutters and open sewers ran milky white and murky brown. Ramshackle homes fronted the rancid sewers over which chai, banana, and coconut vendors sold their wares. The worn dusty shrubbery, trees, oxen, earth, and skies gave the sensation that the region had never known wealth of any kind.

The man from Hospet commented that Americans did not travel India, particularly Andhra Pradesh. The few tourists that did pass through to Puri rode express trains rather than slow buses over these torturous roads. "They fear the people, the filth, the smells," he said.

I suspected he was right. Americans took one or two showers a day, seemed to fear excrement, and demanded modern sewage systems. Yet, I silently questioned the Indian practice of polluting one's own backyard.

Many of the thin, desperate-looking faces of Andhra Pradesh were Adivasi, the indigenous people of India. Some fifty million Indians belong to these tribal communities, which maintain traditions separate from Muslims or Hindus. Many trace their lineage to ancient Australoid hunter-gatherers from sub-Sahara Africa who also had brown skin, low foreheads, and flat noses, but straight rather than curly hair. Though considered uncivilized and primitive by casted Hindus of Dravidian and Aryan descent, Adivasi are not considered impure like the Dalit, and have lived more or less undisturbed for millennia. In so doing, their languages and customs are often not understood by much of Indian society.

Unlike aborigine or tribe, Adivasi connotes a people whose long autonomy was disrupted during the British colonial period, but never restored. Exploitation and land dispossession under a feudal-like taxation system led to unrest and deprivation that continued well into the twentieth century.

At Vijayawada, a mob of rickshaws surrounded me. I escaped to the canteen for food and chai, but upon exiting, the mob found me. I admitted I needed a ride to the train depot. Two drivers out-competed the others for the fare. One had an auto-rickshaw, the other a cycle-rickshaw. Their fares were the same, but I chose the one whose survival relied upon daily pedal pumping.

A uniformed officer approached and motioned in the air as though signing a document. "Police," someone muttered. Upon a slip of paper the man wrote: *Government rickshaw will take you to the railway station for ten rupees*. I rode the government rickshaw, and at the station the driver charged twenty rupees. I had no energy to argue. Outside the station, urchins with clothes black as coal ran past. Families wearing tattered homespun wraps lay upon thatch mats. A young boy with left leg ending in a dull nub at the knee scooted by. After standing in long lines I learned no northbound seats or berths remained on any train in the next week, or the one thereafter. Second class unreserved was my only option.

While waiting, a Muslim approached with the usual questions. He sought a contact in the States and a way out of poverty—perhaps me, he suggested. He was kind and gentle, as are many Muslims, saying all gods are one and it matters not what we call ourselves, for we are all brothers in this world and must help each other as best we can. He sang a lyrical song as we stood on the filthy landing, beneath which rusted trains passed on weed-covered sidings. When finished, he wrote his address on a scrap of paper.

"Perhaps you might help me once home," he said. "If ever you need anything here, I will happily help." With that he shook my hand, and was gone.

My emotional reserves utterly spent, I fell asleep on the

platform. The crowds stirred when the East Coast Express rolled in. As I awoke, chaos erupted. Throngs of shouting people crowded the second-class doors and struggled to climb inside. Both unreserved cars, one for ladies only, were crammed to capacity with women and men. One angry woman leaning from a window shook her fist at any men trying to board the women's car. As the train moved forward, the last of us squeezed inside. We were pinned so tightly against each other that were any man to faint he would not fall over. We swayed as one around sharp bends and jostled as a single mass over rough track.

At the next stop a few debarked, but more boarded and the car somehow grew fuller. A small tin sink attached to the wall formed a recess. I climbed on to sit in the nook, hoping it would hold my weight. Though my legs grew numb and sharp screws and exposed metal tore at my clothes and flesh, I caught occasional glimpses of passing fields and breaths of fresh air. More passengers boarded at each stop. They piled bags onto the sink, which forced me into the mass of ripe bodies.

The crush became too much. At the next stop I tried to pull my bag from behind the door, but the damp bodies were packed too tight to allow any exit. We reached another town, and I fought against the growing surge. At a third stop I at last squeezed out as the train whistled. I sucked fresh air in great gulps as the cars chugged forward.

The remote village where I landed did not exist on my map. Across the street a bus was just leaving, going north they claimed, and I jumped aboard. It rolled south until we turned to follow tracks stretching to the northern horizon. How quickly circumstances can change, I thought. Sometimes the simplest things—such as a seat and space to breathe— bring immeasurable joy. Through my window, the sun set over flat fields. We rode into the evening, everyone still and quiet, watching the driver avoid over-laden trucks barreling southbound amidst the sound of blaring horns.

We arrived in Kakinada. A group of young men, boys really,

took a keen interest and gathered round me at the small bus depot. The boys set a chair for me next to the officer who watched over the place. They had never met an American, and their wide brown eyes stared. They asked questions in broken English, and I told them of home. They played with my camera and asked to be photographed. I was hungry, but a bus was soon due.

"Don't worry," one said. "Another will come. Go eat."

The town constable arrived and sat by my side. A woman sitting nearby had never seen a camera, and inspected mine. I sat dumbfounded, grateful for their kindness and hospitality.

When my bus arrived the boys swarmed it, staked a choice window seat for me, and marked my spot. They returned and I was able to board in leisure. They gathered outside the bus like old friends, waving good-bye over and over in a send-off farewell. I wiped the tears away while waving at the excited boys. Hours before, I had never felt so far from home. Now, I almost felt as though leaving home, such was the welcoming nature of these townsfolk. Moments later my bus delved into the darkness for the journey to Visakhapatnam.

Bodies lying on thatch mats and rags littered the Visakhapatnam bus stand's grimy floor. Despite the late hour, rickshaw drivers smoked and chatted, most eager to make a few rupees. I wanted to see what lay about the village. One cycle man followed me as I walked.

"Five rupees. Five rupees," he said.

"No, no. I want to walk a bit. I've been sitting six hours."

"Okay, two rupees, two rupees."

He followed until I climbed in. We rode half a block, and then he turned into a hotel two minutes away.

"We have no rooms," said the clerk.

"Are there other hotels?" I asked.

"I am sorry, sir. There is only one."

To wander further seemed useless, so I walked back to the bus station. In the corner and along crevices of the building were red stains where men spit their betel nut amongst colors of other uncertain origin. People snored and coughed. A baby cried. From the toothless gums of an old bald man came noises like rubber soles squeaking on tile. Three young boys in rags walked in, pointed to a spot on the cold floor, and lay down to sleep.

Along the far wall of the bus station, in a dirty stained space, I wrapped my scarf about my head and curled up on the sarong I laid upon the concrete floor. Men passing through the open door at first stared at me, but soon no longer seemed to care.

At five in the morning an old man yelled and banged the wooden benches with his stick. Bleary-eyed and stiff, I joined a nearby queue. Before first light, a local bus with bench seats and broken springs pulled in.

We made stops at various outlying villages as Andhra Pradesh yielded to the state of Orissa, yet ways of life were unchanged by borders or centuries. Orange Tata trucks laden with bricks, timbers, and machines beneath flapping burlap covers flew past. At the border, trucks lined the roadside for miles but our driver barreled through in the opposite lane. The drivers slept, smoked cigarettes, or urinated in the bushes.

The staging area at Bhubaneswar bustled with life. Passengers ate at shops labeled with "Meals" signs, music blared, scores of buses revved their engines, and Indians milling around the main building waited for long-distance connections.

After fourteen hours I found Puri, a pilgrimage and resort destination for West Bengalis. Along a wide swath of road swarmed bicycles, rickshaws, pedestrians, cows, and vendors selling sweets, omelets, and chai. Hindus strung lights for another Shaivite festival. Pilgrims gathered by the thousands around Jagannath Temple. I watched as snake charmers drew crowds by tying vipers into knots for them to wriggle out of. Indian tourists sat on cool sands and walked through swirling ankle-deep waters. They regarded beaches, like the fields, as public toilets.

A withered husband pulled his wife in a wooden cart and motioned for food while she begged with fingerless hands. Bells clanged, beggars sat in the road, and rickshaw men watched with scarfs about their necks. As always a cycle-wallah found me, and I directed him to the main temple. I spotted a guest lodge, but he said they would not rent to a foreigner. I protested but let him lead past crumbling storefronts. As we moved into open darkness, I insisted we return to the crowds.

"No, no," he said.

He pedaled towards a line of concrete blocks. They looked expensive and boring, I thought, but told the driver to stop. I checked the desk of one.

"Yes, we have rooms," said the clerk. "But no, I cannot give you one." He insisted the foreigners' area still lay half a kilometer farther east.

Giving up, I watched scenery roll past as we traveled away from the pulse of Puri, towards the place where westerners resided. When we arrived I took a room with fair price but no window. Soon I found myself in the restaurant with plates before me. I devoured vegetable curry, butter chapati, and mango-flavored soda.

Enjoy yourself, the menu read. *These are the good old days you are going to miss in ten years.*

31

FULL CIRCLE

The bus stopped hard, reversed, and shuddered one last time. Calcutta. "At eight the traffic jams start," the taxi driver said. We passed boys and men bathing at old-fashioned hand pumps upon the sidewalks. Brown bodies wearing blue or red briefs lathered up in full view of passersby. A scattering of hotels near Sutter Road lined narrow streets crowded with vendors and beggars. On every corner a chai man staked his spot. Stay long enough, and you learned who sold the sweetest.

All rooms were expensive, basic, and booked. Desk clerk attitudes ranged from apathetic to disdainful. One man wearing a red-checkered headscarf and white cotton dhoti promised a single room. He led down one street, over, across and around another, until I forgot the way back. He brought me to the Dolphin Hotel, which had a triple that I must share when someone else came along.

"All fulled up," said the desk clerk at another.

I found a two hundred rupee double with paan-streaked spittle-stained yellow walls and toilet stopped up and stinking. Sounds of the city—car horns, a child's laugh, a heated argument–drifted upward while I sat shirtless in the heat upon grimy hotel sheets.

When dreaming of India while making initial plans, I had envisioned a more austere version. But, as with Tibet, I found the same despair as anywhere, only more of it. India was like an imperfect child I wished were different, could not change, but still loved dearly. At times I could not wait to leave India. Once escaped, I knew I would long for her exoticism.

Calcutta, long overwhelmed by waves of immigration, embodied all India's problems. The homeless lived on sidewalks with their few possessions stacked in rows. Many lay in the open upon thatch mats or rags, begging for money and food, sometimes sending a child or two to the train station or foreigners' hotels or other profitable haunts. A few attached a plastic tarp to a wall, which they unrolled when midday sun glared. More fortunate ones found a spot in the dirt along the sidewalk for a makeshift cloth canopy that provided shelter for a cook stove and blankets. Masses lived and died inches from thousands of passing feet.

Some found work, such as the men within small shops filling orders for bags of flour, rice, and lentils. Coolies carried the sacks onto lorries or hand-pushed wooden carts. Others pounded pieces of steel or cleaned thin wires with toxic chemicals. Little old men hunched over sewing machines within dark holes in the decrepit walls.

From such neighborhoods poured a steady unbroken stream of Bengalis carrying all manner of wares along the main road, around a tight bend, and across the steel spanning the Hooghly River. Above, greasy men suspended by thin ropes brushed silver paint onto black smog-stained struts. Cars, trucks, and rickshaws belched thick exhaust into the air. Buses cruised by with people hanging from both sides. Below, barges and ferries sliced flat tea-colored waters. The ribbons of humanity surged into Howrah Railway Station and beyond.

Rickshaw men dodged buses. Disjointed out-of-tune wedding processions clomped down filthy streets. Chai men dispensed advice. Mother Teresa's faithful nuns helped the sick and dying. Edifices of the British Raj slowly crumbled. On every corner lurked a man with underground offerings.

"Want something? Change money, hashish, opium. Very good, cheap."

One had a deep scar across the brow, another–yellow milky eyes. Sometimes a woman in sari called out with drugs for sale. When a withered old man offered opium, I wept. The sight of someone's grandfather subsisting in such a manner was too much to bear.

When my time came to leave the city, the travel agent could not find my train ticket. "Come back tomorrow morning," said the little man in the cramped office, where there was only enough space for a school desk and two child's chairs. I felt uneasy about the returning "tomorrow morning" instruction, but there was no other option. Sure enough, the next morning he was nowhere to be found. I learned where the agent lived and sought him out, to no avail. At nine he appeared with the same wait-listed ticket, except someone had scrawled S-3 51 on the tattered envelope. This seemed promising.

Minutes later I sat in idling traffic amidst a thousand other black and yellow taxis. Over the past three months I rarely worried about delays or timetables, but with my first reserved rail seat in hand, getting to Howrah Station on time felt imperative. At last we crossed the Hooghly River.

Pandemonium reigned inside the rail station. Mobs of children searching for spare rupees grabbed my arms and legs and tugged my shirttail as I maneuvered to the platform bearing the Delhi-bound train. Signs were scrawled only in Hindi or Bengali. At platform 8 a train shunted in and a mass of people converged. Cars were marked with chalk: S-1, S-2, S-3. I found my seat on car S-3 and waited.

A surge of clamoring passengers stowed suitcases as they moved through the compartment. The train budged forward nearly on time. As I should have expected, someone pointed out that I sat on the wrong car. When the conductor appeared a few hours later, he reassigned me to a seat in another carriage. In my new berth sat three men. One in white dhoti sat cross-legged by the window, a burly bearded Muslim slept in my seat, and another older man puffed hand-rolled beedis.

I roused the Muslim and settled in beside him. Green rice fields rolled past, as did the rest of the day. Gazing through the window, I knew I was not ready to leave the land I had grown to love. As challenging as many days had been, there were still villages and temples and forts and abandoned cities yet to explore, and more buses, trains, rickshaws, tongas, tempos, and boats to take me to them. I still wanted to visit Darjeeling and the northeast, travel among the Tibetan refugees around Dharamsala, and see Sikh culture at Srinagar.

Yet, all journeys must find their end, including this one. During my time in India I had encircled the whole of the country. This yearlong odyssey was part of a much larger exploration, which slowly looped around the world. At times I likened myself to a bald, toothless baby unsure of his steps, who grows up on a farm, travels the world, then as an old man tends flower gardens on his farm and ages into a bald, toothless man unsure of his steps. Always the circle.

On this grand journey my time and money ran short, and the way home would not be easy, it seemed. Continuing westward was risky. Recent outbreaks of plague in the western Indian state of Gujarat and consequent six-day quarantine with no exceptions had slowed all overland travel. Worse, Islamic militants had ambushed six Westerners in northwest India a few years prior. The terrorists beheaded one and shot the rest.

Across the border, several provinces in Pakistan were prone to smuggling and violence. Kidnappings, bus burnings, car bombings, and random gunfire frequented Pakistan's capital city, Karachi. A special permit was required to reach China via Khyber Pass on the Karakoram Highway, which did not open for three months and often closed without notice.

To the west of Pakistan lay Afghanistan. Travel to Afghanistan was not recommended, and barely possible. All non-essential American personnel had been evacuated, and no diplomatic missions or assistance were available. No American airlines were permitted in Afghan airspace, and one faction declared that all unapproved aircraft would be shot down.

To the west of Afghanistan lay Iran, which did not issue visas to Americans. Iraq was off limits. From Turkey onward the violence lessened, though winter weather, language barriers, and a looming war in Eastern Europe posed obstacles.

The anxiety settling into the pit of my stomach was not about the potential dangers ahead, however, but my readiness to leave India. I wanted to learn from the lepers, beggars, silk and carpet salesmen, sadhus, snake charmers, rickshaw drivers, schoolchildren, touts, hotel proprietors, and waiters I had met and had yet to meet. I yearned to see life through the eyes of Buddhists, Hindus, Muslims, Sikhs, Jains, Parsis, Christians, and Jews and know something of their gods, though had barely scratched the surface of the lessons that such faiths offered.

Walking through Nepal showed me I could accomplish anything I put my mind to. Traveling across Tibet shattered my illusions. Encircling India exposed me firsthand to every major historical religion–except the Chinese philosophies of Taoism and Confucianism, which I knew prior to departure were not my salvation. Yet, I felt no closer to knowing what I believed than when I started. Maybe my ancestral home might have something to teach, I thought. Europe had for centuries been a bastion of Lutheranism, my family's religion. If the answers were not in the East, perhaps they awaited closer to home.

My train rolled on as afternoon faded into night. Sometimes a man came through the coach and asked whether we were hungry. He brought aluminum trays stacked one on the other filled with rice, chapati flatbread, dal, and curd. At night we pulled up the bunks and lay in our spaces.

The air turned cold and whistled through cracks in the window. The old Muslim snored above. Somewhere within the rhythm of the wheels, I found sleep.

With a station stop, flurry of activity, and sun in the eyes, morning wake-ups on the train are rarely voluntary. The porter offered poori–an unleavened South Asian bread–with gravy, but the chai men were slow to appear and the day could not truly begin until they did. A few stops later, one boarded with a large silver kettle and poured a perfect, sickly sweet glass. The Muslim still slept above; the other rolled a beedi. The third, in white dhoti, spoke unbidden.

"It is, of course, all the fault of the Britons."

"How do you mean?" I asked.

"We were the envy of the world once. They came to us seeking riches, wealth, spices. We sent them home with boats so full they sank rounding Africa. We had tradesmen, weavers, carpenters...but the British put them out of business, impoverished them—so their own London craftsmen might have work. They stole our riches and exploited us...this is why British women sleep in the slums...guilt, you see. The French, too, who use us a playground."

I blew on my tea, and waited.

"I'm not bitter," he continued. "No. They gave us the railroads...a common identity...technology. They were no less fair than the Mughals. And the Aryans. It's all part of our history. And we shall endure. We always have."

The train rolled onward. The Muslim slept through the afternoon. The other man chain-smoked his beedis. I watched fields turn from green to brown. Hunched-over men and women planted the spring crop of rice—bright green shoots against broad ochre checkerboard fields.

Near Agra we slowed, losing time on the sidings while awaiting the mainlines. We waited an hour, then another. The sun set orange behind decaying buildings and rubbish piles covering the ground. Men squatted upon the rails with a pail of water in hand, and watched trains shuttle past. I crawled into the top bunk and closed my eyes.

Someone shook me. I stepped into night air of Old Delhi, where even at midnight activity abounded. I breathed in the city, memorizing her aroma. There would be no new discoveries in this land, I thought. A rickshaw bleeped. A cow sauntered past. Somewhere, a room awaited.

PART III

Captain, shake off this trance, and think of home—if home indeed awaits us…

- Homer, *The Odyssey*

32

THE LEGACY OF OSMAN

At a travel agency on Connaught Place, I found a one-way ticket from Delhi to Istanbul for three hundred dollars, less than half what I expected.

"Interesting choice," commented a British woman on my pick of Aeroflot, Russia's national airline, "as they can be a bit dodgy." Another Brit told me about a time he flew with Aeroflot when his plane was rerouted. "The crew came round," he recalled with a smile, "to collect donations for more petrol."

Despite stories of aging Tupolev jets barely reaching their destinations, I withdrew sixteen thousand rupees from a Hong Kong Bank branch and walked round Connaught Place with pockets bulging. The agent rang up the purchase, but I was waitlisted. A runner dashed to the airport, and an hour later returned with my ticket in hand. The die was cast. I retrieved gear I stowed at a guesthouse three months prior, got a haircut, bought a new shirt, had my boots polished, and prepared to travel through Eastern Europe in winter rather than India during monsoon season. The decision was a bittersweet one.

"Move forward!" said my head.

"Not yet," whispered my heart.

Four days later, I floundered amidst a wave of chaos and confusion surging outside Delhi's Indira Gandhi International Airport. Ragged lines of travelers hundreds deep extended from every counter. A man implored me to check one of his bags as we clawed our way forward. At immigration, everyone waited. An Indian in front caused a commotion when he realized the line he stood in for an hour was for foreigners only. Other frustrated travelers began shouting out.

In time my flight filled, and hours later, unbroken snows of Russia passed beneath the airliner. The bulky hairy males onboard wore revealing tank tops or half-buttoned shirts. Tall, thin Aeroflot flight attendants in red uniforms strutted like runway models. I watched the Russians with mild amazement. I grew up amidst the propaganda of the Cold War, and flying through Russian airspace and seeing the 'enemy' in person had once seemed improbable.

Clusters of tight villages and black ribbons of road gradually broke the snows. At Moscow, the thermometer read eighteen degrees below zero. The sky was gray and still. Inside the airport, young women paraded about like the flight attendants.

We continued from Moscow, in the heart of Eurasia, to Turkey, on Asia's southwest edge. The Black Sea appeared through thick cloud, and soon afterward, the Russian crew bid us good-bye. At the Istanbul airport, I changed money at the rate of three hundred fifty thousand to the dollar, and walked away with seventeen million Turkish lira.

Outside the airport, I found a bus bound for downtown Istanbul. Everything had changed. Groups of Indians no longer congregated on street corners and in the roads. Gone were beggars, piles of garbage, and unending poverty. Boxy vehicles followed painted lane markers upon tidy paved streets, which held an orderly European feel. Turkish men wore bushy mustaches and neat appearances, as in India. However, unlike the plump Hindu women hiding beneath sari swirls, slim Muslim women wore snug tops and chic jeans.

I longed, suddenly, for the chaos of India.

"Aksaray," someone said.

I stepped from the bus into the Aksaray neighborhood as rain fell from a gray sky. Beneath a bridge, a man sold pastries from a tray hung around his neck. A tram rolled past. I stumbled aboard and with help found a hostel and four-dollar bed in the Sultanahmet district. The Sea of Marmara spread to the horizon beneath endless white caps. Red, yellow, and blue houses covered the shores. Twilight faded to murky darkness.

Winds rattled the windows as a Danish traveler's raspy snores roused me from jet-lagged sleep. Though the clock said eleven, the hostel was dark and deserted. Outside, clouds hung low over the Bosporus strait. There was no hurry to get out and about, so with hand pressed against the shower tile I let near scalding water stream over my drooped head for forty minutes. Many Indian hotels had showers, but not once did hot water pour from them, only cold. Some had a knee-high tap from which warm water could be coaxed. On occasion, bathing consisted of a bucket filled with lukewarm water and ladle.

I recalled that except for a few cricket matches and single-channel foreign language satellite encounters, I had not watched television in eleven months. I had used one western-style toilet in the past five. The television and toilets I could live without, I thought, but nothing compared to a hot high-flow shower.

Revived, I stepped into the heart of Istanbul. Minutes from my doorway loomed the imposing Blue Mosque. Across Sultanahmet Square stood the mosque of Hagia Sophia, for a thousand years the largest cathedral in the world. Both dominated the skyline. At the crossroads of two continents, the cosmopolitan capital of Istanbul was as eastern in flavor as western. Merchant ships waited upon waters of the Golden Horn for empty berths. Turks filled the streets and bazaars. Upon the grand plazas surrounded by larger than life mosques, carpet salesmen beckoned passersby to corner shops.

Istanbul's European half lies at the southern tip of the Balkan Peninsula, the lands through which I prepared to journey. Threads of history weave the Balkan nations together like a patchwork quilt, though the seams have shifted through the centuries. Like all Europe, the story of the Balkans is one of revolutions, rebellions, conquests, defeats, and disputes. In *A Long Row of Candles,* C.L. Sulzberger notes,

> The Balkans, which in Turkish means "mountains," runs roughly from the Danube to the Dardanelles, from Istria to Istanbul, and is a term for the little lands of Hungary, Rumania, Jugoslavia, Albania, Bulgaria, Greece and part of Turkey, although neither Hungarian nor Greek welcomes inclusion in the label. It is, or was, a gay peninsula filled with sprightly people who ate peppered foods, drank strong liquors, wore flamboyant clothes, loved and murdered easily and had a splendid talent for starting wars. Less imaginative westerners looked down on them with secret envy, sniffing at their royalty, scoffing at their pretensions, and fearing their savage terrorists. Karl Marx called them "ethnic trash." I, as a footloose youngster in my twenties, adored them.

Also a footloose youngster in my twenties, I yearned to understand them. To do so, I thought I must start at the beginning. I knew that Egyptian, Babylonian, Assyrian, Syrian, Hittite, and Greek civilizations rose and fell around the rim of the Mediterranean Sea long before the birth of Christ. Even the Greeks, whose ideas and inventions shaped the core of Western society, were absorbed by the Romans.

In the fourth century nomadic Goths, Huns, Visigoths, and Vandals from the wind-blown steppes of northern Asia swept into Europe and displaced the peasants who had tilled the soil for millennia. After the Roman Empire collapsed, Europe entered an economic recession known today as the Middle Ages.

An altered lay of the land emerged. Austrian Habsburgs, Russian Tsars, Turkish Ottomans and other feudal monarchies struggled for supremacy through annexation, alliances, and wars. New ethnicities formed by the intermingling of invaders and indigents laid the foundations, and rough boundaries, for modern-day nation states.

In the midst of Europe's medieval crisis, the last of the universal religions, Islam, was born. Muhammad's ideas spread in time to present-day Turkey. Under the Turkish ruler Osman, for whom the Ottoman dynasty is named, the Muslim family's lands first expanded. Ottomans described themselves as *ghazis*– those who wage Holy War against non-Muslims–and strove to bring as much land as possible into their Islamic realm. Non-Muslims were assimilated as *dhimmis*, protected subjects.

A belt of territory from Morocco to the Bay of Bengal gradually fell under militaristic Muslim rule. The Turks' massive public works, magnificent mosques, disciplined army, and fourteen million subjects compared to Spain's population of five million earned European respect tinged with concern. And for good reason. Turkey's Ottoman Empire would control the fates of all Balkan nations for the next six centuries.

"Hullo," boomed the carpet dealers as I walked past. "Where you from?" Each one asked all manner of question, feigned interest, and then brought the conversation around to his carpet shop.

"Let me help you spend your money," one suggested.

"How long in Istanbul?" another asked. "How many carpets did you buy?"

"Come to my shop," they all said. "We have some tea. No buy, no buy. Just looking. Looking free!"

Outside my hostel on market day, stands crowding the cobblestone streets were covered by boxes filled with fruit, bright tomatoes, yellow lemons, cabbage heads, grape leaves, cheeses, peppers, oranges, fresh fish, and salamis. A stroll through old Istanbul led over the Golden Horn via Galata

Köprüsü bridge, and ended where men daily unloaded tuna, mackerel, sardines, and trout from the Sea of Marmara. From boats moored at water's edge, other men sold sandwiches for a dollar. When a passerby approached and ordered a meal, the merchant tossed a tomato slice and fish filet from flaming grill onto two slices of bread—with backbone included.

Sultry sounds and savory smells emanated from shops and restaurants. Young couples played backgammon at calf-high tables. When a patron motioned, someone brought a glass hookah with hoses running in all directions and set a glowing coal atop the apple-flavored tobacco.

In one shop, when a muezzin's chants sounded from a nearby minaret, the proprietor lunged for the stereo and switched off the Turkish pop. No others I saw heeded Allah's call. The young backgammon player's two inch-long cigarette ash still hung in a gentle gravity-defying arch. Smoke flowed non-stop from the hookah smoker's nostrils.

Despite the prosperous and progressive feel, Turkey's economy languished. The Turkish lira was rated least valuable currency in the world. Inflation averaged forty percent per year. Over the next few days the exchange rate would fall by six thousand lira to the dollar. I spent forty million in a week.

Much about Istanbul had changed since the city was established and named Byzantium after the Greek king Byzas. Yet, it also appeared that much had not changed. A thousand years after being founding, Constantine the Great renamed the city Constantinople and made it the new capital of the Roman Empire. The walls and seafront protected Christian Europe from invasion until Mehmed the Conqueror transformed the vanquished city into a beacon of Islamic culture.

He converted the Hagia Sophia, a Christian Orthodox basilica since 360 CE, into a mosque. The Blue Mosque was later built, as was Topkapi Palace, from which Ottoman sultans ruled for four hundred years. Twentieth-century visitors continued to clamber inside the palace for glimpses of St. John the Baptist's arm and occipital bone, locks of hair from Muhammad's beard, and a staff belonging to Moses. Not until

Turkey moved the capital to Ankara after the First World War did the name again change. This time it was based on the tenth-century Greek phrase "is tin polin" meaning "in the city."

Black waves from the Sea of Marmara smashed against seawalls. Slender minaret silhouettes pointed heavenward. Moored tankers and merchant ships awaited berths. Silent gulls rose and fell atop rolling waves and watched ships rack to and fro in search of space along the quay. As lights of the city twinkled on, throngs of black-clad commuters streamed onto ferries, which swept them across the Bosporus.

I paused for Turkish coffee at an outdoor café where men wearing white aprons lured passersby inside. When I stepped indoors to pay the pasty-faced proprietor, an accented voice called.

"Hey man, where you from?"

Oversize black spectacles perched beneath a receding hairline, while curly locks covered the collar of the speaker's denim jacket. He was Arabic, he said, but grew up in the States. His wife split with him just before he went abroad. Sick of "all that," he left his life behind to move around for a while.

"Hey man, where ya headin'?" he asked.

"Maybe catch the tram downtown."

"Nah. Don't waste your money. C'mon. I'll walk you down there. Show you the water and fish market."

At the market he made a few phone calls. Since his wife had filed for divorce, he had been sending her postcards to rouse some jealousy. In response, she filed a petition demanding his appearance at court in two weeks. There would soon be a warrant out for his arrest.

The Arab and I each had other business, but agreed to meet later. I walked past Sirkeci, over the Golden Horn, through Cihangir, and into the Taksim district. It was time to choose my northern route through the Balkans. At that time, the former Eastern Bloc nations of Bulgaria, Romania, Hungary,

Slovakia, Poland, and Czech Republic had only achieved independence from the Soviet Union within the past decade. On the other hand, war-torn Yugoslavia quickly disintegrated and might not exist in a few years. One fragment, Bosnia, was mired in civil war and another, Kosovo, soon would be.

I lacked an address but held a vague notion of the Yugoslavian Embassy's whereabouts. When asked, a bread vendor pointed to where I had just come. A taxi drove me in a needlessly long loop and dropped me where I could have walked almost as fast. He took a million Turkish lira before saying something about "Ze police" and speeding off. I found the embassy within a barricaded fence topped by barbed wire.

I punched the buzzer. A man with deep scowl and eyes full of suspicion peered out. A woman materialized too, and asked what I wanted.

"Okay," she said when I told her I needed a Yugoslavian visa. "Let me see your passport."

I pulled it out. "Do you have sixteen million Turkish lira?" she asked. Since I did not, she handed me a form.

"Come back another time," she said. "We are closed now anyway."

I raced through falling rain to the Sultanahmet coffee shop where I earlier met the Arab. He led to a brick-walled pub below street level. Half a dozen wire stools and a five-foot long bar filled the room. A couple puffed cigarettes near a glowing cast iron kettle. The bartender smiled, and poured two cold draughts. The Arab and I clinked our glasses, and we settled in.

He relayed how he had met a woman in Morocco. She kept staring at him. She didn't speak any English, or he much Arabic. Two men approached and sat down with them; they were plainclothes police officers.

"She is a bad woman," one of them told him. Undeterred, he saw Nami often in Marrakech. Though she was Muslim, she didn't follow the stricter guidelines, particularly regarding sex.

She urged him to accompany her to Istanbul, which he agreed to. After wandering around a few days, he decided he preferred Morocco. They tried to change their tickets, but the single flight per week was booked out. Stuck in Istanbul and tired of Nami, he sent her on errands to have more time to himself. When they got back to Morocco he planned to put some distance between them. She, however, wanted him to meet her family near Fez, and he was worried they might pressure him to marry her.

"Get a slave," one Moroccan friend had said when he first hit the country, meaning a wife. They will do anything for you, his friends said. "Cook, clean, and attend to every need. If you can afford to support them, you're allowed up to four."

He thought the Turkish hash was worth avoiding. "It's rubbish compared to the quality in Morocco," he said. He was thinking about smuggling a kilo or two back home. He did it before. "Here's how," he said. "Put it inside a balloon. Swallow it just before your flight. Eat nothing else. Then wait a day or two. That's how I made a little extra cash in prison too."

The beers went down easily and the music sounded good. He had a change of heart. "Tonight Nami will get what she's been wanting!" he exclaimed. I wished him luck, and slipped back into the rain.

In the morning I made a last stop at my recently discovered favorite bakery, for it was time to head north, into the heart of the Balkans. An Arab-dubbed episode of *The Flintstones* aired as I paid for a mass of pastries costing pennies. A tram went to Aksaray, and the metro from there. At Esenler, a Mercedes-Benz bus waited. When I boarded, a man in sweater and tie came around with sodas and tea that he set on folding tray tables. On occasion, the phone in front rang and the driver barked into the mouthpiece.

The sea stretched westward. We entered Thrace, the flatlands north of Istanbul. Pastures bordered by hedgerows of barren trees yielded to transmission towers and concrete modern block apartments. Rain fell from cloudy, gray skies and lent a dour mood to the drab winter landscape.

On the outskirts of Edirne, a line of taxis waited. I

preferred a shared dolmuş mini-bus, but the fixed route was unclear. A man pointed, and then waved a car down. The men inside asked questions I could not understand, but I got in anyway. They then left me on a shop-lined boulevard. I chatted with a member of the police about a possible hotel location using the few words of German I knew before heading north and settling on a hotel empty but for me.

The Selimiye Camii, Eski Cami, and Üscerefeli Cami mosques filled the skyline. Mobs of Muslim pilgrims clustered at the edges. With the setting sun, evening chill arrived. It was then I knew my threadbare clothes could not cope with an Eastern European winter.

At a pub on the edge of town an older gentleman seemed genuinely thrilled to meet me. We talked for hours over dollar beers and a dinner of white cheese, tomato, and pepperoni. A Turkish version of *Wheel of Fortune* played on the television. Following a decade in the military, Euckun lived in London for twelve years. His father had trained with the Turkish army in America in '36. Euckun had owned three pubs in town, but was too busy for all three, so sold two. His newest interest was computers. He planned to turn the third floor of the bar into an Internet café, the first in town serving alcohol.

Euckun walked me to the corner. I promised to visit when I returned. With teeth chattering and body shivering, I found my empty hotel.

33

PLOVDIV

With breath freezing, I waited on the curb beneath thick sky for a shared dolmuş to chance past. When one flashed its lights I waved the driver down. The mini-bus paused at two Turkish checkpoints. On the Bulgarian side of the border, four more checkpoints awaited. At each one they scrutinized the visas in my passport, but let me pass. Only a couple cars from Kuwait and a few trucks bound for Istanbul traveled the road.

After the last checkpoint a small collection of taxis waited. They wanted ten thousand Bulgarian leva, around five dollars, to nearby Kapitan-Andreevo. The fare seemed high, so I walked instead. I chatted with a thick-necked Bulgarian and his friends hovering around a Mercedes-Benz sedan with the hood propped open. The idea of an American wandering the south of Bulgaria amused them.

"For exercise," I explained, patting my stomach. They laughed still more.

Inside a café a group of squat Slavs drank morning beers as *Long Dong Silver had a long ding dong* played over the speakers. I sat at the bar and ordered coffee and a hamburger, which turned out to be a hotdog on thick bread with red and green sauces and pickle-like slices. The slender thirtyish bartender in black mini-skirt and tight woolen leggings was a welcome sight after three months in India.

I indulged in three games of pool with a twenty-year-old Bulgarian Army soldier. With no common tongue we communicated using hand signals, fortunate that the game of 8-ball constitutes its own universal language. I paid my bill, which cost less than a dollar, and headed outside.

Chirping birds, cool warmth beneath dazzling sun, and brown snow-free grasses gave hope for an early spring. Men crossed the road upon wooden carts laden with sticks or stones and pulled by fuzzy burros. The spring planting season beckoned. At the curb, a young woman wearing three-inch platform shoes and striped track pants waited with a half-dozen men. A bus turned the corner, rounded the dirt path, and pulled up before us. With cigarette dangling, the gray-haired driver in imitation leather jacket watched us climb in.

"Svilengrad?" I asked. He shook his head from side to side.

"Da, or Ne?" I asked to be sure. *Yes, or no?*

He shook his head again. As in India, and unlike much of the rest of the world, nodding up and down meant no, and shaking the head from left to right meant yes; except Bulgarians did so more vigorously.

"Da," he finally grunted. *Yes.*

Impassive faces stared at bare fields rolling past. The young Turkish women were stunning; Bulgarians less so, with harsh features and sallow eyes. They knew hardship and bread lines that the Turks did not, and seemed tired in a way that felt different from Indians.

"No autobus to Plovdiv," the portly woman in Svilengrad said, and upon a piece of paper wrote "*0393–14:30*" while repeating "Haskovo, Plovdiv, Haskovo, Plovdiv…" She meant I must find the 0393 bus at half past two, and first go to Haskovo, from where I might find transport to Plovdiv.

Aboard the bus to Haskovo, the fields bordered low-lying foothills of the Rila Mountains. Men tossed seed onto fresh plowed fields with flicks of the wrist. Two farmers, picnicking in a field upon a blanket, feasted on meat and bread. Others drove burros that hauled carts stacked with firewood. An industrial town came into view, dominated by ten-story concrete bunkers, abandoned factories with broken windows, and plywood-covered doorways. The pale afternoon light lent a gray pallor to the gritty monotone streets and cars of Haskovo.

I learned that a bus to Plovdiv left in two hours, so I wandered the central square. Locals crowded the outdoor cafés despite mid-winter chill. Bulgarian Cyrillic lettered every sign, making navigation difficult. Also, most locals spoke German as a second language, instead of English. I jotted the Cyrillic word for "hotel" on a scrap of paper for reference. After finding none, I bought a Lebanese pocket sandwich with bologna and vegetables and returned to the bus station.

I pointed at the bus that stood idling in the lot. "This one to Plovdiv?" I called.

"Ne," said the driver. *No.* He pointed to the space where his bus sat, and put up five fingers to indicate that the Plovdiv bus left at five o' clock. To be certain I boarded the right bus, I memorized the Cyrillic word for Plovdiv, and waited. When a bus departed a few minutes before five o' clock, a powerful feeling overtook me. As the bus rumbled past I glanced at the signboard in the window. The letters greatly resembled the word for Plovdiv. A man standing nearby looked at me.

"Plovdiv," I said.

He motioned at the bus pulling out of the lot. *Already gone.*

I showed him my timepiece, which read five before five. He smiled and showed me his watch, which read 5:35.

"When is next bus?" I asked.

"No more. Last."

He indicated we might try to catch the bus in his taxi, and I agreed. He raced through the streets, and then found the highway, where open fields stretched to the horizons. The effort was futile, for the bus was truly gone.

The taxi driver insisted we continue to Plovdiv, but I resisted and we turned around. He crisscrossed Haskovo in search of a friend who spoke English. We rode in the shadow of the nuclear reactor cone rising from a hill above the town. Factories stood idle within barbed wire, and rusted machinery sat useless. He drove up into a residential area with no houses, only mammoth twenty-story rectangular communist-era apartment blocks one after the other. His friend wasn't home so we visited a café before returning to the bus station. The driver insisted again that we find this mysterious person.

"No meter," he said, and turned it off.

We stopped at a playground, and he finally found his son who explained what I already suspected. Foreigners paid four or five times as much as locals for hotels, and it was cheaper to go to Plovdiv by taxi then stay in Haskovo. His son knew a dormitory at a university in Plovdiv where I could stay. I agreed that the taxi driver should drive me there.

He wanted payment up front, but I paid half in advance and would pay the balance on arrival. Yet I trusted him. Darkness fell as his four-speed sedan screamed past villages and purple mountains fading to black. In Plovdiv, hundreds more proletariat concrete block tenements sat side by side. After querying a local taxi man, we pulled to the roadside at an isolated spot. My driver and I walked along a dark path towards a group of the blocky tenements. A young woman pointed into the blackness. When we reached one of the buildings, my driver stepped inside to ask if they had an open dormitory. They claimed they did not.

A young man passing by and speaking some English said he knew of other dorms. He suggested I should try there, and he would take me. I thanked my driver, paid him what I owed, and followed Mario into the darkness. We walked atop a foot-wide pipe spanning a rushing stream, and then stepped across a long, narrow railroad bridge. We leapt across occasional black holes where pieces of the bridge had broken through. If a train came I was to climb to the outside railing and dangle over the dark waters.

On the opposite bank we tried another high-rise. "They give us some problem there," Mario said, so we checked half a dozen others. All full. Or, no one wished to let a room to an American.

Plovdiv had a handful of unaffordable high-end hotels and, reputedly, one moderate option called the Turisticheski dom somewhere in the old part of town. I thanked Mario and climbed into a taxi with a man who knew no English except one word–*center*. He stopped at a swank hotel, and I pushed him on.

"Center, center," I urged. At a narrow cobblestone dead end he cut the motor and turned towards me.

"Center," he said.

I stood in chill night air amidst a collection of closed shops and restaurants with no idea where to turn. At the second-century CE Roman theater I bore right, then turned here and there along unlit cobblestone streets where aging wooden buildings lined their edges. I began eyeing parked cars in which to spend the night. It would be bad if the owner came out early, though a white Peugeot on blocks looked promising.

The street ended atop a hill at the ruins of Eumolpias, a second millennium BCE Thracian settlement. The modern city spread towards the hills. My spirit sank as I retraced my steps past towering walls and through the stone arched Roman gate of Hisar Kapiya. I again got lost amongst narrow, winding unmarked streets.

Outside a corner pub where music seeped into the street, two men chatted. I enquired about the Turisticheski hotel.

"Oh-ho, slowly now," said the white-haired one on crutches with bundled left foot buried in plastic wrap. I repeated my query.

"Ah, that is closed. But let us see."

His friend and I walked fifty feet to the west, and there sat the hotel, dark and locked. My surprise upon finding the hotel hidden amongst winding streets and landmarks labeled in Cyrillic turned to alarm upon realizing it was closed. I thought of the white Peugeot.

"Well," said the white-haired one when we returned. "You'll just have to stay with me. Come along."

He limped up the hill, almost to the ruins, with his friend and I following. He reached an old building and fumbled with a key while turning the lock in the moonlight. The white Peugeot sat ten feet away.

We climbed a narrow stairwell to a dirty landing and entered a cramped room with one bed, small cluttered desk, chair, 1950s-era console television, and bits of rubbish and clutter. He switched on an antique wooden radio and sound warmed the room. A charcoal of Jesus wearing a crown of thorns hung on one wall. He showed me several books in Bulgarian, all pertaining to God, churches, and Biblical prophets. He handed out cigarettes and I waited while he puttered about and fed the dog that wandered in. Then he explained the plan. He and his friend were going back to the bar until three. I could sleep, and he would be quiet when he came home so as not to wake me. Then, they were gone.

I moved my eyes across the faded nineteenth-century wallpaper, cobwebbed corners, rubbish, and old rags along the floorboards. To urinate I had to use the wooden dry sink. I didn't know how to address the other bodily function should that need arise, though he had motioned to a small cup on the floor by his bed. Lights of the city glowed beyond the cracked windows. The dog decided to join me and scratched on the door until I let him in.

My eyes closed and I hovered on the brink of sleep until a knocking-about on the steps brought me to full consciousness. A burly man, long unshaven, with greasy unkempt black hair and one shoe untied, flicked on the light and stared at me.

I explained who I was and where the white-haired man went, but it was impossible to communicate. He asked questions in Bulgarian I could not understand. He lit a cigarette, turned on the radio, and sat back, looking at me. I didn't exactly mistrust him, but didn't like him in the room and wanted to know who he was. Every so often he asked more questions and I lost patience.

He kept motioning for me to sleep, and though not easy with the music blaring, I closed my eyes. The sound of a zipper brought me back. My rucksack sat on the floor beneath his chair. I had not forgotten about it, but didn't move it, preferring to see what happened. He looked at me, hand about to drop inside.

"What the hell are you doing?" I hollered. He placed my jacket atop the rucksack and tossed the bundle onto the bed.

I got out of bed and sat atop the covers. With face in his hands, smoking another cigarette, he sighed every so often. We had reached an impasse. With no heat in the room it was too cold to sit beyond the blanket for long. Outside would be worse.

I prepared to leave. He motioned. I motioned back that I had nowhere to stay. He waved me into bed, turned off the light and radio, went across the landing to another room, and closed the door. Sometime in the night I heard white-hair come in, and I scrunched closer to the wall.

Sparrows chirped as white-hair fiddled about and clomped downstairs. Sunbeams shone onto the wall, orange then yellow then white. I left a note and slipped out, though from the way he talked the night previous I could stay on if I wanted. Downstairs, I pushed against the front wooden double doors—which were bolted shut. The rear door was open, but led into a grassy yard surrounded by the high walls of adjacent buildings with no way out. A dog barked and a voice called the animal back. Trapped, I climbed upstairs to wait.

After half an hour I knocked on one of the doors. White-hair's friend from the bar opened the door. The burly, unshaven man—last night's intruder—lay in a bed on the far side. The room was otherwise empty but for a few bottles in one corner and couple of rags in another. White-hair's friend put up his finger and slicked his gray hair back. He put a taupe sport coat on over his teal sweater, donned a worn pair of Nike running shoes, and led me downstairs and into the cobblestone streets. A few moments later we entered the Church of Constantine and Elena, where he lit two candles. He made the cross three times as we approached gold-painted scenes of Jesus. He looked at me, smiled, and motioned us outside.

"Bulgarian church," he said.

The burly, unshaven man bumbled along from behind and caught up as we made our way through the city center.

"Autobus," said white-hair's friend. At last I knew where we were going.

"Coffee?" he asked.

I bought us each one and we sat while the men smoked. Then white-hair's friend got up and motioned to the bus. For a moment I thought both of them were coming too, but they only shook my hand and waved good-bye.

From my smoke-stained seat I watched the legs file past. A Turkish woman with a mouth full of gold sat beside me. The little bit of English she knew was enough to hammer out the essentials. She was bound for Sofia on her way to Macedonia. Melting snows dotted brown fields as the bus climbed into the Rila Mountains. After cresting the snow-covered pass the driver opened the throttle wide. Utilitarian high-rise buildings of Sofia appeared in the valley below. The Turkish woman flashed her life's savings at me and was gone.

In Sofia, while walking south on Maria Luiza Boulevard, I memorized some Bulgarian.

"Imate li svobodni stai?" I repeated. *Do you have rooms available?* Upon hearing this, I hoped the hotel proprietor would shake his head from side to side and say "Da." *Yes.*

"Kolko struva," I would reply. *How much does it cost?*

Turning left onto Slivnitsa I recognized the Cyrillic word for "hotel." I pushed open a red wooden door, climbed the stairs, and pressed a buzzer. A white-haired, softer, handsomer version of former Russian president Boris Yeltsin answered. I pronounced my memorized words and lo, he and his wife understood! They ushered me into a high-ceilinged room and stripped and remade the beds while I watched. I didn't understand a word they said, but they were beautiful and kind.

A huge wooden table covered by a green and blue tablecloth crowded the center of my room. An elderly couple sitting across the hall in the kitchen smoked and discussed life. Four others rented adjoining rooms, including three ethnic Albanians—two from Kosovo and one from Macedonia—and a Romanian. They were all surprised by my nationality, but friendly and welcoming upon making my acquaintance.

Freshly showered, I sat at the old wooden table with a loaf of fresh bread, cucumber, tomato, and chunk of white cheese, all for a dollar. I marveled at the vicissitude of life. One day there was frustration and agony—the next brought everything I needed.

34

BALKANS

When I tried to tell the old couple at the hotel my intentions of circling through the heart of the Balkans, they rang a young woman up on the telephone and motioned for me to speak with her. The young woman on the phone spoke a smattering of English. She told the old man my plans; he mumbled to the ceiling while the old woman smiled. "He wishes you good health," said the young woman. I knew that upon my return to Sofia I would surely stay with this kindly couple.

The nondescript bus office sat on a narrow side street rather than at the busy parking lot from where the other buses left. When I approached the Skopje-bound bus, the driver was already hurling Bulgarian at those queued outside. The moment he finished, a chorus of huddled indecipherable mini-conversations ensued among those in line. Eventually we clambered aboard. Cigarette smoke soon filled the bus.

As we passed through mountains of the Rila, snow appeared by the roadside. On the Bulgarian side of the border, officials gathered every passport for inspection and lined us up in the frozen air with our bags by our sides. The man in front of me was taken aside and his belongings searched, but they let him go. When they eyed me, I sensed a mix of suspicion and curiosity.

On the Macedonian side of the border, they again searched the bus with flashlights and lined us up like prisoners awaiting condemnation. The Macedonian guard questioned the same man the Bulgarians had. The guard nodded at the portable electronic keyboard the man carried. He played a few notes, then a minor chord. We laughed. Even the guard seemed to see the absurdity of standing in the frigid air of the Rila.

Borders suppress invasion and infiltration and maintain control and autonomy, but also promote distrust of neighboring peoples and those different from us. Nowhere were these consequences more evident than in the Balkans, where even fortified borders could not contain centuries-old enmities.

After returning to the bus, the motor's droning lulled me to sleep. When I awakened, high-rises jutted into the night sky. A few passengers stumbled into the darkness when the driver yelled something I could not understand, though I heard "Skopje" in the tirade. I stayed aboard and waited half-asleep for the bus station to appear through the window, but soon realized the crux of Skopje lay behind me. As I lurched my way to the front, a chorus of Bulgarian erupted. After explaining my mistake, the driver pulled to the roadside near Tetovo. Someone indicated I should take a taxi.

"No," I protested. "No taxis!" We continued to Ohrid.

Beyond the window, a round moon played over the snow-covered Šar Planina Mountains that straddled Macedonia's turbulent northern border. The snowy peak of Titov Vrv gleamed in the moonlight. Kosovo lay like a ticking time bomb ten miles northward, and war-torn Albania a dozen to the west. These were the lands that Philip II of Macedon ruled, and from where his son, Alexander the Great, set out to conquer the ancient world.

After the driver awakened me, a woman ushered me into frigid night air, as she too was getting off. She indicated that a

Skopje-bound bus would leave from the spot in a few hours. I must change money to do anything, however, since I carried only dollars, Bulgarian leva, and Czech crowns. With the bus station locked and nothing else around, the woman motioned for us to walk towards a nearby taxi, the only transport in sight. We crawled inside, and she explained my situation.

"Is okay," the driver said. "You stay with me. I have office, until bus."

Cauro, the driver, let the woman off, and I followed him into his sparse dispatch office. I sat with two other men, both seemingly content to smoke cigarettes at four in the morning here in Kičevo–twenty miles from the war zones of Albania and Kosovo. One of the men brewed thick Turkish coffee.

One asked why I was in Macedonia. The best answer I could offer was my longstanding desire to visit the volatile historical homeland of Alexander the Great.

We talked of the strife so common among the men's brethren. No one seemed to agree upon the division of boundaries. Kosovo appeared in the news almost daily. The Bosnian conflict simmered. A Macedonia-related struggle seemed likely. Yugoslavia had disintegrated.

"Ah, Balkans," Cauro said of his people, looking to the ceiling and shaking his head. "Crazy people!"

Long ago, the lands of present-day Bulgaria were part of the Kingdom of Macedonia. The Bulgars, an invading semi-nomadic warrior tribe, in the seventh century CE founded the first Bulgarian Empire, which laid the framework for Bulgaria's national identity. Two centuries later, Bulgaria conquered Macedonia. In time the Ottomans defeated Bulgaria and Macedonia along with Serbia. Thus began five centuries of Turkish rule.

The Ottoman Empire's five hundred-year Muslim reign over the Balkans was benevolent in light of Islam's historically militant nature. Though overtaxed and denied any role in government, non-Muslims were not forced to convert.

Christianity survived in isolated monasteries. Folklore bridged the generations and kept local languages and customs alive. Through it all, Balkans remembered their past. From Robert Kaplan's *Balkan Ghosts*,

> Macedonia, the inspiration for the French word for "mixed salad" (*macedoine*), defines the principal illness of the Balkans: conflicting dreams of lost imperial glory. Each nation demands that its borders revert to where they were at the exact time when its own empire had reached its zenith of ancient medieval expansion...In the Balkans, history is not viewed as tracing a chronological progression, as it is in the West. Instead, history jumps around and moves in circles; and where history is perceived in such a way, myths take root.

As Ottoman power waned, the glue that had held the region together for centuries came undone. The Turkish retreat led to a tinderbox needing only a spark to ignite, which alit with an 1815 Serbian revolt. With seeds of nationalism sown, Greece next declared independence. Russian troops intervened in Bulgaria's liberation. Fearing a new Russian satellite, the West made southern Bulgaria subject to Turkey, allowed the Austro-Hungarian Empire to rule Bosnia and Herzegovina, and kept Macedonia part of the Ottoman Empire.

Serbia, Greece, and Bulgaria all wanted Macedonia for themselves. During the First Balkan War they defeated Turkey. The Second Balkan War erupted when Bulgaria attacked Serbia and Greece. After Bulgarian defeat, Serbia and Greece divided Macedonia among themselves. Next, the First World War erupted when a Bosnian Serb nationalist assassinated an Austro-Hungarian archduke as retaliation for the takeover of Bosnia and Herzegovina.

During the Second World War, a new version of Yugoslavia was resurrected after the first one disintegrated. Serbs, Croats, and Slovenes hated each other, yet were joined by Bosnians,

Macedonians, Montenegrins, Herzegovinians, Dalmatians, Slavs, and Kosovars.

In 1991, Macedonians voted for independence. Slovenia, Croatia, and Bosnia-Herzegovina next declared autonomy, which led to a bitter civil war in Bosnia. In Kosovo, most of the world including myself did not yet know that a massacre had just happened. Serbian and Montenegrin minorities in Kosovo were Christian, while ethnic Albanians were primarily Muslim. The Yugoslavian government wanted all ethnic Albanians out of their country.

In two weeks, Yugoslav forces would invade Kosovo in order to expel those of Albanian descent. NATO and the American Air Force would respond by launching a sustained bombing campaign a few miles from Camo's taxi dispatch office. Eight hundred thousand Kosovan Albanians were about to flee, and some ten thousand civilians would be killed. The Kosovo War would dominate newspaper headlines as I traveled north into the heart of Eastern Europe.

I traded Camo a five-dollar bill for 250 Macedonian denari. He suggested I take the train, which left at five o'clock. One of the men drove me to the station as a brilliant full moon set over Kosovo. The morning train followed the Vardar River towards the Aegean Sea past brown mist-covered farmlands nestled amongst snowy mountains. The sun rose over simple red-roofed villages. Laughing schoolchildren awaited the train or walked to school.

Skopje straddles the Vardar halfway between Sofia and Tirana, Albania's capital. As everywhere in the Balkans, waves of invaders including Slavs, Byzantines, Bulgarians, Normans, and Serbs arrived in Skopje following the Roman collapse. The Ottomans came in 1392, and held the city until 1912.

A fifteenth-century Turkish stone bridge led into the old city towards the market area. Serbs, Turks, Greeks, Macedonians, and Bulgarians filled the streets. Minarets pointed to the sky, and men in skullcaps played backgammon and drank tea. Such scenes underscored an enduring Turkish influence. Inside an old Orthodox church, two priests chanted. Locals filtered in and out and lit slender wax candles that they set into broad crocks of sand. On occasion the elderly woman weeping next to me stood to cross her heart.

Old Skopje was overshadowed by "new" Skopje that emerged following the earthquake of 1963. Aid from other areas of Yugoslavia funded a modern urban skyline of concrete construction. Already the buildings were stained and crumbling due to lack of funds. Though cracked, the dome of five hundred-year-old Mustafa Pasha Mosque remained mostly intact and served as a reminder of a more durable and once glorious past. The city's people, wandering beneath towering hulks of ghostly oversize buildings, exhibited little vitality or zest. For me, Skopje lacked the charm of many places I had visited.

I did admire eleventh-century Cyclopean walls while climbing to hilltop ruins of Fort Kale. As the sun sank, a burst of orange splayed upon the land. The outskirts of Skopje spread into the hills, beyond which the icy Šar Planina Mountains hid troubled lands of Kosovo. Beneath lavender-pink skies, I watched the eastern hills turn purple-orange, then black, in gathering twilight.

35

ANCIENT ENMITY

The train to Thessaloniki, in Greece, did not depart until four in the morning. I had enough Macedonian denari for a coffee and beer and bit of food before heading to the frozen, unheated train station. A bearded man moved around the waiting room yelling crazily at the ceiling in some Cyrillic tongue. Then he whacked passengers' chairs and my foot with his stout stick. When the armed guard moved us to another room the bearded lunatic struck my rucksack. While another guard studied my passport, several men flooded the room and confronted the man. He pretended to have done nothing, but the men dragged him down the steps by his feet.

The crazed man returned and found a loud friend resembling the actor Al Pacino in his angriest foreign language role. They engaged in arguments-cum-discussions deep into the night. Somehow the half-dozen other vagabonds managed sleep, but unable to lie down in the rigid plastic chair, I sat in frozen misery.

At quarter past four I walked upstairs into frigid night air to wait on Platform Four for the Belgrade train. After boarding and stretching out on the soft cushioned couchette, I did not stir until roused at the border by a Macedonian guard.

We moved a mile forward into Greece, where in morning sunshine guards there collected passports before allowing us to continue past farms and vineyards over rolling hills and swollen streams. Jagged snow-covered peaks shimmered in the distance as industrialized outskirts of Thessaloniki appeared. There I disembarked and made my way downtown. Upon the squares, old men played chess. Young Greeks sipped cappuccinos and frappes at street side cafés. Svelte Athenian-faced women wearing snug slacks and short black skirts strolled waterfront promenades.

Along ancient stone walls beneath Mediterranean sun, streets grew narrower and houses smaller. On the upper slopes, crumbling castle-like edifices overlooked forested hills and the harbor. Merchant ships steamed into port past red-tiled roofs that covered the hillsides. The Aegean Sea stretched towards the horizon where snowy mountains shimmered beyond the blue waters.

At a stone arch in the old crenelated wall, I entered an outdoor café. There it cost me six hundred Greek drachmas, about two dollars, for spanakopita and thick, sweet coffee, plus nine hundred more for a Greek salad. Later I indulged in a lamb gyro with tomato and onion on grilled pita. While sitting in warm sunshine I savored the salad's strong feta, and thought about the restaurant I sat at in New York City's Chelsea district eleven months earlier. It was then I promised myself I would one day eat such a meal–not in a Manhattan neighborhood–but in Greece proper. Eminently satisfied, I remembered why we must never let go of our dreams.

In addition to sampling fine cuisine, by detouring to Greece I also hoped to gain some perspective. Centuries of conflict between the Ottoman Empire and Balkan nations had constituted a religion-oriented struggle for control. As Anthony Pagden details in *Worlds at War*, the basis for this conflict derived from the ancient tension between Asia and Europe, which began long before Muhammad's migration to Medina or the birth of Christ.

Although Asia and Europe lie upon the same landmass, the idea that Asia is separate from Europe began with the Assyrians. They were an Eastern people, who in the second millennium BCE distinguished between the *ereb*–lands of the setting sun–and *Asu*, or Asia–lands of the rising sun.

The Greeks, a Western people, noticed that gods and philosophies in the east differed from theirs. They considered the Aegean Sea and Sea of Marmara and Black Sea as the border between Asia and Europe. Concepts of East and West, Asia and Europe, evolved from this early Greek perspective. After Peter the Great, Tsar of Russia, extended his empire, the Ural River became the new boundary between Asia and Europe, which endures as part of the seven-continent model.

Those in the West shared a common identity they saw as different from, and in their opinion, superior to that in the East. The Greek historian Herodotus understood what it meant to be Greek, which he described as "a shared blood, shared language, shared religion, shared customs." Though altered since antiquity, that identity formed the basis of European thought.

Herodotus knew firsthand the tension between East and West. He was born in Greece the same year that Persia launched the first full-scale attempt by an Asian force to conquer Europe. Such overreaching imperialism was what the Greeks most feared and despised in the Persians. In Herodotus' day, Greeks were bound by the city-state and governed by the people and guiding principles of democracy: openness, accountability, and equality before the law.

Herodotus described the Persian Wars as a two-part drama in which a far more powerful Asian people took on a weak, but more virtuous, Western one. The first war ended at Marathon when the Athenian army defeated the most powerful force in the ancient world. The victory marked a turning point for Greece and triumph for democracy, a new concept of the time.

The second Persian War ended the same as the first, this time at Salamis, despite Persia possessing the largest army ever seen. The greatest naval battle in ancient times was won not by soldiers but by sailors with much to gain from democracy. Persian troops, on the other hand, were in Greek eyes not warriors but slaves fighting against their will.

The victory at Salamis altered forever the future of Europe. Had the Greek city-states become vassals of the Persian Empire, there would have been no democracy, Greek theater, Plato, or Sophocles, and the outpouring of Greek ideas in the fifth and fourth centuries BCE that formed the core of Western civilization would not have happened. As Pagden emphasizes in *Worlds at War*, this initial struggle between Greeks and Persians laid the foundation for the ancient enmity that inspired the Crusades, contributed to both World Wars, and persists in the ongoing 2,500-year ideological war between Islam and Christianity.

Upon my return to Sofia, I learned the Yugoslavian consulate wanted forty-five dollars and an onward ticket to Budapest or Zagreb in exchange for an entry visa. The fee seemed manageable, but obtaining the onward ticket proved impossible. After biding my time in an underground coffee shop, I bought a ticket to the Bulgarian city of Koprivshtitsa. When the conductor's whistle blew, my train moved past frozen snow-covered fields beneath thick gray skies.

Near Koprivshtitsa I disembarked and rode a waiting bus over winding mountain roads to a cluster of wood and stone buildings nestled amongst the Sredna Gora Mountains. While standing in the cobblestone street, an elderly Bulgarian-speaking woman motioned. I followed her through the maze of narrow medieval lanes to an upstairs room in her early nineteenth-century home. A nearby pub with roaring fireplace and wooden walls served coffee, Zagorka beers, thick bread, and bob—a white bean soup. Locals in the corner drank rakija, a plum brandy, and smoked cigarettes.

Morning snowmelt dripped from the eaves, but spring came slowly to this land. I tried to buy a ticket north to Veliko Târnovo, but the agent rattled off a string of words and turned away. A woman helped by showing me the timetable. When I asked again, the agent gave me a ticket. Later I realized my crude Bulgarian had inquired only about the time of departure, not whether a ticket was available.

I shared a compartment with Dido, a twenty-year-old Bulgarian soldier stationed on the Turkish border. When his mandatory one-year service ended in a month he faced a new dilemma—finding work. Meanwhile, he headed home for the weekend and looked forward to visiting his girlfriend in Sofia. He gave me his camouflaged military cap as a souvenir. Dido disembarked, and a tall blonde in skin-tight vinyl pants and four-inch platform heels entered the compartment. Though her eyes strayed towards me, she spoke no English nor I any Bulgarian.

At Veliko Târnovo I stepped into warm sunshine. Atop four flights of stairs beyond a questionable looking door sat a woman behind a desk. She had a room. When that was settled I set out to slake my thirst. While drinking Zagorka beers for a quarter each, I watched mini-skirts, tight sweaters, and long shapely legs swarm the twelfth-century streets.

After morning coffee and banitsa, a baked cheese pastry, droplets fell from husky clouds. The train moved on through open farmland and past red-roofed villages. When high-rises crowded the landscape, the train called at Ruse. I set my sights on Hotel Balkan, but upon finding the address it became clear the hotel no longer existed. Hotel Helios, the only other accommodation in my price range, wanted thirty-seven thousand leva. I showed the woman the twenty thousand I had left. She shrugged, and returned to her paper.

The last train north had left hours ago and Bulgarian train stations were locked at night, so I took the room. I indicated I would return with more leva. She shrugged again. On the square, each of the dozen exchanges had closed. I dreaded trying to explain my situation to the woman, and drank fifty-cent beers instead. On the way home, I noticed a blinking automatic teller machine. I sighed with relief as leva popped out at my command. I bought a massive loaf of bread for fifteen cents, and returned homeward. The night clerk at Hotel Helios awaited my return.

In the morning, I left Bulgaria behind. Her people lived in the shadow of their past. The corruption-riddled Communist Party had returned to power, organized crime was on the rise, and independent travel was discouraged. Greece warily eyed Macedonia's independence. War loomed in Kosovo. Yet Romania, across the border on the road ahead, sounded far worse. I could barely wait to get there!

36

PARIS OF THE EAST

We waited seemingly forever at Giurgiu for border police to clear our train. When at last the *Bucharest-Istanbul Express* rolled out, a broken countryside unfolded. Rubbish piles and destroyed vehicles littered run-down villages crowded by abandoned machinery and massive long-dormant concrete factories. Armed guardhouse sentries manned every corner of barbed wire-enclosed compounds. Impoverished peasants rode horse-drawn wagons. Mesmerized, I watched the stream of communist-era manifestations flash past.

Border delays pushed our arrival into evening hours. The sun dropped behind a murky bank of cloud as we approached Bucharest's Gara de Nord Train Station. By the time I slipped out of the money exchange, a long line stretched from the packed room.

A Parisian ambiance permeated tree-lined boulevards and looming public monuments, but the grittiness, abundant street hustlers, and lack of affordable accommodations made the city challenging. Men were quick to offer taxis and money changing. I took a wrong street, one too dark and empty, and backtracked to busier boulevards. Hotel Grivița had closed, but I found Hotel Dunărea.

"Quit," a passing man said.

Across the rain-dampened street at Hotel Cerna I held my breath, for the place seemed too plush.

"About ten dollars," said the bored concierge.

Though the hotel was swankier than any I had rented in the previous eleven months, the price had plummeted the past few years along with the value of the Romanian leu. Ten years prior one leu was valued at nine to the dollar, but the currency's collapse plus forty percent inflation had substantially decreased its worth. Now, thirteen thousand lei equaled one dollar.

A man waited outside the hotel entrance. He offered a woman, a Madam, he said. As you wish, he shrugged when I declined. Little had changed since journalist John Reed in 1915 noted, "Ten thousand public women parade, for your true Bucharestian boasts that his city supports more prostitutes in proportion than any other four cities in the world combined."

I spent my lei instead on a Turkish kebab, and wandered the train station vicinity where the hard-faced downtrodden congregated. I purchased an oversize bottle of Gambrînus beer for thirty cents and put it in my pocket for later consumption. Outside a deli, men insisted I change money. By law Romanians could purchase only one hundred twenty-five dollars in foreign currency per year, which enabled a thriving black market.

I asked one moneychanger what he would give for the eight thousand Bulgarian leva from Ruse I never spent. He preferred dollars or Deutschmarks. I wouldn't mind losing the leva, but changing hard currency on the street felt too risky. "I must check something," he said, and went to find a calculator. I found his routine mildly amusing. I ducked inside the deli to look for cheese, but the woman spoke no English.

On the street, a new man waited with a thick wad of lei. The first one appeared from the shadows with a small crowd behind him, one of the men dressed to the nines. They made a commotion, yelled something to the moneychanger, and said something about dealing cocaine. A burly one told me to stay put. They brushed my pockets and fished for a wallet.

I tried to move off, but the burly one yelled again to not move. He kicked my foot to show he meant it. I wondered how far they would go. I suspected they planned to hustle me, but never expected them to rob me. This seemed a violation of some unwritten code of the road. In northern India and other aggressive cultures, touts got whatever they could but rarely inflicted harm. Theirs was a game of wits, of how well they could con you and how well you could decipher the ruse and escape with currency and ego intact.

Bucharest was different. Money changing wasn't a game; it was serious black market business. The contrast between non-harming Buddhist-Hindu tradition and cold atheistic communism rang strikingly clear.

I cursed and yelled as they surrounded me. My heart had never pounded so hard. The street had otherwise emptied, so I hollered louder to draw any attention. The hotel door lay only fifty meters away, around the corner, so there was not much ground to cover. I maneuvered so that for a moment no one hovered behind me. I remembered the oversize Gambrînus in my pocket. Grateful for a weapon, I raised the heavy bottle in the air and, screaming vulgarities like a madman, prepared to bash it on the head of the one closest. This gave them pause. I took two steps backwards, and as the burly one lunged, I made a beeline for the hotel.

The man from earlier still stood at the hotel entrance. Well? His expression asked. I shook my head. I had seen enough excitement for one night.

City sounds filtered upwards from the street and into my room, and morning light soon followed along with a thick cup of espresso. Despite confusing markings in the metro I came to the surface. There was no sign of the Croatian Consulate, until I realized I walked right past the nondescript building. A man carrying a briefcase strode inside and rode the lift upstairs.

I followed on the circular stairs, and confirmed my suspicion that the building had been converted to a flat. Businesses moved and consulates closed, especially in post-communist Eastern Europe.

I turned north to try the Yugoslavian Consulate, which was due to open in half an hour. I hung about outside, then walked through the consulate's high gates past the armed guard and into the outer offices. I waited an hour and a half before the woman returned with my passport in hand.

"I'm sorry," she said.

"Why?" I asked, curious why they refused my visa this time.

"We must have permission from Yugoslav government. Could take two weeks. Or two months." Unbeknownst to me, Yugoslavia was about to sever diplomatic ties with America. It seemed my route north must bypass Yugoslavia.

Afternoon slipped into evening as a bloody sunset and later rainy skies roiled over the city and cast surreal lighting onto upper stories. Few seemed to notice, hurrying as commuters did to buses and trains. At one of the surprisingly good pizza joints surrounding underground metro entryways, I savored a Ciuc beer as the skirts flowed past.

Bucharest was filled with people, bustling energy, fantastically battered yellow trams, and crumbling side street architecture. There was also near-poverty and local pride despite sky rocketing inflation. Someone has called it "Hell on Earth," another "Paris of the East." Neither description was entirely inaccurate. An understated elegance underscored the edginess, in the way it might feel inside an upscale bordello. She was, without doubt, a city I would return to.

In the morning, to show I noticed, I stared back at the man in black leather coat looking me over. "Problem?" he asked. I shook my head. Later, he spotted me again.

"Hey mister," he called. "Wait a minute. Do you have problem? Need to change money?"

I harbored a twinge of unrequited retaliation towards the

moneychangers. "I have a problem with you following me!" I called. Anyway, I felt in no mood for games.

At the train station I bought a first class express seat and soon sat in a private mini-universe of luxury. At midday we called at Brașov. Within moments a man approached with a room offer. I agreed to look, and climbed into a taxi with him. I winced as the meter exploded, but at Radu's home a pleasant surprise awaited me in the form of a fold-out couch, ample hot water, and kitchen access. After the taxi driver got his cut of the ten dollar per night tariff, I walked downtown.

Tight rows of Teutonic homes lined streets around Piaţa Sfatului square but gave way to wider spaced dwellings beyond Şchei Gate. Shops and restaurants filled the lower floors of baroque-faced buildings, and made the former German merchant colony in the foothills of the snow-covered Bucegi Mountains a tourist haven in summer. In late winter, however, locals prevailed amid a pleasant, albeit chilly, climate.

The day warmed as I wandered past old city walls to Saint Nicholas Church. Outside the black-spired Orthodox church, a bent woman hovering near the gate held close the coins I placed in her hand. Inside, my steps echoed through the deep gloom. A priest behind a table prayed amongst candles and stacks of books. I stared into the silence.

At home, Radu cooked dinner while I relaxed to the sounds of Romanian radio. He called me into the kitchen and handed over a mug and shot of ţuică–a potent homemade plum brandy. He described sights around Brașov, how he and his wife often took food and drink into the mountains for summertime picnics, and aspects of his life in Romania.

He paused when I asked about the drab unmarked barbed wire encampment I saw on my walk–with soldiers pacing the gates and armed guards in enclosed glass and steel towers watching passersby. "That was a base for the Brașov Securitate. The secret police," he said. "There we were taken to be questioned. Or worse." Then, he fell silent.

37

SORANA'S ROMANIA

In the morning, after Radu brought a present of buttered toast to my room, I walked the long way towards where he said I should catch a bus. In the window of one a sign read *Bran*. Minutes later, I rambled through the countryside.

"Is this Bran?" I asked suddenly of the young Romanian sitting next to me, forgetting she likely spoke no English.

"Yes," she said. "Wait. Next stop."

Soon after, a whitewashed castle rose into the sky, and we both stepped off the bus. When I started to take a wrong road, she offered to walk me to the castle entrance. From there, Sorana went her own way.

A guide appeared from the shadows. She spoke minimal English and my Romanian was non-existent, but we both knew a bit of Spanish. As we walked, the guide described the castle's history using Spanish and smatterings of English.

I had read that early tribes, which the Romans called Dacians, populated present-day Romania for centuries. As slaves imported by the Romans intermingled with the conquered tribes, a Latin-speaking people emerged. Nomadic

Huns, Avars, Slavs, and Bulgars swept through from the fourth to tenth centuries CE. In the thirteenth century invading Magyars, who settled neighboring present-day Hungary, took control of the Romanian province of Transylvania.

As my guide explained, the king of Hungary offered free land and incentives to Germans as a way to settle and help defend his sparsely populated Transylvanian flank. The five thousand Germans who accepted became known as Saxons. The Hungarian king later allowed Saxons to build a stone citadel at their expense, which led to Bran Castle's origins on the border of Transylvania and Wallachia as a toll station for German merchants.

Resistance to Ottoman expansion brought forth figures such as Vlad Țepeș, a ruling prince in the mid-1400s. Țepeș was known as Dracula, after his father Vlad Dracul, a knight of the Order of the Dragon. Țepeș hated the Turks, and was credited with killing tens of thousands. He later inspired novelist Bram Stoker's novel *Dracula*.

The guide looked around, and motioned me into a side room with trophies and furniture stacked high. She pulled hand-knitted woolen sweaters and hats from a trunk. She asked if I would I please buy one? She needed lei to feed her family, it seemed, so I bought slippers for my mother. Downstairs in the thawing gardens an older gentleman cleared winter debris. As we passed he rattled something off in Romanian before mentioning lei, and indicating I should give him some.

"Vait a moment!" called the woman at the exit who had taken my ticket. She led me into a side room where stacks of sweaters, mitts, and caps surrounded a slew of women waiting to sell wares. And a dozen deserted souvenir shops near the entrance sold, what else, but piles of woolen sweaters and hand-knitted goods.

Another bus continued to the village of Râșnov, where I wandered over a snow and ice covered country road through pine forest. Ancient stone steps near an unmarked courtyard climbed to the crumbling thirteenth-century ruins of Râşnov Castle. From the hill's crown, the Făgăraş Mountains stretched to the west; to the east snow-covered Carpathians reached into clouding skies.

The red-roofed village nestled below. Villagers awaited buses and hailed passing cars. One woman denounced a man pushing his bicycle. The woman's good-natured husband tried to convince them to forgive their differences. I followed expressions and hand movements and tone of voice for clues. As usual, much remained a mystery to me, though haggard faces on many passersby seemed indisputable evidence of poverty and desperation.

At six o'clock I met Sorana in Râşnov on the square beneath the clock tower. We climbed to the White Tower. On the next ridge remains of the Black Tower, another fourteenth-century guardhouse, stood charred and abandoned after its stores of gunpowder long ago blew the roof off.

After the Ottomans were defeated, Transylvania fell under Habsburg rule. The remainder of Romania later declared independence, and entered the First World War with the unsuccessful goal of taking back Transylvania. After the Second World War, the Soviet Union arranged the return of Transylvania to Romania. The next year, Romania's monarchy was abolished. Soviet troops withdrew, but communism still dominated. With the aid of the Securitate, the secret police, Nicolae Ceauşescu seized power.

Sorana and I found a local beer joint. She talked of life under the dictator. "Everyone had jobs and wages and a flat," she said, "though no one prospered. There were often no fruits or vegetables in the stores, yet no one starved. Life was difficult, but not impossible."

Only after forty-five years of communist rule and twenty-five under Ceauşescu's firm grip did the iron curtain finally fall. The spark ignited when Father László Tökés spoke against the dictator. The gathering grew into a demonstration. After police made their first arrests, the unrest spread to Bucharest. Army soldiers and the Securitate soon confronted huge crowds.

Tanks and armored cars cleared the squares, and the Securitate buried the dead in mass graves. The turning point came two days later when the army went over to the side of the demonstrators.

Robert Kaplan in *Balkan Ghosts* describes these days, ten years prior to my visit.

> No country during Eastern Europe's year of revolution in 1989 baffled the West as Romania did. Those first grainy scenes, broadcast with Romanian television's own antiquated equipment, revealed a physical world in which World War II had just ended, filled with soldiers in greatcoats and fanned helmets reminiscent of Russians at Stalingrad. The atmosphere was wintry, Slavic. Yet the people were dark, almost South American-looking; the language was a Latinate one, in some respects closer to the ancient Roman tongue than modern Italian or Spanish; and the violence, along with the religious rites that surrounded the burial of the victims, bore a theatricality and ghoulishness that revealed a people driven by the need to act out their passions in front of a mirror, over and over again.

Ceauşescu and his wife attempted to flee the nation, but were arrested, tried together by an anonymous court, condemned, and executed by firing squad.

"After the Revolution, life grew harder," Sorana said. A decade after the dictator's fall, disillusioned Romanians still floundered. "Many are impoverished," she said. "The number of thieves and thefts is growing. The desperation is deepening. Some survive on seventy dollars per month."

She talked of her struggles, on one hand fortunate to receive a college education—under Ceauşescu she would only have been permitted to complete high school—and on the other faced with bleak job prospects. A sixth grader at the time of the Revolution, she had known hunger. "It is a matter of opinion whether life was better before or after," she said, "but there is good and bad in both."

She would like to go abroad for work, but visas were hard to come by and Romanians were not openly welcomed by any nationality. Due to his Romanian citizenship, one friend had been denied even a transit visa to visit friends in Sweden, much less a working one. To open a business was nearly out of the question, for it required capital to begin any operation. More than that, signatures were needed from countless firemen, police, and authorities that all demanded a form of legal bribe.

"Even if I could open a shop," Sorana said, "the taxes would be so high they would overwhelm me. I have no money anyway."

She wouldn't mind continuing her studies at the university level, but though her school offered a scholarship, tuition was unaffordable. It was important that she learn several languages to break out, which was why she liked to practice English. Ten years after the Revolution, she still faced an uncertain future.

A fifty percent inflation rate affected even visitors like me. The exchange rate slipped daily, and I should have changed money as I needed to, not all at once as I did upon arrival. I knew Radu preferred hard currency, but I did not want to be stuck with thousands of lei worth less even than the Bulgarian leva I had carried to Bucharest.

The next morning, I met Sorana beneath Braşov's clock tower. At the Black Church, a fourteenth-century German Lutheran Gothic cathedral, whitewashed flying buttresses soared high above the main hall. Faded murals showed how city walls once fortified the medieval core, while the fortress and hillside towers kept watch. Through Şchei Gate, a wooded path led along the southeast wall to Cetatea Braşov, a sixteenth-century citadel built to defend Saxon merchants from invading Turks.

After lunch at the fortress we pondered wall and ceiling frescoes at Saint Nicholas Church. Under communist rule images of monarchs were banned, but the portrait of King

Carlos and his queen on horseback survived because clever townsfolk painted a moustache and beard on the queen and told visiting bureaucrats the scene depicted two unknown soldiers.

Martyrs of the revolution had ranged from students to elderly peasants. Soldiers shot most of them. Many lay in perfect white-tomb rows at the Heroes' Cemetery. Sorana's childhood schoolhouse stood nearby. She described how bullets flew when she sat at her sixth grade seat, sixth desk from the corner.

Inside an Orthodox church in old Şchei, a black cloth draped over a painting in the vestibule reminded churchgoers not to eat meat, milk, or eggs on Wednesdays or Fridays during Orthodox Easter. Sorana broke her fast when I bought her a hamburger-filled sandwich. Sometimes, hunger trumps ritual.

In the church cemetery, above ground tombs of white concrete marked with white crosses covered the hillside. At one, covered by pine needle boughs and dry flowers, lay her grandfather, who had passed three weeks before. Sorana did not like visiting alone, and said she welcomed the company. When her grandmother died two years prior, he bought his plot and had all the essentials etched into the cross except the date of his death. In a few days Sorana's father would clear away the wreaths. Next spring, her family would plant flowers atop the graves.

Grassy slopes led towards forested hills and mountaintops. Red roofs of the village nestled below. A thin wisp of smoke curled upward near the colorful spire of the church. A dog barked and the gentle peal of playing children echoed in the distance. These sounds soon faded, leaving a silent stillness.

When two elderly mourners in black approached, we continued into the Carpathian foothills. Birds sang though snow still clung to hillsides and meltwater rivulets ran along the muddy country road. Winter sun gleamed through oak and maple silhouettes. Overhead towered cliffs of white rock called Solomon's Stones. Sorana told of the legend which held that a Roman soldier, pursued into the wilds by enemies, leapt from one crag to another to avoid capture. He tumbled into a ravine, and later the stones were named after him.

Near a cluster of nineteenth-century homes we sat upon a wooden bench to watch three girls play a game. We were in no hurry, content to enjoy the afternoon. I found both strength and serenity with Sorana. She urged me to stay on longer, and I considered this. Her slender physique and shoulder-length brunette hair complemented wide brown eyes which hinted of dreams and longings that might never be sated. There was a sadness about her, and also a comfort in her company. I found myself tempted to linger.

In evening hours we searched for her friends in a crowded smoke-filled bar. After a round of Bergenbiers we found another spot with no available tables, and then settled into a third. Tripe soup, frying sausage, peasant's hog soup, and mititei–minced meat rolls–filled the menu along with cow soup, cock schnitzel, sheep pastrami, and moss hog grilled. There were also items called slack time and chop outlaw frying. I ordered the chop outlaw frying, hoping it resembled the fried pork chops my grandmother made.

"It's over," said the disinterested waitress, Romanian for no more. I ordered green beans and potatoes, also as my grandmother made.

After I paid the bill, we stood in frigid night air. On our lengthy daytime walks she complained once or twice of the silence that interrupted our conversations. I explained them away as my having spent a year alone in multiple countries with minimal English spoken. What I did not say was that getting too emotionally close to someone made parting unbearable, especially when my rucksack got tossed into a new hotel every few nights. In pushing my feelings deep, heartfelt words came reluctantly, for I knew the road waited and I would soon be back upon it.

Yet, Sorana said she understood the freedom I coveted. It allowed me to come into town, sightsee, meet new people, do as I wished, go where I wanted—and leave when I chose. She moaned that she had to stay in Braşov, unable to go as she pleased. That was a part of her infatuation with me; she longed for the carefree life I symbolized, which she might never know.

As the hour neared midnight the time came to say good-bye. She presented a cassette tape of Romanian music she had compiled, and a small bag of chocolates as a gift from her mother.

She dragged out the good-bye, but finally I was firm. I promised to write, and said good-night. As I watched her walk away I recalled reading that when people are unhappy they turn mean, and when content they are kind. Spending long hours with Sorana, and buying her meals and treats with no expectation of anything in return, had taken a chip out of my armor. I would miss her. And, I thought, maybe I am even happy.

38

SIGHIŞOARA

In the morning, after Radu brought coffee and buttered toast with cheese, I told him my plans. He shook my hand, and promptly peddled his bicycle to the train station to find a new tenant. I stopped for a final cheese salad sandwich before buying a bus ticket from a curbside kiosk. On the number four, passengers punched their tickets in a contraption on the wall, unlike in most countries where the conductor did so. As I studied the process a man approached. He seemed official so I handed him my ticket. He glared at me.

"You must punch it," he said. As I stood up, he flung a barrage of questions. "Who are you? Where are you from? Do you speak English? Let me see your documents!"

Another man arose and spoke to him in rapid Romanian. The first said nothing. At the next stop both stepped off. As they dropped from sight my accoster still stood silent upon the sidewalk while the second man gestured. Who were these men? Such were the mysteries of travel.

The train rolled through fields brown and flat. Distant hazy mountains brooded beneath gray sky. Smoke clung to the air from small grass fires and burning cornstalks that fertilized fallow fields for spring plantings. Whitewashed steeples peeked above red roofed villages nestled in hidden valleys.

Outside the Sighişoara train station a young woman asked if I needed a room. "Ten dollars with breakfast," she said, "in the old part of town." Her father, John, rode in the passenger seat of her car. Patronella drove us into the narrow medieval hillside streets. In their kitchen her mother, Maria, offered tea and asked questions. As Patronella made up my room her eighty-year-old grandmother smiled, laughed, tousled my hair, and pinched my cheeks. She spoke to me in Romanian as though I understood every word.

On my way out for a walk, they invited me to sit down. Before I could respond, Maria ladled omelet soup with greens and fried eggs and milky broth into a bowl. Salad, sausage with hot mustard, fries, and sweet pickles came next. Afterward they handed me a goblet of homemade wine. Maria mentioned that the grandmother craved something sweet, so I darted upstairs and brought down the last of Sorana's chocolates. Maria scurried upstairs to give one to Patronella's eighteen-year-old sister, Marionella.

After dinner I strolled among mammoth churches and baroque houses lining cobblestone streets. The brisk wind blew. A wooden tunnel from the 1640s sheltered a long uphill flight of steps. Atop the hillside, I wandered through an old graveyard near the church. The town, both old and new quarters, surrounded the promontory. Untouched and awaiting exploration, this extraordinary medieval village in the heart of Romania was the European town I had long envisioned.

Awake at five thirty, a sumptuous breakfast was served. In addition to hot tea, there was sausage with mustard, home baked bread with a cheesy substance, and sweet homemade jam. Eggs appeared, fried in boiling oil, and aubergine–an old world purple eggplant-like fruit. After the meal we stepped into the chill dawn of morning to pick up Patronella's friends,

Maria and Harold, who needed a ride to visit the German Consulate at Sibiu.

Patronella had been driving a year, but at age twenty-two, still took curves too fast and overtook horse-drawn carriages too close. Her Dacia, the ubiquitous national car of Romania, was relatively new yet so cheaply made it felt like the famously austere Serbian Yugo. Coiled springs in the seat jabbed my back. Neither the speedometer or odometer worked. Passenger side doors could only be opened from the inside. The driver seat was permanently raked backward at such an angle that Patronella required a huge fluffy pillow to not be lying horizontally. Harold sat behind her with his legs spread wide and the seat between them. I wondered what else the clunker lacked.

A ball of orange to the east rose above low-lying hills, and then disappeared behind scuttling clouds of midnight blue. Frost covered last year's brown hay pastures and withered corn stalks, and white chimney smoke hung over the villages. After nearly an hour Patronella pulled to the roadside. Maria and Harold spoke no English, but the occasional Romanian word similar to Italian or Spanish was often enough for me to grasp the essence of a situation. I knew that something was wrong.

"She has forgotten her papers!" cried Patronella.

They debated amongst themselves before turning the car around. We returned to Sighișoara to find the documents, and by mid-morning reached Sibiu. Patronella asked several people the location of the consulate. When we tackled a traffic circle she panicked, for she had never driven in a city before. As we hurtled towards oncoming traffic she asked if I would drive, but it was too late. She cut a car off and missed the hood by inches, but somehow threaded her way through without misfortune.

At the consulate a mob massed at the entrance. Many Romanians of Saxon descent wishing to visit their German homeland also wanted to stay for the opportunities Germany offered. It was difficult for any Romanian to secure a visa. All visitors needed a reference and letter of recommendation, and as a German, Harold was Maria's. A fixer standing nearby offered to arrange their documents for them.

Once the fixer finished and the papers were submitted, we had to wait so walked the cobblestone streets straying in random directions. Something seemed unsatisfactory with each eatery, though it was never clear what. We at last settled on a place frequented by Gypsy children seeking handouts, which served mititei, fries, and bread.

Afterward we returned to the consulate, where Maria and Harold were told they must return at three in the morning, take a number, and wait through early morning hours to get inside. At one in the afternoon a crowd of people still stood outside, remainders of those who had arrived at three the morning previous.

On the return we paused in a remote village to visit Maria's sister. At the second-hand shop where she worked, I bought a German leather jacket for six dollars. We continued to another village, well off the beaten path. Patronella located a rusty old-fashioned key, and we climbed via wood-covered tunnel to a massive fourteenth-century walled church atop the hill. Patronella turned the key in the heavy door.

In earlier days, when enemies invaded, villagers sequestered themselves inside for protection from the siege ahead. Nearby stood remains of an old chapel, faded wall paintings still visible, in which villagers congregated while building the main church. But for a few wires and one partially paved road, the surrounding village looked as it did five hundred years before. Wooden carts pulled by horses and bullocks transported residents. Smoke curled upward. Cocks crowed and dogs barked. Not a single auto was visible anywhere. Here, I thought, is the essence of old Romania.

On my last night in Sighișoara, at a bar advertising beers for three thousand lei, a young couple mistook me as German. "We are pleased to make your friendship," Anka said. She was in law school and planned to become a prosecutor. Anka lamented the poor state of the economy and challenges of survival. Andre knew minimal English, but wanted my address. After I bought the first round they switched to vodka. Andre asked me to buy more. "Because I am your friend," he said. I did, but went my own way when they headed to a disco.

Historically, Hindus in India resigned themselves to the poverty daily surrounding them. Modern Romanians saw the prosperity their western cousins enjoyed and never hesitated to point out disparity. Perhaps resentful, many seemed to feel entitled. Yet when a Romanian went on hunger strike—so the cruel joke went—no one noticed. After the revolution ended, the world no longer watched.

Overnight, snow covered the fields and hilltops in a thin veneer of white. When I awoke, Maria served homemade cheese, pig fat, aubergine, and plenty of bread.

"Is poor man's breakfast," she said.

She showed me pictures. Each Christmas, the family butchered a pig and used every part throughout the year. In the cellar too were four casks of homemade wine made by John. Maria once worked in a textiles factory hunched over a sewing machine, until illness struck. From a drawer she produced a walnut-sized mass they took from one of her organs.

I bid her good-bye and made my way to the train station, where I bought a ticket to Cluj-Napoca. The sky was raw, the air bitter. Snowflakes fluttered from a steely sky onto the frozen tracks as I arrived.

My destination was Budapest, but getting there no simple matter. One could not purchase tickets at the train station, only at the main office. I caught a trolleybus to downtown. A clothing store stood where the office should have been. I found the relocated office uptown. With only enough lei in hand to make Püspökladány, I would need to exchange currency somewhere inside Hungary and buy an onward ticket once over the border. At least I had passage out of Romania.

Streets of Cluj-Napoca brimmed with shapely twenty-year-old university co-eds. A massive Orthodox church loomed near the city center. Inside, devout Christians crossed themselves three times, kissed a stone at the center, and prayed at the fore or from the side. I sat in silent contemplation of the simplicity of home, so far away. When on the road where no one speaks your language, the simple act of purchasing an international train ticket can prove exhausting.

I filled my remaining hours at a 24-hour bar adjacent to the train station by drinking cheap beer and editing hand-scrawled half-written stories. There was little else to do. The dark-clothed men peered at me through smoke-filled haze, hard faces and leathered hands all.

Fresh snow lay on the asphalt, and probing headlights of a passing Dacia illuminated more falling from dark skies. Even while sitting by the struggling heater inside the waiting room, my feet felt encased in blocks of ice. How long ago the heat of south India seemed, for which my thin clothes were far more appropriate. I put my cold damp socks on the heater to dry, and waited as the clock ticked slowly towards midnight.

39

AH, BUDAPEST

I waited on the platform until I could bear the cold no longer, and then ducked into the station to warm my clumsy hands near a heater upon which a Gypsy lad slept. In the second-class waiting room, snoring Romanians awaited their trains. Based on the prevailing odors many were in need of baths. Some wore homespun, and all seemed dressed in whatever motley collection of clothing they could muster. Most carried little baggage though a few had sacks at their feet filled with handfuls of goods. When a whistle blasted I dashed to the platform, where my idling train sat.

When we reached Oradea on the Romanian border three hours later, someone switched on the blinding overhead light. The two young women in my compartment had only been able to purchase tickets this far. Though authorities had told one she could obtain onward passage from Oradea, the conductor seemed reluctant. They were not sure what to do. When the conductor came again they were able to secure seats. Both beamed with relief. I again regretted I only had enough lei to buy a ticket as far as Püspökladány.

When we continued into Hungary, I slept hard. Hungary marks a transition from the Balkans to Central Europe. The Danube River separates Hungary's eastern plains, the Nagyalföld, from the western Dunántúl. Celts farmed the plains for centuries, until conquered by the Romans. Then Huns led by Attila swept through. Tribes of the Magyar followed. In the year 1000, Hungary's first king was crowned. Medieval Hungary controlled present-day Transylvania and Slovakia, but the powerful kingdom still succumbed to Ottoman rule. After the Turks were expelled, the Habsburg Dynasty of Austria filled the void. A deal was later struck that created an Austro-Hungarian monarchy, which endured until the First World War.

As first light spread over the Great Plain, farmlands and occasional villages stretched evenly to the horizon. Part of me hoped we had passed Püspökladány so I could be that much closer to Budapest. Another part wondered what would happen if we had. While contemplating this, the conductor entered. He demanded my ticket. His creased brow and stern tone meant only one thing: we had passed Püspökladány.

Minutes later I stood in a deserted station as the train pulled away with a blast of the whistle. The station had no facility for changing cash, and I was still a hundred miles outside Budapest. I shouldered my worn bag with icy fingers, and walked towards town. At a small open air market merchants set out apples, bananas, pears, breads, pastries, and vegetables. I wondered how long I would go hungry. At a kiosk I showed the young woman a dollar bill. She shook her head, but pointed. Fifty meters farther along, I laughed. Near an automatic teller machine stood a bank and change booth, both open in a few hours. I returned to the train station with five thousand Hungarian forint in my slowly warming hands, enough for a ticket to Budapest.

At Budapest, an information office booked my room in the nine-bed hostel dorm, and even drove me to the doorstep for free. The hot shower was a godsend and the first since Veliko Târnovo. I attempted to launder my clothes, but the facility was out of soap so I walked instead to the city's core. Upscale shops resided within distinguished stone buildings. After coffee and a croissant I wandered to the great curve of the Danube. Trees, benches, and twittering birds lined the river's edge. The architecture, well-dressed denizens, window displays, and cultured atmosphere suggested prosperity.

Budapest's Romanian roots are evidenced by a surviving aqueduct and amphitheaters north of the Óbuda district. Following Turkish and Habsburg occupation the residential community of Buda merged with Óbuda and the industrial sector of Pest to form Pest-Buda. At some point the name reversed itself and Budapest, more romantic than Warsaw and more cosmopolitan than Prague, became known as the "first city" of Eastern Europe.

On the Buda side, history abounds. Wooden buildings and cafes lined cobblestone streets. Tour groups crowded thirteenth-century Matthias Church. From within each cluster a loud German, Italian, or on occasion English voice explained the cathedral's history, richly painted ceilings, and exquisite artwork. Sometimes a tour leader clapped at someone in the group to get his or her attention despite the multilingual *Silence please in this sacred shrine of Hungary* signs posted throughout.

A handful of cut rate opera seats remained, so I purchased one for the evening's performance. Gilded ceilings and plush carpets adorned the gold and brass lobby and opera hall. The orchestra played and curtain fell to reveal a glamorous medieval Hungarian set. Two young people fell in love. An older, less attractive suitor also had his eye on the damsel. The older suitor offered flowers and his affections. When the lass refused, commotion ensued.

That night the village men gathered and the young lover got his rival drunk. The older suitor passed out, so the men carried him to the home of the young girl where he caused trouble for her parents. As morning broke the whole troupe poured onto the stage, including the young man who disarmed the drunkard, much to the delight of the girl's father who welcomed the young man with open arms. Not a word was spoken; all music, dance, and movement.

Hostels, I had learned, can be lonely respites. The jovial groups, peals of laughter, and closeness of couples accentuate the loneliness of a long journey. I preferred the solitude of single hotel rooms, but for the sake of economy, made an exception in Budapest.

As I sat on my bunk, wondering what to do with my evening, into the dorm room walked a slim, stunning beauty. I looked at Patrick, my new Irish friend, in mild astonishment. I had never stayed in a unisex dorm room before. On occasion hostels did provide unexpected opportunity, I thought.

Elissa was assigned the bunk above mine, placed her belongings there, and left. Later, as I was getting ready to go somewhere and do something, she returned.

"Want to get some pizza?" she asked.

"Sure," I said. "I'll go."

Across the street at a quiet bistro we chatted over brews. From Sacramento, a lifelong gymnast and member of a judging committee, she worked at a bar on weekends. She was part Mexican which explained her brunette hair and deep, dark eyes. Rather than waste money taking odd classes towards no degree, she dropped out of college but was thinking about law school. She decided to take two months to see Europe and now was here, loving Budapest and everywhere else. Two hours before I met her she had bought a ticket to Prague, having decided it was time to move on.

After dinner we visited the 24-hour bar below our room. In my naïveté I had never heard of such a thing at a hostel, but there it was. Wine was cheap—three dollars a bottle for Hungarian red. The pool table was uneven and the felt worn through; the cue stick had no chalk or tip, just a blunt wooden end. After the first bottle I bought a second. An Estonian, Tania, joined in a few games, but insisted in her matter-of-fact manner that we play by British rules. If I scratched, she got two shots. Once someone called the 8-ball, all successive shots on the eight must be towards that same pocket.

Tania soon moved on and Patrick joined us. He had left rural Ireland and ended up in Italy for a year, working at a horse farm. Everyone had a story. Elissa and I switched back to beer, putting them away easily, smoking cigarettes, and playing some combination of American and British billiards with a bowed wooden stick.

Around four in the morning Patrick went to bed, but Elissa and I had clicked. Some pheromone-induced attraction coupled with Eastern European romanticism led in directions unimagined eight hours earlier. In early morning hours in the heart of Budapest we were two sloppy lovers, impassioned and carefree.

The hostel required check out by nine or payment for another day. At eight a gaggle of bustling co-eds entered the room and organized their belongings. We were in a bunk assigned to one of them, so we dragged ourselves with our two hours of sleep into the morning. I felt dreadful about disturbing Patrick and the odd English bloke during wee hours of the morning, though neither seemed to have noticed. Elissa needed to pack, but our hangovers and lack of sleep slowed us down.

Elissa and I found a fabulous coffee and pastry shop downtown across from the Opera House. We sat a while, smoking unfiltered Hungarian cigarettes and eyeing the extravagant décor. Brass fixtures and luxuriant wallpaper adorned the walls; attractive chairs surrounded elegantly decorated tables. Creamy cappuccinos and thick slices of chocolate cake brought me slowly around, and the morning seemed not quite so murky.

The night prior we talked about finding this coffee shop. This morning she asked what I was doing today, and I said it might be fun for us to venture downtown before she caught her train to Prague. She breathed an odd sigh, or so it seemed, but said okay. She seemed somewhat distant, or perhaps sleep deprived and hung over. It was hard to say.

We checked our email at an Internet café. News from home was otherworldly, like watching a movie. I imagined all the people and events, but it was as though they were not part of my life, only a sequence of events playing in some cinema. People were moving forward with their lives regardless of whatever adventure I might be living out.

Elissa didn't feel well and returned to the hostel. I meandered through grassy parks and across medieval squares, burning away my energy and giving my mind time to work. After returning to the hostel I talked with two Americans who just moved into the room. They studied at Edinburgh, Scotland, and had two weeks to travel Europe. I hadn't heard unbroken English or seen a tourist since Istanbul, nearly a month ago, and now in Budapest they were everywhere.

Elissa found me again. We walked outside and embraced. What I perceived as a distance between us had melted away. It seemed she had been hung over after all. I looked into her deep, dark eyes as we said our good-byes. Then, she was off to Prague.

After so much walking I hoped for sleep, but in the hostel bar a band's hardcore music pounded my room despite the sign at reception reading *Quiet Please after 10pm*. I gave up on sleep and wandered downstairs to the noisy bar. The lead singer, seemingly influenced by MTV, wore an unbuttoned leather shirt and long, stringy hair.

The past few nights a Hungarian kid frequenting the place had been hunting an English-speaking girlfriend. He was young, comical, mostly harmless, and overeager. When a young woman sat behind us he asked me to help with his English if he had a chance to talk with her.

He wrote her a note: *What would you say if I told you I love you? Just a humor from a silly Hungarian boy.*

He showed me her reply: *Love is a strong word. And besides my boyfriend is sitting just to my left. I'm flattered. Mindy from Detroit.*

"Does she like me?" he asked.

"She has a boyfriend she probably likes a lot," I explained. "She might have liked you too, but she has this boyfriend."

"So she likes me?"

"Sure."

He wrote me a note: *What can I do to get a girlfriend on this night? I do not want to be lonely. Do you know which rooms are staying nice girls?*

I wrote back: *There's not much to choose from here. You could knock on all the doors and see who answers. There are all guys in my room now.*

It was true. There was just Patrick, the odd Brit, and me. Finally the band packed up. No more *Guns n' Roses* covers. In the room I read a little, and when the Brit closed his eyes I switched the light off.

"Turn that back on," the Brit commanded for no apparent reason.

Early in the morning the light was still on, though the Brit slept. And Patrick was still missing. The note from reception hanging on our door asked that he speak to the manager. The gear on his bed hadn't budged in two days. No one knew where he was. Ah, Budapest, I thought.

40

HOME OF THE HABSBURGS

I pulled my rucksack on–literally falling apart at the seams though I sewed it together in Bulgaria–and debated my next move. Prices in Budapest were higher than I feared, or perhaps I just spent more than I intended. Either way, my dwindling cash heightened the need to find an affordable flight off the continent. I checked the travel agencies, but all flights from Paris to New York were full. One agent suggested I visit the Air France office.

"Yes," the Air France agent confirmed, "all flights are booked until the sixteenth, though one seat is available for twelve hundred dollars. There is also a flight today for New York, departing Budapest, for three hundred dollars."

"And if I buy the three hundred-dollar ticket but don't use the Budapest to Paris portion?" I asked.

"Then they will cancel the Paris to New York segment," she replied.

With no feasible option on hand I bought chocolates, a newspaper, Danish pastries, and a loaf of bread before boarding a train bound for Bratislava, the capital of Slovakia.

With no Hungarian forint left, but in possession of a few Slovak crowns, the day looked promising. Shortly after the rims hit the rails we rounded the Danube Bend, passed through the Carpathians, and followed the river north. We soon hummed over plains of southern Slovakia. After an hour the landscape turned urban.

"Bratislava?" I called to a man. With all signage in Slovak, it was hard to know.

"Áno," he replied. *Yes.*

I hopped off to find the YMCA, a supposed ten-minute downhill walk. I looked around but saw only flat ground around the small, nearly abandoned station. A man on the platform convinced me that one of the street trams would take me to the main station, Bratislava hlavná stanica. To get a ticket I must pump coins into a box on the sidewalk. I had only small denomination bills, and the station's sole employee refused to make change. I pondered the coin-hungry box. When the number three tram arrived, I boarded without a ticket to see what happened. Nothing did, and I bounced jubilant into Bratislava hlavná stanica.

I found the YMCA that, against the odds, still existed. I spotted an employee.

"Do you have any rooms? Beds?" I asked.

"Hotel?" the woman responded. "No. Finish. Over."

Back at the main train station, I filled my water bottle in the WC and ate a fat hot dog while pondering my options. Sounds of cities flipping through the overhead split-flap drew my attention. I swallowed the last of my hot dog and minutes later found myself aboard a full train racing across the Austrian countryside towards Vienna.

Inside the Viennese train station bathroom, I changed into long underwear for free, courtesy of the kindly cleaning lady, and at the kiosk exchanged a twenty dollar bill. The man kept sixty schillings–almost five dollars. I left my bag in a locker for another thirty schillings. I recalled that Elissa had planned five days in Vienna but had to leave after two because her daily budget, nearly twice mine, couldn't handle the expense.

In the Viennese train station waiting room, two snoring drunks sitting beside me reeked of urine. Another one stumbling in caused a ruckus. A homeless woman gazed upon me with empty eyes. I watched groups of backpack-wearing school kids stream to and from their trains. I felt a tinge of envy. It seemed so easy for them. Escorts told them what to do and where to go. Mother and father likely provided all the money they needed.

I wandered with my few schillings through cold damp streets lettered in Germanic script. At last I found the two-hundred-bed dormitory.

"I'm sorry," said the man behind the glass. "We are all booked up."

I found another warm, inviting hostel down the road, but that too was full. There was a third I could not find, which no one could direct me to. The handful of unaffordable high-end downtown hotels cost hundreds if not thousands of schillings.

The night air grew bitter. I huddled inside the other train station on the west side of town. Once the last train of the night left, the station closed until morning. I sat inside, worried. I had grown weary of such nights in strange cities without any shelter. Such was the case when I was stranded overnight in downtown Baltimore, curled up on the street in Belfast at twenty degrees, marooned at the bus station on the Mexican coast, asleep on the concrete bus station floor in rural India, and frozen in the frigid train station at Skopje.

At one in the morning a uniformed guard entered the station and barked at me and another bum who had wandered in. Back in the street, worry turned to fear. Not one hostel, restaurant, or café was open. With the right gear I might have walked all night, but with threadbare clothes and my frame so wiry after months on the road, I wondered how long I could stay on my feet. My teeth chattered. With nowhere to turn, I headed down the least windy street.

A beacon of light appeared amongst the closed shops. Inside, Austrians drank beers and ate fast food. Music played and images flickered on a muted television. I found a table and ordered a two-dollar coffee. The cheapest meal, a thin piece of meat on small dry roll, cost three dollars. A hot dog was more.

If I paced myself I might last the night, I thought. That is, if they stayed open and didn't kick me out. Despite frequent glances from the two staff, I held my ground. Outside, awnings shook in the wind. I preferred not to spend all night in the restaurant, particularly since they overcharged on every item I ordered, but it was their prices or the cold. The hours dragged. After a long spell I ordered the next cheapest item I could find.

As pale light on the building opposite slowly brightened, a weightiness welled behind my eyes. Through teary eyes I saw the value of coming to Eastern Europe on the heels of Asia. In India I was among the richest of men. In Austria, I was one of the poorest. My remaining funds would get me home, if I lived until then like a pauper. To touch both extremes with the whole of my heart in the span of months was to know a little of life. Hours before, I feared for my safety. Now, my feet were frozen but my core was intact. I was hungry, but not starving. Not young, but not old. Not wise or completely ignorant. Not rich, but not yet broke. Alone, but not lonely.

Daylight filled the empty streets. The staff, happy to see me go, were the only others I saw awake at six on Sunday morning in Vienna. The wind sliced through the streets and drippy drizzle fell from gray skies, yet my mind ignored every discomfort as I walked amidst the architecturally extraordinary home of the Habsburgs. I staggered through the streets, overwhelmed by the immensity.

The dynasty's origins trace to a Swiss fortress built in 1020 by a count who named the edifice Habsburg Castle. The count's seventh generation descendant moved the family to Austria, which they ruled for the next six centuries. They were as influential as the Ottomans, who also controlled swaths of Europe from the thirteenth century onward. So grand was the Habsburg Empire that its demise was the second of four events that redrew maps and shaped twentieth-century Europe. The first had been the collapse of the Ottoman Empire, which led to the splintering of the Balkans. The rise and fall of the

Habsburgs led directly to the First World War. Both empires helped sow the seeds for the Second World War.

During the Habsburgs' centuries-long reign, they built one of the most stunning cities on earth. Few others could match Vienna's unparalleled grandeur. I wandered for miles through the drizzle, subsisting on the prior night's bread, while finding my way over cobblestone streets of the old districts. Around every corner, on every block, a visual masterpiece awaited savoring.

A great tolling interrupted my awe. The tremendous bells of St. Stephen's Cathedral pealed unlike any I had ever heard. Hindus ring bells when they pass a shrine, "to wake the gods," as one Hindu explained to me. The steeple atop St. Stephen's and all cathedrals proclaim the glory of God and remind the pious of His greatness. Gaping at the massive church as bells echoed through the magnificent city, I could almost believe He listened.

41

SLOVAK PROLE

I needed a haircut, shower, shave, clean clothes, and sleep. My socks were disintegrating, my clothes reeked, and my right boot was falling apart. My return to Bratislava fortunately lifted my spirits. Wood-frame homes and shops lined the cosmopolitan center's cobblestone streets amidst a smattering of churches and parks. Only six years old, Slovakia was Europe's youngest country and the world's third newest, yet castles and Saxon-founded thirteenth-century medieval towns dotted the countryside.

History credits geographer Isaiah Bowman with delineation of the nations that arose from ruins of the First World War. Some newborns such as Poland and Hungary represented a single ethnic identity. In other cases, Bowman lumped lesser-sized populations together because he believed small countries lacked the resources to oppose larger ones seeking expansion. Such was the case with Slovakia. Slovak intellectuals had courted the Czechs, also dominated by the Austrians, with the idea of a single entity. Thus, the territories of Moravia, Ruthenia, Bohemia, and Slovakia united as Czechoslovakia.

In time, urbane Czechs alienated the rural Slovaks, so Slovakia declared autonomy. Following the Second World War, a second Czechoslovakia arose. Slovak nationalism again revived, however, and the federation peacefully dissolved six years before my visit. Slovakia and the Czech Republic seemed destined to remain separate countries.

While asleep in a Bratislava train station waiting room lounge chair, armed guards woke travelers and asked for passports. They kicked some out, including the man next to me. I slept hard on the train, until at daybreak a conductor speaking rapid Slovak entered the compartment. It took time to realize we had passed my intended stop, Košice. He demanded I pay the fare to Trebišov, the next stop, in addition to a fine.

In Košice at last, the hostel I sought no longer existed. At another place, I took a room. A corner café served Turkish coffee with segedínsky guláš—pork, sauerkraut, and sauce—plus a side of white bread. Raindrops drizzled down from gray skies. Colorful shops lined wide cobblestone streets in the shadow of St. Elisabeth Cathedral. I regained elements of my humanity: a hot shower, new socks, razors, a fresh pen.

During the evening in my room I sewed my rucksack together, dined on brown bread, and drank Steiger beers as my Aunt Fay's husband Steve Marko might have done. He and Fay inspired my travels across Nepal, Tibet, India, and Eastern Europe. Slovakia, in fact, was where Steve's ancestors originated. His paternal grandparents lived in Nitra, which I passed not long after leaving Bratislava. His maternal grandparents derived from Košice and lived in the city at a time when Slovaks still fell under Hungarian domination. In the early 1900s, they immigrated to Pennsylvania.

I raised a Steiger in his honor. Had I never known him, I would not have sat in Košice with a rucksack so road-weary it needed sewing. Thanks to Fay and Steve, my rucksack and I would not spend our lives yearning for the adventure it seemed we had been born for.

Chirping birds and cool underlying winds lent a touch of

early spring to the morning. After an easy ride to Prešov, dark skies to the west turned angry. I sat in the hollow silence of St. Nicholas Cathedral before ducking inside a store to buy beer, brown bread, and white cheese. The beers, at ten crowns, were cheaper than any food and filled the stomach almost as well. Rains fell and the air turned crisp as I hurried to my hotel in the ex-communist proletariat part of town.

Lights flicked on and off in the concrete high-rises beyond my window. Music filtered upward from the bar below. Tourist centers were for shops and restaurants, but Prešov was a working town. For a time, I too was a Slovak prole.

Thoughts of Fay and Steve reminded me of my impending return home. Anxiety about reuniting with Tamara enhanced my reluctance. I worried that upon my arrival, we would fall into our old patterns. I felt an urgency to detail my concerns about our past, and explain what I wanted for any future union. With such thoughts in mind, I wrote her a long letter. As I feared and perhaps expected, she responded in fury.

An outbound bus left for Plaveč at quarter before six, from where a connection might depart to Muszyna, in Poland. Sometimes departures left early, so by the appointed time I knew there was no bus for me. I wondered whether the *informacie* officer gave me the wrong information or if I misheard him, and either way wished I were still sleeping as blue-gray light filled the morning sky.

A man trying to help made a *choo-choo* sound and pointed. It seemed a train departed for Kraków in half an hour. The fare ran six hundred crowns. I had one hundred forty-nine on me, but for one hundred forty-seven could make Nowy Sącz, beyond the border, then exchange dollars for Polish zloty and purchase an onward ticket.

Sun burst through morning cloud and filthy windows as the express rattled northward. At Plaveč, the custom agents and police checked my passport but let me cross. When the conductor came through and said I must get off at Muszyna, I could not fathom why.

"Is this Muszyna?" asked a blonde Slovak who poked her head out of the neighboring compartment. I had no idea, so she made inquiries and translated what she learned. "This is Muszyna," she said, "but train bad today. Only today."

She asked directions as we scurried around the corner to a waiting bus. We passed villages along back roads of idyllic, unspoiled southeast Poland. Despite her limited English we discussed her homeland and mine. After a time I dozed, and when she woke me we dashed off to another train. A long-legged blonde joined us in our compartment. At Nowy Sącz, both women agreed I should find the conductor to purchase an onward ticket. But, I had no Polish zloty, no way to get any on the train, and not enough time to dart into the station before departure.

The abundance in the Polish language of unpronounceable words nine and ten letters long with a single vowel among them made orienting the train station a challenge. I facetiously wondered whether Poland used all its vowels by the twelfth century and had no more to go around.

In Kraków at last, young women wearing short skirts and intoxicating perfumes filled the streets. The hotel had no more beds. Every accommodation in Eastern Europe seemed full, closed, or overpriced. I backtracked and lost my way but spotted a sign that read HOTEL, which seemingly meant something in Polish other than a place to spend the night, for I could find no accommodation anywhere nearby.

Lights of Kraków alit as sun set behind Wawel Castle. Colin the Canadian and Demian the Irishman joined me in the eight-bed dorm that I eventually found. We drank beers in a dark place frequented by a few young Poles. Three hulking men in black guarded the tiny, filthy bathroom located off an outside courtyard. On the way back to the hostel we got lost and just made curfew.

During the night, American and NATO forces bombed

Serbia, as they had threatened since I reached Turkey. Demian talked of indiscriminate Serbian snipers shooting civilians and Europe's embargo against Bosnia, though, "Serbia is armed to the teeth and Bosnians have nothing," as he explained.

"Europe doesn't want a Muslim state on the continent," Demian claimed, "just as Europe didn't want the Jews." This is why, in his opinion, the European powers had done nothing against Christian Serbians or stopped extermination of Islamic Bosnians. The United States helped, to its credit, by dropping supplies at night with pinpoint accuracy. Europe's fascist leanings, as the Irishman saw it, meant white Protestant Catholics but no Jews, Gypsies, Romanians, or any other ethnic minorities were welcome on the continent. "All of Europe opposed the Jews, but only Germany did anything about it," he theorized.

Certainly, Adolf Hitler did rally around racism and anti-Semitism, believing Germanic peoples to be the purest form of Aryan and in his definition the "master" human race. The first concentration camps primarily held political prisoners. Before long, the Soviets had moved hundreds of thousands of non-political Poles to labor camps. German camps quadrupled to over three hundred and imprisoned slave laborers, Jews, criminals, homosexuals, Gypsies, and the mentally ill. In Hungary, the fascists that Hitler put into power deported hundreds of thousands of Hungarian Jews to Polish extermination camps. Likewise, hundreds of thousands of Czechoslovakians were murdered in Nazi death camps. The Jews of Kraków were moved into a walled ghetto, and then sent to Auschwitz and Płaszów. The system that began as a political tool culminated in mass genocide.

Colin and I found a bus for the ride through southern Poland's rolling countryside. We stopped at Auschwitz, where tons of human hair, toothbrushes, shoes, and other human detritus filled some of the otherwise empty cellblocks. I was fortunate to have befriended Colin the night prior, for Auschwitz is a place more easily coped with in good company. Words do little justice for such a place. After Auschwitz, sightseeing seemed superfluous.

After Hitler invaded the Soviet Union towards the close of the Second World War, the tide turned against Nazi Germany. Soviet counter attacks comprised the largest land battles in history. When the Soviets liberated Poland and Hungary, the war ended. Poland contributed the highest number of troops to the Allied effort after the Soviets, Brits, and Americans. Poland also lost nearly one fifth of its citizenry–over six million–half of whom were Jewish.

Similar to Greek historian Herodotus' observation about the Persian Wars millennia before, the Second World War was the second act in a two-part drama. The Second World War was also the third of four momentous events–after the rise and fall of the Ottoman Empire and the Habsburg Empire–that altered maps and reshaped twentieth-century Europe.

We returned late to the hostel. After a somber room-picnic of cheese, ham, beer, and bread, we bought tall black cans of bitter beer, *piwo*, and distracted ourselves by watching young Poles flow around Rynek Główny, the largest medieval square in Europe.

The next morning Colin and I explored Wawel Castle, built in the thirteenth century at the behest of Casimir III. Plaster heads on the receiving room ceiling struck us as odd and inexplicable. We studied leather walls in the chapel and pondered the haunting sounds of a lone lute player. Just south lay Kazimierz, the old Jewish suburb. Once numbering seventy thousand Jews, most were exterminated at the Płaszów concentration camp. Perhaps one hundred Jews remained. This is the story depicted in the film *Schindler's List*.

Rain clouds moved in, so we paused for coffee at a café before returning to Rynek Główny. Young Poles strolled about, listened to live music, and chatted in beer gardens. Palaces, churches, and historical townhouses surrounded the thirteenth-century square. We flowed with the throngs.

As evening fell, pyrotechnic explosions marked the start of

an avant-garde performance. Much Polish art reflects Poles' longtime desire to escape the yoke of some foreign domination or oppression. Men wearing suits and headsets pushed four strangely clad gesticulating figures on wheeled scaffolds through the crowd. A screaming insane man squawking a horn atop a mammoth bicycle-like contraption moved past. Next a half-naked blonde was pushed in on another scaffold. She disappeared. There was a war. The suits climbed towers that the others wheeled out. The scaffolds returned, now with figures on top wearing steel masks who vanquished a human in white wraps. Then, it ended.

For me, the true highlight of Kraków's artistry lay half hidden in Czartoryski Museum. There I came across a small, dim second-floor room. Only one painting hung on the wall. Without taking my eyes from the portrait, I walked in and sat upon the bench.

The Italian master Leonardo da Vinci painted four female portraits, including *Ginevra de'Benci*, *La belle ferronnière*, and the *Mona Lisa*. I found myself gazing in awe at the fourth, *Lady with an Ermine*. I had long wondered what set masterpieces apart from lesser efforts. As with most wonders, no book or reproduction could substitute seeing with one's own eyes the mastery of form and technique that so few possess. Not until forty-five minutes later, when a middle-aged woman discovered my refuge and broke my trance, could I pull myself away.

42

HOMEWARD

The train station in Wrocław reeked of stale urine and desperation. Drunken Poles stumbled into each other and staggered into walls. An elderly one-legged man sprawled on the spit-stained floor. One old woman slept on her battered suitcase near a row of men with heads bowed. A mumbling homeless woman inspected the contents of each rubbish container and others asked for zloty.

Another with his head swathed in bandages sat beside me. A mesh skullcap kept the bundle in place. He drew stares, but sat as though nothing were out of the ordinary. He struggled to work pieces of bread through the bandages and into his mouth using bruised, lacerated fingers. "Auto accident," he claimed, and then asked me in Polish to watch his bag.

Armed soldiers in camouflage fatigues woke the sleeping drunks and forced them to move on. Some refused. Confrontation brewed, until the ruffians gave in and braved the cold. The man with the bandaged head returned to his seat. When a barely noticeable announcement played over the speakers, he pointed to the sky.

"Your train," he said.

I cozied into the solitary compartment until in wee hours, with rain dripping from the windows, a uniformed Polish guard threw open the door to check my passport. Soon after, I continued into Czech Republic.

At daybreak, the train called at Prague's Praha hlavní nádraží station. After deciphering the underground rail, I found a half-hidden hostel. With all beds filled until later, I took a long walk along the cobblestones. Blustery Czech cold replaced the spring-like warmth of Kraków. At Staroměstské náměstí, the Old Town Square, vendors set out their wares amidst a three hundred sixty degree panorama of history and architectural genius.

In ancient times, Celtic Boii inhabited the region known as Bohemia, which upon my arrival comprised much of present-day Czech Republic. When the Romans arrived, most Celtic Boii retreated across the Alps. In the sixth century, invading Slavic tribes merged with any remaining Celts.

The fourteenth-century reign of Charles IV culminated in a Czech golden age that saw construction of Charles Bridge, Charles Square, much of Prague Castle, and the founding of Charles University. The Thirty Years' War, which devastated Europe in the seventeenth century, began in Prague and marked the start of a long period of plague, Germanization, forced Catholicism, and dark age in Czech history.

In the twentieth century, the signing of the Munich Agreement without Czech involvement turned Czechs away from the West and towards the Soviet Union. This shift in loyalty enabled a Soviet takeover of Czechoslovakia.

As part of a pact between the Soviet Union and Germany, Eastern Europe was divided into German and Soviet spheres of influence. The Soviet realm included Poland, Hungary, Czechoslovakia, Romania, and Bulgaria. British Prime Minister Winston Churchill claimed the region had fallen behind an Iron Curtain of control. Creation of this Eastern Bloc, and the proliferation of communism, marked the fourth significant influence that shaped twentieth-century Europe.

Whereas throughout European history monarchies and dynasties had used religion as a political tool, the Soviet Marxist-Leninist brand of communism advocated for the abolition of religion. Karl Marx considered religion's contributions over the centuries unimportant and irrelevant to humanity's future, and argued that religion had been invented as a reaction to suffering and injustice. Vladimir Lenin considered religion an opiate of the masses, and the primary tool which ruling classes used to exploit their subjects. Both men advocated for atheism.

The policy that endured throughout Soviet history was that religion would be tolerated by the state, but gradually eliminated from society by the Communist Party. This philosophy extended to the Eastern Bloc nations. With the beginning of the Cold War, a new line was drawn between East and West.

Organized religion was proving to not be my answer. The absence of faith was not my choice either. I needed meaning in my life, and knew that neither the Soviet social experiment nor atheism were my solution.

The second blue moon of the year revealed itself as a murky shade of orange while rising over the twinkling lights of Prague. A blue moon—by definition the second full moon in a calendar month—appears every other year or so. Far less common are two blue moons in the same year, which happens once every nineteen years.

In addition to being astronomical events, blue moons also refer to events in life that rarely occur. This journey across Eurasia reminded me of the double blue moon, in that a yearlong adventure around the world happens only so often. All the more reason I wanted it not to end.

I remembered that one year ago, a full moon rose over Real de Catorce when I encountered the heralds in the abandoned church. The reminder that I had failed to find any answers or make any choice on this journey darkened my mood.

I lifted my spirits at a locals-only beer hall. No music, no atmosphere; just long tables filled with Czechs drinking half-liters of Staropramen for twelve crowns. A local informed me of my good luck in finding the beer hall. He too wanted to open a bar. They started to paint the walls, he recalled, but the paint came out pink instead of red. Maybe someday, he mused.

Around the corner at U Kiliána, the attentive waitresses hustled and drinks flowed. An old man sat alone at the opposite end of the bar. He wore a coat and tie, white slicked-back hair, wedding ring, and permanent smiling frown. After washing down the borscht with a few half-liters of beer, he donned his black hat and overcoat and puttered out the door. The march of time, cycling of the seasons, and phases of the moon all endure for eternity. Life, love, the old man, my journey–these must end.

On Easter Sunday I arrived in the tranquil Bohemian village of Český Krumlov. The vegetarian eatery served red wine, šopský salát–a Czech specialty salad–and chléb–bread. Upon a hilltop in a meadow overlooking the valley and village, birds twittered and bees buzzed. The day marked the anniversary of a year on the road. The prior Easter I visited the abandoned church in Mexico. Memorial Day and Labor Day were spent in Alaska. A Halloween sandstorm trapped me in Nepal. I suffered through Thanksgiving on the harrowing journey out of Tibet. Christmas and New Year's I spent in India. On St. Patrick's Day I imbibed in Hungary. Then, Easter came again as I savored my last hours in Czech Republic.

A London-based band played in the downstairs pub of the hostel. One with deep lines and hollow eyes resembled Rolling Stones guitarist Keith Richards. He chatted up the young woman pouring the beers, but she wasn't interested. In the morning, someone new lay in the bed next to mine. For the past few nights a Bloomsburg University co-ed studying abroad in London had slept there. Now, Keith Richard's doppelganger snored beside me.

In morning darkness I slipped out of the hostel to catch a bus to České Budějovice. Only a snack shop at the station was open. From there, the slow local train stopped at dozens of way stations. In Pizeň, Czech for Pilsner, nothing was open. I found a grocery mart that opened at two, and bought bread and cheese before attempting the tram. With the ticket boxes all broken I rode black, without a ticket, but made the bus station.

A bus with a signboard reading *Praha-Paris* arrived at the station. The conductor looked over my ticket and asked me something in Czech. Having bought the ticket in Prague and with everything closed for Easter Monday, a problem might be disastrous. I shrugged. He dialed someone on the bus phone. I waited. After a few moments he glanced at me and nodded. I climbed aboard for the journey across Germany. Soon, I fell into a deep sleep.

In the night I dreamt a band of thieves robbed my traveling companions and me of all our possessions. I told the band's leader I didn't want to lose my journals. He nodded, so I pulled my notebooks from the heap. When I spotted my exposed rolls of film I stuffed those into my pockets. Then I saw my money pouch and passport, and grabbed those when no one watched.

I had crossed too many continents and questionable countries to lose everything. Though placid at the dawn of the twenty-first century, most of Western Europe's history had not been so peaceful. After upheaval spurred by nomadic invaders wound down at the close of the first millennium, religious and political jockeying for position, power, and property spurred a thousand years of war. The rise of the Ottomans had planted one seed of conflict. Another was sown when construction of Habsburg Castle began in present-day Switzerland.

Thirty kilometers east of the castle, the earliest known thread of my own story began in 1580 when Felix Zander, my direct ancestor who lived ten generations before me, was born.

In the centuries that followed, Europe's religious wars drove many members of my family and thousands of other seventeenth and eighteenth-century Swiss and German Palatinates from their homeland along the Rhine River to William Penn's colony in the New World. For the remainder of my journey I would follow my ancestors' route, from southwest Germany to the Netherlands and from there towards my grandmother's 1820 stone farmhouse and the fertile Pennsylvania farmlands and rural villages of Dryville, Topton, Kutztown, and New Jerusalem.

When I awoke, the bus paused at a grand square with magnificent majestically illuminated buildings lined by tall nineteenth-century brick homes. A weathered Renault and signboard confirmed our arrival in Strasbourg, capital of France's Alsace region. My experience in Germany resembled what little I knew about my German ancestors—only a smattering of dates, place names, and stories about people I would never meet.

While aboard the bus, I wondered whether the spiritual benefits that religion brings to humanity have outweighed the pain and death that witch trials, Inquisitions, and wars have wrought. The battle between Christians and Muslims flared with Ottoman expansion into the Balkans. The rise and fall of the Habsburg dynasty led to the First World War. Opposition to Gypsies, Jews, Muslims, and other non-Aryans underlay the genocidal catastrophe of the Second World War. Then, communist principles rejected all religion.

In Asia, I investigated firsthand the choices at my disposal, but felt no connection to the rites and rituals that any faiths require. While crossing Europe, I uncovered the impacts of religious and political turmoil upon my own lineage, and felt further removed from religion's dogma. Even after journeying across much of the Eurasian landmass, I wondered what organized religion could offer me.

Perhaps the most meaningful Western bricks and mortar

church-going experience I remembered was the hour I spent in a 1759 Quaker church with my Aunt Fay. It was one she visited on occasion with her husband Steve. The handful of Quakers in attendance meditated and contemplated. No one spoke. Birds sang outside the open wooden windows. They were the choir. A locust whirred, a fly buzzed past, a wasp rasped the stovepipe, and butterflies flittered through one door and out the other. These were the apostles. When a woman to the side gave a signal, everyone arose. Congregants shook hands. No one preached. No one proselytized. There was no minister, offering, or service. No one tried to manipulate anyone.

Despite such positive attributes, I knew that even the Quaker model did not meet my needs. I was looking for something else. Organized religion, it seemed, was simply not my answer.

43

CITY OF LIGHT

"Gare du Nord?" I asked. The bus driver took another drag of his cigarette and pointed. I discovered that trains in fact departed for downtown Paris from nearby Gare de l'Est, not the Gare du Nord station.

Dark blue and orange clouds swirled to the east. Trees sprouting bright green leaves shaded quiet boulevards. Birds twittered from budding branches. Grassy parks and manicured gardens of tulips, pansies, and crocuses lay around every corner. An earthy, rain-tinged bouquet hung in the air.

When I spotted a woman walking her dog, I stopped. The realization that I stood in the heart of Paris, the *city of light*, illumined my soul. That was not just a woman. That was a French woman. That was a French dog!

I walked beside the Seine, down the Quai d'Orsay, past the Pont des Invalides and Pont Alexandre III, along Place de Invalides and Rue de Grenelle, and into Saint-Germain-des-Prés. Each shop specialized in something—wine, bread, cheese, tobacco, perfume. I paused inside a cathedral before buying a thin baguette and chunk of cheese for a park bench picnic.

I encircled the Sorbonne. Established in 1253, the university served as theological center of a city long dominated by religion, yet had also stirred controversy. The Sorbonne recognized English King Henry V as France's rightful ruler and refused to support former Protestant French King Henri IV. It condemned Joan of Arc, opposed eighteenth-century philosophers who challenged the church's thinking, and taught students who battled police during the Student Revolt of 1968.

Inside Nôtre Dame Cathedral, on the island of Île de la Cité, the tourists congregated. They filled the church but it was too massive even for them, with fabulous stained glass windows beneath soaring spires and flying buttresses. Parisian history began two millennia ago in the middle of Île de la Cité, which sits in the center of the Seine River—for a thousand years the city's defensive moat, drinking fountain, laundry, bathtub, and main highway. Set in the square in front of Nôtre Dame, at Kilomètre Zéro, sits a brass compass from which all distances in Paris are measured.

In the fourteenth century, Charles V moved his court from Île de la Cité. In the sixteenth King François I built a royal palace on the Right Bank. With the theft of twelve paintings from Italy, François started a royal art collection that grew into hundreds of thousands, all housed within the future Louvre Museum. François also brought the *Mona Lisa*, and a young Leonardo da Vinci, to Paris. By the time the royal court moved to the extravagant new palace at Versailles, the area around the Louvre had become the new heart of Paris.

I walked northwest past the Louvre along Avenue des Champs-Élysées to the Arc de Triomphe, which Napoleon conceived to commemorate victory in battle. Here, twelve roads merge to form a junction known as Place de l'Étoile, the Square of the Star. The arch aligns with the Arc de Triomphe du Carrousel outside the Louvre, and the Grande Arche de La Défense to the west.

I turned south, past the Eiffel Tower. Commissioned for the 1889 Universal Exhibition, Gustave Eiffel just made the two-year deadline. Not everyone appreciated his fin de siècle effort. Guy De Maupassant noted that he liked dining at the Eiffel Tower because it was the only place in the city where he did not have to look at it. Where writers opposed it, artists praised it, including Utrillo, Dufy, and Pissarro. I for one gawked in awe at this icon of Parisian elegance.

With the hostel room divided in two sections and the rear full, I took a bunk in the empty outer portion. Others filtered in from each corner of the Empire: two Mikes from Canada, Tony from Ireland, and Jason from Oz. I bought fresh bread and a can of ravioli for six francs, plus a bottle of French red for six more. As we drank in the room two American co-eds entered. Following confusion about who should go where, we finished the Scotch and, drunk on life, headed into the streets.

I led the group to the Eiffel Tower, stunning by day but at night defying description. The elevator brought us towards the top as twinkling city lights spread to the horizons. I led onward to the Arc de Triomphe, itself ablaze. The others tired but I wandered the city of light alone and enraptured. In a corner café I rested.

"Is this your first time to Paris?" the young brunette beside me asked.

"Yes," I sighed. "I always wanted to visit in spring."

"It is lovely."

I smiled. "And the people. So beautiful."

"The French are snobs," she said.

"I adore them!"

"They're so arrogant," she declared.

A chill breeze swept through the window. She edged closer.

"Where are you from?" I asked.

"A place you probably never heard of."

"Oh. Where are you staying?"

"The city's booked full," she said. "I'll probably drink cappuccinos 'til dawn then take the train to Brussels."

"But this is the city of romance!" The clattering of hooves upon cobblestone outside the café distracted me. "I suppose I could keep you company if you wish."

The furrows in her forehead softened. "Really?"

We stepped into rain-dampened streets. "Do you smell that?" I asked. "The smell of spring." Sparrows twittered among the treetops. "Can you hear? The sound of spring!"

She looked around. "I don't hear anything. Which way?"

Something in the spring air suddenly inspired me. "I'm sorry," I said, "but I have something to take care of," and dashed into the night.

Dawn broke over the soaring spires of Nôtre-Dame. I waited until they unbarred the heavy wooden doors. I walked inside and stood near a small shrine dedicated to Joan of Arc. She had led the French army to multiple victories late in the Hundred Years' War before the English burned the nineteen-year-old at the stake as a heretic. Twenty-five years later she was martyred and declared a patron saint of France.

"One life is all we have and we live it as we believe in living it," she said, "but to sacrifice what you are and to live without belief, that is a fate more terrible than dying."

As the tourists streamed past, I contemplated why people choose a particular faith. Some cling to religion to fill a void. Others need a moral compass. Many crave emotional comfort or inner peace. Upon starting this journey, I had feared that this universe has no god, no purpose, and no meaning, and that only an empty void awaits us after our brief lifetime. I looked towards organized religions for answers.

Hinduism says all paths lead to the same goal, like choosing one of several routes to a mountain summit. Perhaps the Hindus are right, I thought. Maybe which ideology I follow matters less than simply choosing and believing in *something*.

Those of faith do believe. Enlightened Buddhists, devout Hindus, somber Sikhs, militant Muslims, sky-clad Jains, secretive Zoroastrians, confident Christians, and chosen Jews do not empirically know whether there is emptiness on either side of life or whether there is a God. Unlike me, they simply believe in their chosen faith based upon their intuitions.

Yet as the Taoists intuited, whatever power created the

universe lies far beyond human comprehension. "I don't know whether this world has a meaning that transcends it," observed French philosopher Albert Camus, "but I do know that I do not know that meaning and it is impossible for me to know."

God is a metaphor for the unknowable, which transcends all human thought. Rites, rituals, gods—even cathedrals such as Nôtre-Dame—are manifestations of intangible abstraction.

The gods that people had created in humankind's image did not inspire me. Following any religion's rules was too dogmatic for my taste. I felt that trying to describe the indescribable was simply satisfaction of the ego. On the cosmic scale, the collective creations of humankind are like a dewdrop, and I an atom on the underbelly of the universe. To accept insignificance rather than succumb to tenets that for me rang hollow was true revelation.

To persevere in the face of nothingness is a difficult burden, I had learned. An employer of mine once confided in me that he hedged his bets with God. "I don't know if there is one," he mused aloud, "but I'm not taking any chances. Why not go to church, just in case?" Like me, he had no idea. Yet his choice was without conviction. To cling to a belief out of fear felt to me like living without belief.

To discover what I believed, I had studied the historical religions to uncover any core messages that resonated with me. What I noticed is that most religions preach a similar message; the style of expression among them is what varies. One universal lesson that every historical religion seems to teach is that love is all-encompassing and all-important.

God is love, claim the prophets. And as my mother had told me twenty years earlier, God is everywhere. Therefore, it follows, love must reside within the twittering birds, blooming flowers, springtime rain, and each of us.

What I wanted, I realized, and what every person wants, is to love and to be loved. In order to give and receive love, we must first love ourselves. Reaching heaven in the Christian tradition and finding enlightenment as a Buddhist, for example, can both be interpreted as letting go of attachments and suffering, and finding peace within ourselves. In a moment of clarity, I saw that any meaning in my life must derive from a healthy combination of self-reliance, self-respect, and self-awareness.

There might only be this single lifetime, but I could accept that so long as I was true to myself each day and each moment. I did not require anyone else's approval to be happy and fulfilled. I did not need to identify with any religion to get what I truly wanted. I only needed to believe in myself, embrace change, and accept others and life as they are. My salvation lay in accepting love—accepting myself, really—as my own savior.

Long lines waited outside the Louvre. I fought my way inside, past crowds clustered around the *Mona Lisa*. The French writer Marcel Proust spent many hours in the Louvre while penning his three thousand-page *In Search of Lost Time*, regarded by many scholars as the definitive modern novel. Proust mentions a hundred artists and dozens of paintings in the one and a half million-word work, one of the longest in world literature.

To be happy, Proust claims, we should shed our pretensions for immortality, renew our taste for life, discover new possibilities, reassess our priorities, and live life joyfully. At age fifty he told a French newspaper that if death were to become suddenly imminent he would do three things in short order: visit the Louvre, journey through India, and throw himself at the feet of Miss X. Four months later he was dead, having never seen India or confessed his unrequited love.

On the topic of travel, Proust notes that, "the real voyage of discovery consists not in seeing new landscapes, but in having new eyes."

I sat in a quiet corner of the Louvre. On my yearlong journey I saw something I had not seen before; felt something I had not felt before. I had learned that love really is the most important thing. Only when we love ourselves first can we love any other. To love any other we must learn to sacrifice, compromise, be selfless, and accept not only the lovable qualities in any other, but also the unlovable ones. We must love unconditionally.

The question posed by the heralds was not about choosing any particular religion, I realized. Their question was about the kind of life I wanted. Did I want a selfish life alone, or a selfless life with another?

For a moment not yet lost to time, I possessed the ability to choose how I wanted to live my life. I had journeyed through India, and now sat inside the Louvre. I felt ready to try to love authentically—meaning openly, honestly, and unconditionally. I composed a new letter to Tamara, and this time I apologized. As Proust might have advised, I threw myself at the feet of Miss T.

44

TWO AMSTERDAMS

In central Amsterdam, five hours north of Paris, a peace rally filled Dam Square then overflowed into adjoining streets. Serbs demanded that NATO stop attacking their homeland. Refugees fled Kosovo while Yugoslavian president Slobodan Milošević deported and exterminated ethnic Albanians. Headlines warned of Russian president Boris Yeltsin's threats for another world war, or at least European one, if NATO persisted.

"Clinton, how many kids have you killed today?" read the signboard one old man carried. A young woman's button pled, *"NATO please don't bomb my father."*

Meanwhile, senior citizens oblivious to conflicts boiling over in the Balkans followed tour guides through Amsterdam's red-light district. Half-naked women posed for potential customers behind full-length glass partitions. Photos of people engaged in lascivious acts covered storefront windows piled high with sex toys. Tourists shopped for psychedelics and reposed in smoke-filled cannabis coffee shops.

The city of Amsterdam, along with Rotterdam and The

Hague, were part of the Dutch nation of the Netherlands. In the 1500s the region fell under the dominion of Charles V, King of Spain and member of the Habsburg family. The Eighty Years' War between Spain and the Dutch provinces started in part as a reaction to Protestant persecution by the Spanish Inquisition. The war led to Dutch independence. Afterward, the Dutch Empire grew into one of the major maritime powers of the seventeenth century.

The Dutch East and Dutch West India Company established colonies and trading posts around the world. Amsterdam evolved from a twelfth-century fishing village into a financial base during the Dutch Golden Age, and became the wealthiest city in the world.

The Dutch founded their first North American settlement at the southern tip of Manhattan in 1614 and named the colony New Amsterdam. Half a century later the colony's Director-General surrendered New Amsterdam to the English, who renamed the city New York. The wealthiest city of the seventeenth century ultimately lent its name to the city that would become the financial hub of the wealthiest nation of the twentieth century. Every empire has its heyday.

Having located no affordable fares from the continent out of Paris, I found a two hundred-dollar ticket to New York from Amsterdam. I exchanged the last of my guilders for dollars, a symbolic end to my journey. The day was cool and rainy, and I was not sad to leave. I arrived a bit early to the airport. So used to filling time meaningfully while awaiting tardy transportation, a few hours at an airport was no problem. Once onboard I waited a half hour, and then another while maintenance crews located a faulty wire amongst the massive bundles. After three more hours, we at last lifted off for the flight from "Old Amsterdam" to "New Amsterdam."

While in flight, I reflected upon the words of William Blake. In *The Marriage of Heaven and Hell* he observes that, "Man has closed himself up till he sees all things through the narrow chinks of his cavern." Soon I would return to my cavern, I lamented, and perhaps forget how to open my eyes wide. I hoped that would not happen. Some lessons I could carry to the end. Picking my way around the world with no compass but my own intuition, after all, was no different from daily life. We must each find our true path—dharma, in the Hindu tradition—that is right for us.

I remembered the message I found inside a fortune cookie at a Chinese carryout. "It matters not what road we take," the slip read, "but rather what we become on the journey." I hoped I had changed, and soon would find out. I knew I no longer saw the world the same. The chinks of my cavern might soon narrow, but I must never let them close entirely.

While contemplating this, my thoughts were frequently interrupted by irate flight attendants. Each time the smell of cigarettes wafted into the cabin and the bathroom fire alarm rang, they repeated that smoking would not be tolerated. When we reached New York, half a dozen police waited at the end of the gangplank as attendants fingered select passengers.

I eased through passport control and at customs drew a burly African-American. They had pulled my tightly packed bag apart in Amsterdam, so I held my breath for the inevitable.

"So whatchyou do?" he asked. I explained.

"And the last time you left the country?"

"The first of October."

"You can go all that time without working?"

"Five hundred a month plus airfare is all I've spent. Just three grand. That's it. No funny stuff."

He eyed me and poked a little at the bag as we talked about the subway. He handed the bag back.

"Go on," he said. "Have a good night and watch yourself on them trains."

As I crammed items back inside, a young woman at the agent next to mine protested. "Well how is it different from marijuana?" the agent responded.

"What are they doing?" she cried. "What's going to happen?" More agents approached.

As the transcendentalists understood, social institutions provide benefits, but at times strive to control us. The state will always regulate. The corporation will always manipulate. Religious tenets will always entice. I saw that defining myself by which religion I follow would severely limit my potentiality. The human experience is much broader than any single ideology. I wanted to avoid self-limiting labels and always follow what I felt in my heart, even if the masses believed otherwise. Religion's focus–like the state and corporation–is too narrow, I realized. Each individual possesses the ability to transcend any institution, ideology, or label, and I promised myself I would always endeavor to do so.

I knew I could not avoid the institutions. I reminded myself that all I could do is embrace self-reliance, self-respect, and self-awareness. I must know myself and seek my true nature. As Thoreau advised, we must live the life we have imagined.

Outside the airport, a young Frenchwoman living in the Netherlands sat with her bulging bag. Florence was a little befuddled, but getting her bearings. After a Jewish woman in front of us at the ticket booth had a problem with her change, Florence and I realized we had missed our train. So, we waited on the platform in the bluster of a White Plains evening.

Another subway train at last appeared. As we sank beneath Brooklyn, Florence highlighted the Dutch influence on New York. Harlem, Amsterdam Avenue, and Van-something station flashed past. We exited at Forty-Second Street. The neon winked. A sharp wind sliced up Seventh Avenue. Even on the muggiest summer nights, Manhattan streets could feel frigid. New York was like a proud, polished apple with a few bruises. She might taste sweet, but sometimes there were a few surprises.

And yet, the normalcy of the city struck me. Nearly every pedestrian strolling beneath the flashing theater house marquees seemed to wear the same clothes and colors. I no longer had to rely on gestures and expressions to interpret the simplest sentence. Everything suddenly seemed too easy.

Florence disappeared into the crowd. I grabbed Chinese

takeout then sought refuge in the bowels of Port Authority Bus Terminal. The next outbound to Baltimore departed in five hours. The thirty others in the waiting room, most sleeping or trying to, hailed from dozens of backgrounds. An energetic Guatemalan asked me about an affordable place to visit.

"You could walk outside to Times Square, for free," I said.

"No, too dangerous," he said. "Many people have said so."

Despite economic disparities between his nation and mine, he had visited Washington D.C., the Deep South, and parts of Canada. His gold tooth flashed as he told of the time in Guatemala City that someone stole all the clothes he owned while bringing them home to his mother to wash.

"That city is no good anymore," he said, "but Antigua is wonderful. El Petén was destroyed by fire and overgrazing, but the lake at Flores is *muy bonita*."

On the pros and cons of travel, Blaise Pascal in *Pensées* writes that all the unhappiness of man comes from one single thing–his inability to be content at staying put, in his sitting room, at home.

Though perhaps true, to refrain from all travel out of fear is to miss many of the great adventures of a lifetime. Even insufficient funding is an inadequate excuse, as this spirited man proved. Had I not spent a month in Mexico and Guatemala the year before, I could not have connected so well with the friendly Guatemalan.

I remembered that I must see and feel and understand a place to best appreciate and feel compassion for the cultures and people that live there. I would likely care less about the bombings in Kosovo and the war's refugees had I not myself been there. I would likely not know that the quetzals and tigers had left El Petén and gone into Mexico had I not traveled there.

When the Guatemalan tried to sleep I broke open my fortune cookie from the Chinese takeout. "Dreams are extremely important," the slip read. "You can't do it unless you imagine it." True enough, though dreaming is not enough.

Often we rush through life, telling ourselves we'll do this next week and that next year. In the end, many of us carry our dreams to our deathbeds. We must always strive to transform our dreams into action.

When I came to and left New York at the start of the journey a year ago, I stayed in Chelsea, chatted with a Basque, ate dinner in a Greek restaurant, and walked through Central Park with mind full of expectation, hope, and wonder. I had intended to finish this journey as I started it, by seeking out the same haunts and activities, as a sort of reunion. It did not turn out that way. My plane was delayed, unexpected contingencies arose, and I waited for a bus home whether I was ready or not.

I realized this was how it should be. Upon my return, the city was not the same as one year ago. Some buildings were new and others destroyed. Nor was I the same. I saw people differently. I wanted to know where they were from and why they were here and how their stories and cultures and lives had made them who they were. Once home I would return to the same people, but they too would be different. Change is inevitable, and a cornerstone of travel. I did not revisit my old haunts in Manhattan as I had planned, but I had new stories to tell, and that is what the adventure is about: finding new ways to see old things.

The night was long aboard the Greyhound, and sleep impossible. I had been there before, waiting or riding in early morning hours upon a bus or train, but I savored those blessed spaces of time in which to think, talk, write, or meditate. I held those moments dearer than any material wealth, for such intangibles are the stuff of humanity.

My mind turned over and over, anticipating all that lay ahead. I decided I had done what I wanted. There were some places I had not seen, but I saw others which I did not expect. I did not visit Franco the Basque's homeland in the Pyrenees, but I did visit Greece as I dreamed of. I did not travel overland through Iran, but I did see Macedonia. I did not visit Kashmir, but I did marvel at Paris. That is the essence of travel, and life itself. I can only be in one place at one time doing one thing, though a thousand other places and activities silently beckon, their calls unheeded. Once I make my decisions I must live by them. I must believe in myself and my course of action, always prepared, of course, to change direction when necessary.

At first light farms appeared among the Maryland forests. A warm orange glow—the first break of dawn—covered trees and shrubbery along the road. For a moment I imagined I rode on another bus in an unknown land. But, I was not in a new place. I was in a land irrevocably different from any other. I was home.

Baltimore felt different than it ever had. I saw individuals struggling as best they could, and centuries-old prejudices that refused to die. Walking the streets, I felt I understood them better than I ever had. In a coffee shop on Charles Street and Redwood I watched morning commuters stream to their offices. I still expected to hear unintelligible jabbering, but instead remembered I did not have to point or ponder indecipherable menus or wonder what people around me were saying.

Tamara picked me up at the metro station. We talked for hours. An air of separation remained, as would be expected. She looked well. She seemed more mature, having thought things through over the past year, as I had. Before my journey, our relationship was a frantic one. The highs were high. The lows were low and seemed to involve large amounts of pain, betrayal, and anger. My fear was that we would fall into our same patterns.

Upon my return we seemed calmer, more relaxed. Our interactions held less intensity and emotion. I had learned how to be apart from her and be happy. I had found satisfaction and contentment in who I was and what I was doing. I did not need anyone, including Tamara, in order to be happy. We had a lot of work to do, that was certain, yet we each seemed undeniably happy to be reunited and ready to try anew.

Two weeks after arriving home, my parents and sister and I visited my grandmother at her 1820 stone farmhouse in New Jerusalem. Aunt Fay and Steve had just returned from a two-month trip to Portugal and Morocco. Though Steve had fallen ill, he insisted they finish their journey as planned. This time, the couple that inspired my travels through Nepal and Tibet and India and Eastern Europe listened as I described my own travails. One dream, at least, would not die with me.

"If you ain't got work," my grandmother sometimes said, "you ain't got nothing." She was right, mostly. After my brief visit home, I returned to Alaska and my job at the lodge. This time, Tamara came too. We moved into a one-room twelve by twelve-foot wood frame cabin without running water that nestled amongst white and black spruce of the outer Alaska Range near the one I had inhabited the prior summer.

A few days after arriving in Alaska, I received a shocking phone call at the lounge where I worked. Liver cancer had unexpectedly taken Steve, at age sixty-six, far too soon. I recalled the Hindus burning their dead upon the ghats of the Ganges, a sight I saw because of him. In time, as the Hindus would do, I accepted that his death was a part of life.

Kelly, who gave me the penicillin that saved me after the journey out of Tibet, stopped by our cabin a few weeks later. She glanced at the handful of souvenirs on a shelf.

"So where you two heading next?" she asked.

"Well," I said, looking towards Tamara, "South America has been on my mind…"

The loss of a mentor is never easy. Steve's death had come as a shock, but in no way curbed the adventurous spirit he had helped stir within me. In fact, his passing inspired me to continue living the life I had long imagined. While able, I wanted to see as much of the world as I could. I wanted to follow my heart, wherever that might lead, and be true to myself.

I remembered the story about the wistful pansy that my friend Glenn had told in the Mexican village of Real de Catorce. Aunt Fay and Steve had encouraged me to venture beyond the garden wall. I had become a rose.

SOURCES

A Field of Buttons. The Economist. April 3, 1999.

Armington, Stan. *Trekking in the Nepal Himalaya*. Hawthorn, Australia: Lonely Planet Publications. 1997.

Barraclough, Geoffrey, ed. *Atlas of World History*. Ann Arbor, Michigan: Harper Collins. 1999.

Chodag, Tiley. *Tibet: The Land and the People*. Beijing, China: New World Press. 1988.

Cotterell, Arthur and Storm, Rachel. *The Illustrated Encyclopedia of World Mythology*. New York, NY: Anness Publishing Ltd. 2010.

Cotterell, Arthur, ed. *World Mythology*. Bath, UK: Parragon Publishing. 2003.

Dalrymple, William. *City of Djinns: A Year in Delhi*. London: HarperCollins Publishers. 1993.

Ehrlich, Blake. *Paris on the Seine.* New York: Atheneum. 1962.

Fallon, Steve. *Eastern Europe on a Shoestring.* Hawthorn, Australia: Lonely Planet Publications. 1997.

Finlay, Hugh. *India: A Lonely Planet Travel Survival Kit.* Hawthorn, Australia: Lonely Planet Publications. 1996.

Forster, E. M. *A Passage to India.* New York: Harcourt Brace Jovanovich, Publishers. 1924.

Fritsch, Peter V. *Pennsylvania Dutch Halloween Scherenschnitte.* Gretna, Louisiana: Pelican Publishing Company, Inc. 2011.

Fuller, Gary. *The Trivia Lover's Guide to the World: Geography for the Lost and Found.* Lanham, Maryland: The Rowman & Littlefield Publishing Group, Inc. 2012.

Gerrard, Mike and Dailey, Donna. *Paris: A City Revealed.* New York: AA Media Limited. 2008.

Harrer, Heinrich. *Seven Years in Tibet.* Penguin. 1997.

Hobbes, Thomas. *Of Man, Being the First Part of Leviathan. Chapter XIII. Of the Natural Condition of Mankind as Concerning Their Felicity and Misery.* The Harvard Classics. 1909-14.

Hollick, Julian Crandall. *Ganga: A Journey Down the Ganges River.* Washington, DC: Island Press. 2008.

Ingrao, Charles. *The Habsburg Monarchy 1618-1815.* Melbourne, Australia: Cambridge University Press. 1994.

Kaplan, Robert D. *Balkan Ghosts: A Journey through History.* New York: Vintage Press. 1993.

Kaplan, Robert D. *The Ends of the Earth: A Journey to the Frontiers of Anarchy*. New York: Random House. 1996.

Keay, John. *India: A History*. New York, NY: Grove Press. 2000.

Lewis, Brenda Ralph, ed. *Great Civilizations*. Bath, UK: Parragon Publishing. 2005.

McCurry, Steve. *The Unguarded Moment*. London: Phaidon Press Limited. 2009.

Mehta, Gita. *Karma Cola*. London: Minerva. 1979.

Mehta, Gita. *Snakes and Ladders: A View of Modern India*. London: Random House. 1997.

Newby, Eric. *Slowly Down the Ganges*. Hawthorn, Australia: Lonely Planet Publications. 1998.

Noble, John. *Mexico*. Hawthorn, Australia: Lonely Planet Publications. 1995.

O'Brien, Cormac. *The Fall of Empires: From Glory to Ruin, an Epic Account of History's Ancient Civilizations*. New York: Fall River Press. 2009.

Pagden, Anthony. *Worlds at War: The 2,500-Year Struggle between East and West*. New York. Random House Publishing Group. 2009.

Pastva, Loretta. *Great Religions of the World*. Winona, Minnesota: St. Mary's Press. 1986.

Polo, Marco. *The Customs of the Kingdoms of India*. London: Penguin Books. 2007.

Rousseau, Jean-Jacques. *The Social Contract*. New York, NY: Barnes & Noble, Inc. 2005.

Schaefer, Stacy B. and Furst, Peter T. *People of the Peyote: Huichol Indian History, Religion, and Survival*. UNM Press. 1997.

Singh, Khushwant. *We Indians*. Delhi, India: Orient Paperbacks. 1982.

Smith, Huston. *The World's Religions*. New York: Harper Collins Publishers. 1991.

Stegner, Wallace and Mary. *Great American Short Stories*. New York, NY: Dell Publishing Co., Inc. 1957.

Tallmadge, John. *Meeting the Tree of Life: A Teacher's Path*. University of Utah Press. 1997.

Taylor, Chris. *Tibet*. Hawthorn, Australia: Lonely Planet Publications. 1995.

Wilkinson, Philip. *Religions*. New York, NY: Metro Books. 2008.

ABOUT THE AUTHOR

Across Eurasia

Toby D. Smith, a financial consultant and writer, lives in Pennsylvania. He holds a Bachelor of Science degree in Zoology, and an MBA, both from the University of Maryland. During an eighteen-year Alaska-based career, he led multiple non-profit organizations focused on wilderness preservation, education, and advocacy. He has driven through fifty U.S. states, traveled across five continents, and visited over fifty countries. *Across Eurasia* is his first book.

11761013R00208

Made in the USA
Middletown, DE
15 November 2018